South Korea

Dissent within the Economic Miracle

George E. Ogle

Zed Books Ltd
London and New Jersey

in association with
**International Labor Rights
Education and Research Fund**
Washington D.C.

South Korea: Dissent within the Economic Miracle was first
published by Zed Books Ltd, 57 Caledonian Road, London N1 9BU, UK,
and 171 First Avenue, Atlantic Highlands, New Jersey 07716, USA,
in association with the International Labor Rights Education
and Research Fund, Box 28074, Washington DC 20038–8074, USA,
in 1990.

Cover designed by Andrew Corbett.
Typeset by Cliff Rohde, Washington DC.
Printed and bound in the United Kingdom
by Biddles Ltd, Guildford and King's Lynn.

British Library Cataloguing in Publication Data

Ogle, George E.
   South Korea: dissent with the economic miracle.
   1. South Korea. Economic growth, history
   I. Title
   339.5095195

   ISBN 1–85649–002–5
   ISBN 1–85649–003–3 pbk

TABLE OF CONTENTS

ACKNOWLEDGEMENTS

I am grateful to many people for helping me to complete this work:

To my employer, The General Board of Church and Society of the United Methodist Church, which provided me with the leave time to do the study.

To the International Labor Rights Education and Research Fund which funded many of the expenses for the undertaking and especially to Bill Goold and Holly Burkhalter for their sage counsel.

To the North American Coalition on Human Rights In Korea and its director Pharis Harvey for sharing with me many of its resources.

To all the Korean friends and colleagues who gave me assistance and inspiration, especially Reverend Cho Wha Soon, Reverend Cho Sung Hyuk and Mr. Whang Yo Wang who set up my schedule and accompanied me to many interviews while I was in Korea. Without their guidance, I would have been lost.

To Mrs. Bethany Laura Rowe who has not only been an excellent typist, but has patiently corrected my many errors.

To my wife and children who shared many of my experiences and helped me along the way with the writing and rewriting of the manuscript.

About the Author

Dr. George Ewing Ogle -- theologian, sociologist and human rights activist -- was educated at Duke University where he took a Masters degree in Divinity in 1954, and at the University of Wisconsin where he received his doctorate in Industrial Sociology in 1973. George Ogle has spent much of his life living and working in South Korea. From 1960 to 1971 he was co-director of the Urban Industrial Mission in Inchun and in 1973 became Professor of Industrial Sociology at Seoul National University. The following year he was arrested and deported because of his work, as well as his public statements on behalf of eight innocent men who were first tortured, and then hanged, by the Pak Chung Hee government. The story of these events is told in his book, *Liberty to the Captives* (1977). From 1975 to 1981, Dr. Ogle was Professor of International Missions, Candler School of Theology, Emory University. He is currently Program Associate, General Board of Church and Society, the United Methodist Church. For the writing of this book, he was able to return to South Korea for an extended investigation.

This book was originally written under the title *Dissent Within the "Miracle": Korean Labor Moves toward Democracy*

INTRODUCTION
*by Professor Ray Marshall**

Dissent Within the "Miracle": Korean Labor Moves toward Democracy is an important contribution to our understanding of the obstacles and opportunities involved in political and economic developments in Korea. Because George Ogle has for many years been a deeply committed participant–observer in efforts to improve the conditions of Korean workers, his thoughtful, informed ideas are therefore invaluable to students of labor and democratic institutions.

Ogle's work is important, in addition, because he presents a very succinct account of the political and economic development of Korea, a country that has emerged as a leading economic power in a relatively short period of time. Indeed, the speed of development of the Korean economy has been unprecedented. Since Korea emerged from World War II with much more primitive conditions, its development is even more impressive than the so called "Japanese miracle." *Dissent Within the "Miracle": Korean Labor Moves toward Democracy* presents a valuable analysis of the strategy used by Korean elites to achieve these remarkable economic results.

But George Ogle's most important contribution is his depiction from personal observation and experience of the extent to which the "economic miracle" was based on the exploitation of Korean workers. Korea's industrializing elites used a variety of controls to depress working conditions in order to accumulate and attract the capital used for economic growth. These labor controls included patriotic appeals, legal restrictions on workers' rights, and official tolerance of long hours and unsafe, unhealthful and oppressive working conditions. Korean authorities used anticommunism to make McCarthyism a kind of official national policy. Any effective effort by workers to organize and bargain collectively was labelled communistic. Perhaps the darkest side of the Korean miracle was the use of sheer physical brutality, fear and personal humiliation to prevent workers from acquiring independent sources of power to protect and promote their interests.

George Ogle's work makes it very clear, however, that economic progress and the suppression of workers' rights are fundamentally contradictory processes. This is perhaps the most important lesson from the experiences in Eastern Europe and the developed countries since World War II. Modern information and military technologies make it possible to control a country from the top, but only at great costs in terms of lost economic efficiency and human degradation. If it is to be

---

*Mr. Marshall is president of the International Labor Rights Education and Research Fund and a former U.S. Secretary of Labor.

used efficiently, information technology is inherently democratizing; it requires that many decisions be made by workers at the point of production. High performance production systems likewise place a great premium on the development of an educated, healthy, skilled, motivated work force. This is so because efficient production systems give workers considerable discretion and flexibility in achieving quality and productivity. High performance cannot be achieved by brutality and fear; it must be achieved by positive incentives. Korea, like the Soviet Union earlier, could achieve impressive economic growth at early stages of development through oppressive labor controls, but world class competitive systems require free and democratic institutions.

It has become equally clear, therefore, that economic growth and political and social stability make it necessary for workers to be able to participate in political and economic processes, as well as in work place decisions. This is so, in the first place because workers with the levels of education and thinking skills required for economic efficiency are not likely to accept totalitarian controls. And in the second place, economic policies are not likely to be successful in any country if they are contrary to the interests of workers -- who constitute the great majority of the participants in any economy. Indeed, there is a very strong correlation between the degree of worker participation and economic performance -- among nations as well as among enterprises.

Experience and logic also show that worker participation is not likely to be very effective unless workers have independent sources of power to represent their interests in the process.

Finally, George Ogle's book makes it clear that the U.S. and other developed counties have a strong interest in working conditions in Korea. This is so because in an interdependent global economy countries and companies that gain economic advantage (however temporary) from depressing working conditions make it more difficult to maintain acceptable working conditions anywhere. There is a kind of Gresham's law in labor protection – bad standards tend to drive out good standards. Labor standards therefore improve managerial efficiency by forcing managers to compete through better management instead of by depressing wages and other labor standards. For these reasons, all who believe in free and democratic institutions should support international labor standards as part of the system of rules for international transactions. In other words, the observance of such generally accepted labor standards as the right to organize and bargain collectively should be the price that Korea and other countries should have to pay for membership in the international economic system. An open and expanding global economy is not possible without rules. Labor standards are at least as important as any other rules. George Ogle's book shows why these rules are necessary to help Korean workers improve their conditions as well as why democrats everywhere have a strong interest in what happens to Korean workers.

INTRODUCTION
by Professor Bruce Cumings[*]

I will have earth cover my eyes before a union is permitted at Samsung.

-- Samsung founder Lee Byung Chul

All I came to Korea for was to make a buck. I don't want anything to do with their politics or unions.

-- An American businessman

We might take these two statements as the alpha and the omega of George Ogle's study of labor in Korea. Industrialist Lee liked to be known as "a Japanese gentleman," and modelled his sprawling corporation on Japan's big firms. Just so, South Korea's successive regimes have mimicked Japanese labor practices -- that is, those of the prewar militarists whom Americans fought against. American business wishes to utilize Korea's cheap (and presumably docile) labor, and not get involved with a lot of messy politics. In so doing, American businessman, and especially the American government, have given critical support to this same authoritarian system.

Dr. Ogle has written a systematic history of continuity in Korean labor and change in the Korean economy. He has situated the story just where it belongs, in a remarkably resilient labor movement going back to the 1920s that has been bedeviled by one dictator after another, each getting full support from the United States since 1945. Those who trumpet the Korean "miracle" can now witness the full reality of a remarkable case of industrialization: cheap labor yes, but hardly docile, as Korean organizers fought time and again for union rights in the teeth of truly horrific repression.

George Ogle has long experience with Korea and a rare "feel" for the ordinary laborer, by virtue of having lived there as a missionary for many years, and, in the early 1970s, of having worked in a church ministry called the Urban Industrial Mission. This mission, and more broadly the many courageous Christian groups that fought for human rights, played an important role in legitimizing union organizing that had long been denounced by Japanese and Korean capitalists as another species of "communism." Dr. Ogle has supplemented that background with a wide reading in the literature on Korean industrial relations. The result is a pathbreaking study of the Korean labor movement.

---

[*]Mr. Cumings is a Professor of History at the University of Chicago.

The account rightly begins during the period of Japanese colonialism, when millions of Korean laborers were deployed at the behest of Japanese overlords to convert Korea (and Koreans) into a cog in the wheel of industrialization and militarist expansion. It was at this time that the postwar system for labor control emerged, in the form of so-called "sampo" patriotic organizations that functioned as company or state unions, organizing the work force hierarchically according to a class system (pp. 21–22). The account continues right up to the most recent period, when Chun Doo Hwan built "purification camps" to beat back a strong labor organizing surge in the early 1980s, and when the Roh Tae Woo regime sent strike-breaking thugs into various factories in the late 1980s to beat workers and demolish their unions. The long night of Korean labor can be summed up in three principles: labor must be cheap, laborers are inferiors who must show deference to their owner superiors, and collective action of any sort means communism (p. 47).

This is no mere scholarly dissertation, however, but a heartfelt, sincere and highly readable account that spans sixty years of history on one level, while giving moving snapshots of people struggling to live and work on another. The contrast between two sons of peasant families, Hyundai magnate Chung Ju Yong and labor martyr Chun Tae Il (who immolated himself in 1970), is finely and pointedly drawn. Dr. Ogle's comparison of the different labor policies of the four largest firms is particularly well done, and illustrates the concerned objectivity that informs this whole study.

But it is perhaps George Ogle's own experience at the hands of the same system that will most impress his readers. In 1974 he had spoken on behalf of several people accused of being members of a revolutionary party, hoping to keep them from being executed. Dr. Ogle was arrested and interrogated around the clock by the Korean Central Intelligence Agency (which became the critical organizer of labor suppression in the early 1970s). His tormenters wanted this Christian minister to admit to being a communist. In the course of the interrogation, Lee Yong Taek (head of the KCIA's 6th section) began an emotional diatribe against the arrested men:

'These men are our enemies,' he screamed. 'We have got to kill them. This is war. In war even Christians will pull the trigger and kill their enemies. If we don't kill them they will kill us! We will kill them!'

As Dr. Ogle writes, "here was a man locked in mortal battle with Satan."

Since 1945 when the United States played the major role in dividing Korea, both Koreas have been "locked in mortal battle." By associating itself with men like Lee Yong Taek (our CIA helped set up theirs), the United States was drawn into a vicious conflict that has sullied the American reputation for fair play and democratic traditions, detonating a predictable "anti–Americanism" among Korea's youth. Nowhere is this more evident than in the history of Korean labor relations; it was, after all, an American general who inaugurated the suppression of authentic labor unions during our occupation of Korea in the 1940s.

Dr. Ogle therefore includes in his book a number of messages to foreign governments, corporations and trade unions. These messages bring his fine book to an appropriate end, where we can all contemplate the mentality of foreign investors rushing off to Korea "to make a buck," and finding themselves participants in a most unsavory system of labor repression.

PREFACE

This book is written from the perspective of one who for nearly four decades has closely observed the struggle of workers in south Korea for economic justice. Twenty of those years were spent in Korea as a missionary of the United Methodist Church. I arrived in Korea in 1954, the year after the Armistice was signed. The destruction of the war could still be seen everywhere. Homes, churches, schools, industries were yet to be rebuilt. By the 1960s, however, things had begun to change. Industrialization and economic development were taking hold. The mood of the people changed from one of despondency to one of hope for the future.

For twelve years I worked as a staff person in a ministry called Urban Industrial Mission (UIM) in the city of Inchun. Our mission included labor education programs and a variety of support ministries for Inchun's factory and dock workers. My Korean colleagues began their probationary period at UIM by doing labor in one or the other of Inchun's many factories. My assignment was to the "factory chaplaincy." Each week my routine was to visit factories to talk with workers or hold lunch–time rap sessions, to call upon union leaders and company managers, and to make pastoral visits to homes and hospitals.

Through the years we at UIM became very close to Korea's industrial workers. When in the 1970's and 1980's the military government and economic planners decided to stamp out the rights of Korea's working people in order to achieve their ambitious economic development plans, the UIM staff was put under constant surveillance. Several were arrested, imprisoned and beaten by the Korean Central Intelligence Agency (KCIA).

I was arrested and deported from Korea in 1974 because of my participation in UIM and because of my call for a public trial for eight innocent men who had been tortured into confessing leadership in a non–existent communist conspiracy.

Fifteen years later, in 1989, my wife and I returned to a south Korea much different than the one we had known. Such tremendous change had taken place that we did not recognize old familiar places. One thing, however, remained unchanged: the government still persisted in trying to stamp out any and all efforts by workers to organize and act independent from government dictates. In 1987 industrial workers throughout the nation had risen up in revolt. The revolt was still going on two years later in 1989 when we visited. During our stay I was able to interview workers, union leaders, managers and government officials about the significance of these labor uprisings. The major content of this book relies upon those interviews, but, of course, I also called upon my earlier experience and my PhD dissertation (1973) from the University of Wisconsin.

Much has been written about south Korea's "economic miracle," and rightly so. The transformation of south Korea in the last three and a half decades has been astounding. While giving full recognition to the economic transformation, in this book I have concentrated on Korea's industrial workers. The very same forces responsible for the economic transformation are also responsible for a subsystem of cruelty that inflicted needless sufferings and indignities upon the working people of the nation.

This book tells the story of the long struggle of Korean workers for human decency and democratic rights. It highlights the revolt which began in the summer of 1987. Within six months thousands of new unions and tens of thousands of workers were organized into a democratic labor movement. From Pusan to Seoul, in large firms and small, Korean workers rebelled against employers and political authorities. Nowhere has the revolt been more desperate and more persistent than in the Hyundai Corporation. Hyundai, known in the West primarily for its automobiles and ship building prowess, is one of a dozen or so huge industrial conglomerates (chaebol) that dominate Korean industry. Such chaebol set the pattern for oppressive control of labor. The depth of worker revolt at Hyundai reflects the magnitude of worker alienation across the country. Over the last three years (1987 – 1990) massive work stoppages, some involving ten to twenty thousand people, have wracked the Hyundai yards in the city of Ulsan. In 1989 and again in the spring of 1990, the government mounted military–like attacks by land, sea and air against the Hyundai workers, but nothing was resolved. Workers remain in bitter defiance of the system.

Worker revolt of this scale reminds one of the uprisings of the Polish workers who initiated the fall of communism and the beginnings of democracy in that country. The significance of the Korean worker revolt might be of a similar calibre. It is a grass–roots spontaneous people's revolt for democracy against a coercive economic–political system. It seeks to transform an authoritarian capitalistic system somewhat as the Polish workers sought to transform an authoritarian communistic system. The big difference is that the Korean workers have revolted against a system that the U.S.A., Japan and the West have established and support, whereas the Polish workers had the good fortune of opposing communism and the U.S.S.R. For the workers of Poland moral and financial support flowed in from the West. Korean workers receive stony silence. Western reports of their struggles for human rights, collective action and democratic participation are colored with adjectives like "radical," "agitator," "extremist," and "communist."

Despite the lack of sympathy from the West, however, the democratic movement in Korea is the most significant break through ever achieved by labor in south Korea and has messages for labor and unions in other capitalistic economies. Just as Solidarity sends a message for democratic values in eastern

Europe, so does the democratic labor movement in Korea witness to a road toward democracy for workers already within the orbit of capitalism. Hopefully this book will help workers and democrats in the West hear and receive the message coming from their brothers and sisters in Korea.

I. INHERITANCE FROM THE PAST

JAPANESE LEGACY

Japanese soldiers guarded every street corner. A corridor of heavily armed guards surrounded Doksu Palace where the King of Korea had residence. Inside the palace, General Terauchi Masatake was forcing the King to proclaim the annexation of Korea by the imperial throne of Japan. This final act of the King did not take long. Terauchi had planned well. Already he had the signature of Korea's Prime Minister, Yi Won-yong. He also had in his hand the royal seal, stolen from the inner-sanctum of the palace. The King registered his objections in a perfunctory way and signed the document.

Terauchi marched out of the palace guarded closely by his soldiers. He had served his emperor well. The Kingdom of Korea had officially become a province of the Japanese empire.

Behind that brief scene of August 22, 1910 lay three decades of humiliation. The French, Americans, English, Germans and Russians each in turn, through military or diplomatic pressures, forced themselves on to a Korea that wanted to stay hidden from sight. It wanted to be the "Hermit Kingdom," as it liked to call itself. The government had tried to fend off the foreigners, but to no avail. Already desperately poor, each effort by the palace to raise funds for defense only impoverished the people more. In the midst of these miseries there arose the rebellion of the Tonghak. Tonghak, or "School of Eastern Wisdom" was a religion and a social movement. It demanded that foreigners be expelled, that taxes be decreased, that land be fairly distributed and the class system abolished.

In response, the Korean government made a serious mistake. To put down the rebellion which covered most of the southwestern province, it called for help from its old friend, China. Japan, fearful of a strong Chinese presence in Korea, rushed its own troops to Korea. It quickly and savagely put down the Tonghak and with the same efficiency drove the Chinese back to their homeland. That was the year of 1895. Thereafter, when the poor of Korea have entered into a struggle for justice, the spirit and the policies of the Tonghak have been evoked.

Ten years after the defeat of China, Japan again exhibited its military prowess. In 1904 they attacked Russia at Port Arthur. Within a year the Russian armies in Manchuria were badly beaten and the Russian fleet was destroyed. The Czar was forced to sue for peace. Russia was removed as an actor on the Korean peninsula.

After the defeat of Russia, the only remaining foreign power that could have possibly challenged Japan was the United States of America. The Americans had "opened up" Japan to westernization when it sent Commodore Matthew

1

Perry and his fleet into Yokohama Bay in 1854. The American fleet continued as a power in the Pacific waters. In addition American missionaries had heavily penetrated Korean society and had been instrumental in developing a close relationship between the royal household and the American government.

Instead of challenging each other, however, the United States and Japan decided on a compromise that benefitted both, but sealed the demise of the Kingdom of Korea. In July of 1905 William Howard Taft (U.S. Secretary of War) and the Japanese Prime Minister, Taro Katsura, met secretly in Tokyo. They signed a treaty in which Japan promised not to interfere in American rule in the Philippines; and the United States recognized Japan's right to rule in Korea.

From that time on Japan took over official control of Korea. For all intents and purposes in 1904, it had militarily occupied Korea when it sent troops northward to engage the Russians. In 1907, at the point of bayonets it had forced the Emperor of Korea to turn over all governmental authority to a Japanese appointed Government-General. The Emperor was forced to abdicate in favor of his son, a mentally retarded young man who could not care for himself. The final scene of humiliation was that of total annexation in 1910.

These historical events are necessary to recount in a book on contemporary organized labor because they have been re-incarnated within today's Korean society. The Tonghak, the "modernization" process instituted by the Japanese takeover, the dominance of foreign powers, and the Taft-Katsura Treaty are all central themes of today's struggles for democracy in South Korea.

Industrialization Begins

The Korea that Japan took over was a society that had changed little over the centuries. There were no big cities, little industry and primitive transportation. Most everyone lived on the farm either as owners of small plots or as share croppers on the lands of large owners. Politically the nation was governed by a King, but in fact his power over the nation was exercised with a light hand and local autonomy was practiced everywhere. Koreans were a people schooled for centuries in the ethics and rituals of Confucianism. Society was structured clearly along class lines. The *yangban* was the ruling class and the *ssangnoms* were the under class, the peasants. Confucian ethics based on the five relationships between ruler and ruled, older and younger, father and son, husband and wife, and friend to friend knit the people together both within and across class lines.

Japan took over Korea primarily for military reasons. By the time it had defeated the Russians in 1905, Japan was already committed to a policy of military expansionism. It saw Korea could not handle the foreign powers and would eventually be taken over by one or the other of them. To forestall that

2

event Japan took action. Its annexation of Korea not only ruled out the threat of a foreign power being close by, more importantly, by controlling Korea it controlled the road to Manchuria with its rich supplies of natural resources.

Once in command, the Japanese military governors of Korea began to modernize the country. Railroads were built, leading northward to Manchuria. Mining industries were opened. World War I opened new markets for Japanese goods. Japanese businesses expanded their plants into Korea. By the war's end they were exporting textiles and chemicals to the combatants' markets.

As Japan organized to invade Manchuria (1931), and China (1937) and the United States (1941), it made increasing demands on the Korean people to join in war production. People were forced from the land to work in Japanese-owned factories. By the late thirties Korean workers under the control of their Japanese masters were producing electrical equipment, machinery, explosives and railroad cars. Korean mines were supplying tungsten, coal, magnesium and gold. Within a matter of three short decades Korea was launched head-first into a militarized industrial society. During those years almost thirty percent of the population moved from the farm to the city. In 1907 there were scarcely 200,000 people in Seoul. When the Japanese left in 1945, the Korean capital had become a metropolis of well over a million. Similar transformations took place in Pusan, Taegu, Inchun, and Kwangju.[1] Total population had grown from about 15 million in 1910 to around 26 million in 1944.[2]

Industrial workers became a distinct class of society. In 1910 industry did not exist. Thirty years later industries of mining, manufacturing, transportation and communication employed about 420,000 workers. Perhaps a quarter of that number were young women and children who labored in the Japanese textile industry.

Japanese companies transferred business to Korea to take advantage of the cheap and docile labor. There was never any labor legislation to protect Korean workers so the employers had a free hand to manage them as they saw fit. If workers became uncooperative, Japanese police were always there to see that the employer's will was obeyed.

The Labor Movement Begins

The stirrings of a labor movement began simultaneously with industrialization. As has happened in so many countries of Asia, the first seeds of socialism and unionism were sown by the colonial power itself. The short lived industrial boom during World War I brought not only Japanese industrialists to Korea but also Japanese workers. These workers, who had been introduced to the ideas and practices of unionism in their home country, frequently protested against their working conditions, and made demands on management. To help enforce their demands they enlisted the support of the

3

Koreans with whom they worked. There was a period during the early twenties when Japanese workers were conspicuous in leading demonstrations and strikes.[3] The authorities soon stepped in. Japanese workers were isolated in their own worker organizations, and given preferential treatment, thus eliminating a possible radical element from among the Korean workers. The Koreans, however, had already learned the lesson. From 1917 to 1928, hundreds of Korean workers became involved in disputes with their employers. The first labor organizations before 1920 were small, local groups that joined together out of idealism, nationalism or a particular grievance. In 1919 "the Labourers' Mutual Relief Association" was formed. It claimed to have a nation-wide membership, but it quickly passed off the scene.

The farmers took the lead in forming the first organization that lasted over a period of time. The Federation of Farmers' Unions of Korea was organized in 1924, and after three years of fair success they were joined by several small industrial unions.[4] The name then became the Korean Federation of Laborers and Farmers. Aside from the farmers, the membership included: transport workers (4,358), cotton cleaners (3,078), printers (4,358), woodworkers (1,354), metal workers (753), leather workers (974), bricklayers (657), rice cleaners (2,584), daily laborers (9,574).[5] Not all industrial workers were affiliated with the Federation, but it was the closest thing to a national union that Korea had seen. It continued in its extra-legal condition until its suppression in the thirties.

In midst of sporadic disputes and chronic tension between employers and workers two strikes occurred in the late twenties that helped create tradition and mystique within the labor movement. The first strike was carried on by workers in the Seoul Electric Power Company. They were one of the first groups to develop a lasting type of unionism. Even today the electrical utilities union is one of the strongest in the country. In 1925 they struck for higher wages, and after only a few days wrested a wage gain from their Japanese employers.

The second strike, however, was neither that short nor that victorious. It took place in the city of Wonsan on the East Coast. It lies in what is now North Korea. In this port city in 1925, the Federation of Labor Unions of Wonsan was organized. It claimed a membership of 1,350, most of whom were dock and transport workers. In 1927, success over a wage dispute so encouraged them that they enlarged their membership and tightened up their organization in case of future need. The need was not long in coming. In September of the next year, 1928, a Japanese foreman beat and flogged a Korean worker. The union seized the opportunity to make demands: the foreman had to be dismissed; workers had to be guaranteed better treatment; and a minimum wage and pension system had to be established. The only alternative was a strike. The Japanese authorities, in order to maintain peace, immediately dismissed the foreman and promised to take the other demands under consideration. In December, the final decision was

4

made. The government accepted all of the workers' demands as just and promised their immediate implementation. But it ordered that negotiations be carried on with each worker individually. There would be no recognition of the union. The ensuing strike lasted from January 14 to April 21. Transport workers in the whole region joined in the strike. Union organizations from all over the country sent aid. A situation where commerce was obstructed and the colonial authority of Japan openly flaunted could not, however, be tolerated. The leaders of the union were jailed and the Federation of Labor Unions of Wonsan was suppressed. The strike was over. All points were lost.[6] Never again under Japanese rule were the Korean workers to rise up in strike as they had done at Wonsan. With the coming of the thirties, war was in the air. Unions no longer were tolerated.

In the anti–Japanese underground, however, industrial workers became an important factor. As their numbers increased, the political left and political right sought dominance within their ranks. The Japanese authorities, ironically, assisted the cause of the communists. They built up the image of the communists by giving them credit for every dispute and every act of disobedience that took place among the workers. Japanese police and secret service intelligence agents were always in search of clandestine worker organizations and were quick to squash any overt action. Regardless of what they turned up or imagined, it was designated as a communist plot. The following account in a 1931 Japanese newspaper gives an idea that agitation among workers was a rather frequent thing. It also credits the communists with initiating the action.

"Frustration of a plot by Korean Communists to declare the independence of the peninsula and establish a proletarian government along the Soviet type was announced by the police July 25 [1931]. Some 300 arrests have been made.....

"Details given out by police authorities indicate that a definite Communist organization had existed in Korea and that it operated extensively under the direction of a committee which, it is alleged, kept its headquarters across the border in Manchuria. This committee is understood to have been affiliated with and to have cooperated with the Chinese Communist Party.

"...Then on May Day of this year, the agitators distributed handbills throughout Korean spinning factories and other centers of labor employment. The police caught some of the handbill distributors and in the course of their investigations immediately obtained clues pointing to the existence of a local headquarters...

"This group apparently set about reorganizing agitators in Korea and had made considerable headway before the most recent raids broke them up again. They sent secret agents throughout the peninsula disguised as laborers and to incite interest in communism and to promote organization of local groups and distributed quantities of literature on the subject."[7]

The Japanese sought to use the fear of communism to bind the Koreans closer to their Japanese masters. The results were, of course, the exact opposite. The prestige of the communists was enhanced so that when liberation finally came, they were known as heroes of the underground.

As the War in the Pacific heated up, the empire called for more and more sacrifice from the industrial workers. The empire's very existence came to depend upon increased output. To help achieve that increase, Japanese employers in Korea instituted the *sampo* system. This was an "industrial patriotism club" in which employees and employer joined together to increase production. Each unit in the firm chose representatives to form a workers' association. The association was given offices inside the plant and provided with funds to carry on program. Full time officers in the association were paid by the company. Together the association and employer established programs of educating the workers, making the production process more efficient and preventing disputes among the workers.

Whether sampo helped the Japanese war effort is uncertain, but one thing is sure: sampo became one of Japan's permanent contributions to Korea's industrial relations system. All subsequent unions have been organized along the sampo pattern. Police-employer collusion and sampo persist as dominant patterns of industrial relations fifty years after political liberation from Japan.

AMERICAN LEGACY

The Japanese surrender to the United States came on August 15, 1945. It was not until 24 days later on September 8 that American troops found their way to Korea. For those twenty-four days the Korean peace-keeping groups maintained law and order in South Korea. In the North, as agreed upon with the United States, the Soviet Union had immediately crossed the border and moved southward to the 38th parallel. They were in a position to occupy the entire peninsula, but refrained from doing so.

The Peoples' Committees

In the South the Japanese waited anxiously for the Americans fearing that Korean revenge for the decades of suffering could explode even without provocation. It never did, however, due in part to the actions of one man, Lyuh Woon Hyung. He was a charismatic leader of great speaking ability and moderate politics. Before the Japanese threw him in jail in 1938, Lyuh had been an editor of a newspaper. He was respected by both communists and the right wingers.

Early in the morning of August 15, 1945, the very day of Japan's capitulation, General Abe Nobuyuki, Japan's Governor-General in Korea, brought Lyuh to his mansion for a talk. Abe agreed to turn over supplies of food, guarantee freedom of the press and not interfere in Korean politics. For his part Lyuh promised to take the initiative to set up political organizations over the country to keep the peace and govern in place of the Japanese. In this way attention was to be deflected from thoughts of revenge against Japanese.

The Japanese freed Lyuh and a cadre of his supporters. Quickly they travelled over each province of the South organizing local committees for self-government. The committees were called "People's Committees" which name unfortunately, both in Korean and English, has a ring of communism about it. Lyuh and friends were tireless. Before the Americans made their appearance, Peoples' Committees were set up in every province and in most cities and towns in the country. The very area of the country, the southwest, that had been the stronghold of the Tonghak (p. 1), now became the major center for the Peoples' Committees. Two days prior to the arrival of the American military, representatives from the Peoples' Committees met in a national convention in Seoul and declared the existence of a government for the entire peninsula. It was called "the Peoples' Republic."

The American military command under General John R. Hodge anchored in Inchun Bay on September 8, 1945. That very day a three-man, English-speaking, delegation from Lyuh Woon Hyung visited the ship to pledge its cooperation with the Americans. Hodge refused to meet with them.

He had been ordered to act as military governor of south Korea until the Americans and the Soviets could reach a permanent arrangement. The People's Committees' claim to be a government and to represent the people of Korea ran counter to Hodge's orders. The curtness and animosity displayed by Hodge and the military rulers of South Korea, however, probably had their origin in a radio-gram received prior to landing in Inchun from the commander of Japanese forces in Korea. It read in part as follows:

"There are communists and independence agitators among Koreans who are plotting to take advantage of the situation to disturb peace and order here."[8]

The radio-gram also warned Hodge that there were "red" labor unions plotting violence. Hodge's refusal to meet Lyuh's party came from a mind already prejudiced against the Koreans. It was ironic that the American "liberators" readily followed the advice of the oppressors. Even more ironic was the decision of the Americans to rely for advice on men like Kim Song Su, a rich land lord, an aristocrat and a collaborator with the Japanese. He reinforced the Japanese general's assertion that communists were about to take over everything. Kim was appointed chair of the advisory group to the U.S. military government. The Peoples' Republic was declared illegal by Hodge and the Peoples' Committees were ordered to disband.

Hodge's refusal to meet with Lyuh was a death sentence for the coalition Lyuh had forged. He and other moderate leaders were put in an impossible position. They could not easily abandon the organizations they had built up through the last months and decades, nor could they very easily repudiate the Americans and continue on the course they had set. The radicals on both sides of the political spectrum now were free to pursue their own course of action. The moderates were trampled by both. On July 19, 1947, Lyuh was assassinated. South Korea plunged into an internal battle of right wing versus the left, with General Hodge, and the American government, giving full support to the right.[9]

Chun Pyung

Shortly after the dissolution of the Peoples' Republic a coalition of workers and communists held a convention in Seoul and organized the "All Korean Labor Council," or Chun Pyung. As they had waited for the Americans during August and September of 1945, workers throughout the country had begun to organize and develop leadership. By the time the Americans were on the scene, many of the businesses abandoned by the Japanese were in the hands of the workers. In some factories the workers appointed their own management and continued production. Chun Pyung was the national federation of these local organizations.

Even though Korea was still a predominantly rural society in 1945, its industrial population was not insignificant. The Japanese had pushed industrialization for almost two decades. The Japanese Government-General reported in 1944 that probably 20 percent of the Korean population, 5 million people, were dependant upon wages earned in mining, manufacturing, communication and commercial enterprises.[10] Chemicals and textile industries were the biggest employers, but companies which produced machinery, electrical equipment, power, transportation and communications all employed large numbers of workers. As the Japanese left, Koreans took over. Sometimes Korean managers who had worked closely with the Japanese assumed control. Sometimes it was Chun Pyung. Chun Pyung was not an ordinary labor union operation. It sought not only worker rights, but also worker control. By 1946 Chun Pyung had established itself in most of the country's industry. Its claim of 574,475 members was an obvious exaggeration, but its claim to represent most of the workers was probably accurate.[11]

Chun Pyung had one great advantage. It could draw upon the tradition and emotions of the underground and the popularity of the Peoples' Committees. For thirty five years Koreans had struggled and suffered to gain independence from Japan. What they got was domination by two even bigger foreign powers. Frustrations were high, and Chun Pyung leaders played on it. They denounced the foreign (American) occupation, pointed to the ideals of the underground, and exalted a future day of true liberation. The people heard their word and responded. Large numbers rallied around Chun Pyung's flag.

But Chun Pyung also had a great disadvantage. It existed under a military government which had radically different ideas for the future and cared nothing for the underground. General Hodge's first offensive against Chun Pyung was to promulgate a set of labor laws. American style conflict resolution through direct collective bargaining between employer and employee was established at the heart of the law. In cases where the two parties could not resolve a dispute, a battery of reconciliation, mediation, and arbitration agencies was established. The eventual undoing of Chun Pyung, however, was the legal requirement that a union had to register with and gain recognition from the government. Only if it registered could a union bargain with an employer, and by definition a union could not be an employer. Non-registered groups that agitated, made demands on the employer or tried to act as employers were in violation of law. For Chun Pyung it was a catch-22. To register and play the game by American rules would be tantamount to accepting Hodge's military government as legitimate. To refuse to register would bring the weight of that same government down on its head. Chun Pyung chose not to register, putting its faith in principles and the allegiance of the workers.

The second tactic used against Chun Pyung was the establishment of an alternative union that would cooperate with the American way of doing things. A first step toward that end took place in a textile mill in Yongdong Po (a section within the city of Seoul). Chun Pyung controlled the workers' organization, but two young men, Kim Ku and Hong Yoon Ok, challenged it on grounds that it was tied to the Communist Party. They organized their own union which they named the General Federation of Korean Labor Unions (known in Korean as *No Chong*), and called upon all non-communists to abandon Chun

Pyung. Two weeks of pitched battle in the factory and throughout the neighborhood followed. Dozens on both sides were seriously injured. The U.S. Army finally stepped in to restore order. Kim Ku, Hong Yoon Ok and their newly formed No Chong gained much attention.

General Hodge, and his chief ally, Syngman Rhee, saw the potential in No Chong. Quickly Rhee-people gained control of No Chong and set off to oust Chun Pyung from its citadels over the country. Their most effective weapon was to operate in accordance with the American laws. This gave them legal sanction and protection. Even in places where Chun Pyung was strong, No Chong could seize the right to bargain with the company by simply persuading a few workers to register with the government as a union.

No Chong had three advantages in its struggle against Chun Pyung: it could count on financial assistance from the management; it could rely on the backing of the police; and if necessary, it could call upon an organized group of thugs to harass or eliminate stubborn opponents. In this way, the same type of power structure, which controlled the working class under the Japanese, wrested control of labor from Chun Pyung in 1945–47.

Railroad Strike of 1946

1946 was the turning point in the fortunes of both Chun Pyung and No Chong. The Korean economy was at a near standstill. The Japanese were gone, but they had owned and controlled everything from the farmlands to the heavy industries. General Hodge's military government had taken all Japanese properties over as a trusteeship, but no one, American or Korean, could make things function in the midst of constant political confusion. In August, 1946, about one year after Hodge's arrival, the Military Government estimated that food costs were one hundred times higher than in pre-war days. Rice was becoming scarce. Wages were at a standstill. The whole American undertaking seemed to be in a state of paralysis.

Railroad workers under the Chun Pyung chose this opportunity for a showdown. Demands were sent to the American authorities for higher wages and rice allotments.[12] General Hodge claims that no "formal" demands were ever presented.[13] Military authorities in their Summation report for September do note, however, that some petitions were received from the railroad workers but they "were not signed."[14] Perhaps Chun Pyung, which scorned American ways, sent their demands by extra-legal channels. Whatever the cause for the breakdown in communication, on September 23, 1946, the railroad workers of Pusan, Korea's second largest city, walked off the job. Chun Pyung called for a nationwide general strike. Through mass action, it hoped to expand its image as a liberation movement and as a defender of the workers' rights.

10

Chemical workers, textile workers, communication workers, along with thousands of students, civilians and farmers joined the railroad union in its protest. At its height some 251,000 workers throughout the country were involved. The center of the strike shifted northward to the railroad and industrial city of Taegu. Police smashed the picket lines and in the ensuing riots three people were killed and many wounded by police gunfire. In retaliation people of Taegu attacked and killed thirty-eight policemen throughout the city.

Martial law was declared and United States' troops were sent to restore order. The American Director of the Department of Transportation described the American military's role in these words: "We went into that situation just like we would go into battle. We were out to break that thing up and we didn't have time to worry too much if a few innocent people got hurt. We set up concentration camps outside of town and held strikers there when the jails got too full. It was war. We recognized it as war. And that is the way we fought it."[15]

Over a thousand were arrested, many were convicted of crimes against the government and sixteen were sentenced to death for their role in the "insurrection."[16] The strike was crushed and order restored. Chun Pyung had suffered a severe defeat. No Chong emerged as the legal union representing the railroad workers. Once the strike had started No Chong moved in and organized a small group of dissidents who claimed they spoke for the rank and file. The Department of Transportation was more than happy to accept that claim. No Chong quickly reached a contract agreement with management, and that contract was declared to be the legal contract covering all railroad employees.

A warrant was issued for the arrest of Pak Heun Yung, the head of the Communist Party and acknowledged leader of Chun Pyung. Pak fled to the North. Ho Hun, the number two man, was arrested, and as noted previously Lyuh Woon Hyung was assassinated. In a matter of a few months the main leadership of Chun Pyung was eliminated.

The final chapter in Chun Pyung's brief life, however, was fittingly enacted among dock workers. Dock workers and stevedores were the center of the great Wonsan strike (p. 4) against the Japanese in 1928. Their position in trade has always given them a lever of power. Realizing this strategic position and popular heritage Chun Pyung had organized the dock workers into a strong, closely knit union. Unlike Chun Pyung strategy in other industries, it had entered into contract with the shipping companies of Pusan, and had actually negotiated settlements in October of 1946 and June, 1947. When, however, No Chong decided to crack this bastion of "communism," it found a legal opening. The contract that Chun Pyung had concluded with the companies had been declared illegal by the Department of Labor, but it had never been renegotiated. Seizing on this, No Chong petitioned the Labor Department for an election to

11

determine the bargaining agent for the dock workers.[17] Shortly before No Chong's call for elections, several of the top Chun Pyung leaders were arrested for complicity in an alleged uprising.[18] Leaderless and unwilling to abide by legal procedures, Chun Pyung lost out. No Chong took over the Pusan docks.

The "communists" were beaten on every front, but in so doing the rightist politicians and union leaders created for themselves habits and patterns of action that were to plague Korean society for decades to come. The ghost of Japanese labor regulation by police was re–incarnated; the use of goons to persuade workers of the "right way" became systemized, and manipulation of legal interpretation to favor government became standard action.

Syngman Rhee

No Chong now became the mainstream of Korean labor. A political ally of Syngman Rhee, Chun Chin Han, shouldered aside the original leaders of No Chong and took over control. With the help of the Americans, Rhee had succeeded in gaining political control of the South. His men were advisors to the military government. He held the loyalty of the former collaborators with Japan who now became the property–class of Korea; he controlled the police and with Chun Chin Han's help he captured the remains of the underground labor movement. By the end of 1947 Syngman Rhee was in full command.

The defeat of the left, however, was never complete in Syngman Rhee's mind. Partly from the realities of Northern militancy, partly from his own paranoia and partly from pure chicanery, he kept the fear of the "Red" underground alive. As the Japanese had done before him, each unwanted event was credited to the communists. The cry of "Communism!" became his most used strategy for stifling opposition. That legacy too was passed on to subsequent dictators.

To help him control the "communists" remaining in labor, Rhee integrated No Chong into the very structures of his own political party which later on became known by the misnomer, the "Liberal Party." No Chong became one of five social organizations within the party.[19] Three of the executive members of the No Chong (from here on referred to as the Federation of Korean Trade Unions [FKTU]) were included on the Central Committee of the Party. Within the government itself, labor matters were subsumed under the Department of Health and Social Affairs, and conveniently enough the head of the Department for the first five years was Chun Chin Han, president of the FKTU.

The FKTU remained as an arm of Rhee's party until his ouster in 1960. During that fourteen year period Korea suffered the calamity of a war and spent nearly a decade trying to get back on its feet. Little was heard from labor unions during those years. Except as a messenger for Rhee, they made no noticeable contribution.

12

Organized labor carried heavy shackles as it moved into the 1960's. Internally it continued to be organized and related to the employer under the sampo system of the Japanese. Legally it was wrapped around by American style labor laws re-issued by Rhee in 1953, the chief intent of which was to bottle up labor grievances in endless legal manipulations. Politically it was in captivity. Rhee domesticated it within his party, but never hesitated to send the police or the thugs against workers if they became obstreperous, or gave him cause to think there was a Red among them.

Student demonstrations drove Syngman Rhee from power in April of 1960. The FKTU had nothing to do with his downfall. It had been used by Rhee in demonstrations supporting him, but it never acted against him. Within the unions there were those who opposed control by the politicians but all too often they were compromised by financial and political dealings with Liberal Party leaders. Union support among the rank and file was minimal.

One day before Rhee announced his resignation, an anti-Rhee faction took control of the union and proclaimed itself independent of all political parties. Rhee men were expelled at the national and local levels. Recriminations and charges of corruption were hurled back and forth. New unions sprang up dedicated to "purifying" the corruption that had become so endemic. Labor disputes, demonstrations and strikes erupted everywhere. The content of the labor demands, however, merely reflected the popular sentiments of the day: punish the corrupt politicians! Give us a better living now! Union leadership, and rank and file, had had no experience in the responsible formulation of policy relative to the economy so they frittered away their opportunity by shouting slogans and making allegations.

The government that took over from Rhee could never get its act together; nor could it secure the consent of the governed. For about a year it blundered along in near chaos. Claiming that North Korea was about to attack because of the social disorder in the South, on May 16, 1961, the military took over government and has ruled South Korea ever since.

A PROMISING INTERVAL

Early in the morning of May 16, 1961 with only a few gun shots and no loss of life, the military seized power in South Korea. People were frightened. The Korean military had seldom been a main actor in Korean politics. No one knew what to expect. There were rumors that the leader of the coup was a communist. General Pak Chung Hee had indeed been part of a leftist uprising in a southern province in 1948. He had been captured and almost executed. His life, so the story goes, was saved at the last moment by an American colonel.

13

Economic Planning and Democracy

His brush with death apparently converted him away from any communist inclinations for one of his first acts after assuming control was to establish an Economic Planning Board that would guide the nation down the path of capitalism. He and his cohorts brought to the task of government a store of managerial skills. They looked upon poverty as an enemy to overcome. Their military minds were practiced in making plans and setting up strategies to defeat an enemy. Pak Chung Hee transferred that approach to the sphere of economics with amazing success. At the same time that he established the Economic Planning Board, he also ordered it to produce a five year plan that would begin the process of overcoming Korea's poverty.

A systematic approach to the nation's worst problem paid dividends from the very beginning. Each year the GNP grew by 8.6 percent; during the decade (1963–72) per capita income expanded from $80 to $225; unemployment steadily declined; and the other economic indices all marched steadily upward. A change in attitude was perceivable even among the people. Where Koreans once were highly critical of their own country and the goods they made, a new pride was born and self–effacement became less of a habit.

The biggest change brought on by the military, however, was in the field of politics. Much to everyone's surprise Pak Chung Hee promulgated a constitution that established a progressive, participative form of government. Citizens were given the right to choose by free vote a president and a parliament. Basic human and civil rights were protected. The young generals and colonels were oriented to the future and echoed the cry of the people for freedom. Many of them had high ideals. Their revolution was to eliminate the corruption of the past, to establish a new society and create better human beings. "...it is our cardinal belief and conviction that economic development and progress is possible only with democratic freedom and initiative," wrote Pak Chung Hee in early 1962.[20] In 1963, under his new constitution Pak campaigned for the presidency. The author heard one of his speeches as he spoke to the people of Inchun. It was impressive. He spoke of pride in one's country and one's self. He spoke of how everyone had to work together. They must build their nation and be dependent upon no one. Though he was not a great speaker, his ideas were on target. For the next eight years Pak and the military acted as though they believed that democratic processes went hand in hand with economic growth.

Rights of Labor

The new administration also meant good news for labor. The new constitution guaranteed the right of workers to organize, bargain collectively and take collective action.

Under Rhee unions had been restricted to the workplace where the employer could easily control them. Pak Chung Hee changed that. Local unions at the place of work would remain, but each local now had to belong to one of seventeen nationwide industrial federations. Textile workers, for instance, were all organized into one nationwide textile workers' union. So were the metal workers, chemical workers, transportation workers and all the rest. Each local or regional union had to belong to the appropriate national union. Registration of a local with the Office of Labor Affairs (OLA) required the signature of the president of the National and in times of collective bargaining at the local level the national headquarters could join in the process.

As each local was required to be part of an industrial federation, so each federation was required to join one national confederation called the Federation of Korean Trade Unions (FKTU). Only one confederation was permitted.

Some say the new structure was really a subterfuge. Rationalizing it in this manner made labor easier to control. Toward the end of the decade and in the years after 1971, that certainly was the case, but in the earlier days, that downward control was not nearly as severe. Others saw the new structures as a move to provide economic planning with labor structures that could grow in a complementary and supportive fashion. In preparation for the second five-year (1967–71) plan, the government's Office of Labor Affairs published a book entitled *Nodong Saop Ohnyun Kyewhek* ("Labor and the 5–Year Plan"). The book reflects a belief that there is a positive correlation between union organizing and economic development. It expresses the government's intention of supporting labor union organization. One paragraph reads as follows:

"In 1960 36.7% of German workers were organized. In Japan it was 36.1%. But in Korea only 6.5% of the nation's 5,176,000 workers are organized. In the future, the path of the developed countries must be followed and more unions organized."[21]

The practice of collective bargaining was also an essential part of the labor–management scene. There was almost no experience to build upon. Nevertheless, its practice was begun and by the end of the period many gains had been made. The actual bargaining process settled down into three patterns depending upon the type of industry. Eight of the industrial unions bargained at the national level. With the exception of the textile workers the employer in each case was the Korean government or the U. S. Army. Railroad Workers, Electrical Workers, Communication Workers, Bank and Financial Workers, Union of Monopoly Workers, Foreign Organization (U. S. Army) Employees' Union, and the Seafarers' Union. These eight accounted for 49 percent of organized workers in 1969.

Three unions bargained on a regional basis because of the type of industry: automobile workers (in the sixties this referred primarily to drivers and helpers on buses and taxes), transport workers and dock workers. The remaining unions bargained locally with management in one enterprise. Local bargaining was practiced in businesses that collectively employed about 30 percent of the organized work force.

Though the units for bargaining were different, the process was the same. Unions had to register with the government to gain recognition. Disputes also had to be registered. For twenty days after registration, there was a cooling–off period during which the government's tripartite services of the National Labor Disputes Mediation Committee were made available. Strikes were legal if no solution could be found in twenty days, and if the government did not declare the industry to be one vital to national security.

Collective bargaining was always a touch and go business. There were no precedents to follow. New patterns had to be devised. Nevertheless, collective bargaining did occur and with some regularity in many places. The law required that each work unit have a Joint Labor–Management Council for bargaining purposes.

Wages were the major item of concern for most unions. The government intended to have the Joint Council in all the large firms. That never was achieved, but in 1965, for example, the Office of Labor Affairs reported that there were unions organized in 892 work places. Of these, 664 had concluded collective contracts and two thirds of those contracts were agreed to in the context of Joint Councils.[22] The FKTU reports that by 1969, 435,296 workers had joined unions and 320,371, or 73.6 percent worked under a collective contract.[23]

During the 1960's the author worked in the city of Inchun with a church ministry called Urban Industrial Mission. Each year we would hold two or three education programs for local union leaders. There would be classes on labor law, union organization and administration, collective bargaining and what to do in case of a dispute. Most of the participants were men and women coming into the labor movement for the first time. The hardships of their own lives evoked a demand for collective action. They brought with them a sense of dedication. Leadership material was not wanting –– only experience and time, and even in the brief period of five or six years one could see new leadership taking hold. When in the 1970's the government turned to dictatorship, many of these same dedicated people were forced out of the labor movement.

Conflict Resolution
The 1960's also witnessed a decided improvement in the way labor-management conflict was resolved. The system of conflict resolution was

cumbersome, but all sides actually tried to make it work. The law required a twenty day prior notice of intent to strike. During the cooling-off period both sides were required to make efforts at reaching a solution. Government mediation services could be called in if needed. In 1965 there were 97 disputes registered with the Office of Labor Affairs. These disputes involved 88,496 workers. Four years later the number of disputes had risen to 112 with more than 205,000 taking part.[24] The numbers are not large, but considering the background and the brief period in which workers were permitted to initiate a dispute, they are an indication of a new consciousness and a new behavior.

Strikes as a result of a dispute were rare. In 1968 when there were the 112 registered disputes only 16 of them ended in strike action. The average length of a strike was three to four days. Only ninety five work days were lost because of the 16 strikes. Sixty of those days were lost in the metals industry.[25]

It is not the frequency of conflict that is important. It is the fact that open conflict was allowed, and to some degree recognized as an inherent part of the process. This pattern, unfortunately, did not last very long. The dictators who took over in the 1970's had no tolerance for conflict. Their's was a system of command and obedience.

One example of a dispute toward the end of the 1960's illustrates how labor conflict was handled. While most strikes went no more than a few days, the case of Chosun Kongsa in Pusan lasted forty days. Because it was so long it gives a good introduction to the many facets of conflict and conflict resolution as practiced in the 1960's.

Chosun Kongsa built and repaired ships. It had been a nationalized industry, but in 1968 was turned over to a private owner. Almost immediately tension arose between the new owner and the union. The company dismissed a number of temporary workers. Since some of them had been employed at the company for quite a while, the union demanded severance pay for them. It also took the opportunity to demand a hefty pay hike of almost 60 percent. The Joint Council met thirteen times and the union president made repeated visits to the company president, but to no avail. On July 2, 1969, the union filed an official dispute with the Pusan City Labor Committee. Five days later, according to law, the labor committee responded that the union could begin a dispute. Immediately a twenty-day cooling-off period went into effect.

On July 25, the union was legally permitted to begin its strike. A previous vote by the workers had given an overwhelming 98.4 percent support to the union's stand, but as is usual, a strike was not entered into immediately. On July 18, the Pusan City Labor Committee performed its function as a mediator. A mediation committee was formed according to Chapter IV of the Labor Disputes Adjustment Law, and the two parties, along with the mediation committee, met in the offices of the city Labor Committee. All attempts at reaching settlement,

17

however, failed. The company president had left for the United States on July 17 in the middle of the cooling-off period and did not return until the strike was well underway, thus making any serious attempts at mediation all but impossible. The president retained full decision-making power on matters of wages and working conditions. Frustrated, but still attempting to arrive at an agreement, the company and union opened an eleventh-hour meeting of the Joint Labor-Management Council. The company expressed its willingness to compromise and offered a wage increase of 20-25 percent. The union, however, contended that the offer was inadequate and the meeting broke up in failure. Strike action was the only route left.

The strike began on August 1. Each worker was assigned one or the other of two twelve-hour shifts so that the shipyards were constantly occupied by five to six hundred men. At first, the days passed rather uneventfully, but then, on August 19, the company proclaimed a lockout and simultaneously began legal action against seventy of the union members for unlawfully occupying company property.

The strike had begun on August 1, but the company had not paid the strikers their July wages. After a month, the workers were without money and were in desperate need, but the company contended that the strike had created such chaos that it could not accurately and safely dispense the July wages. On August 31, the company distributed the following announcement to the workers:

> With regard to the workers' wages for July, because the union has carried out strike action which has included both permanent and temporary workers, it has become impossible to calculate or pay July salaries.

> If for the next five days there is no strike and the offices and factory are completely vacated, July wages will be paid on September 6. But if there is even one person left, then the company cannot consider the atmosphere appropriate for figuring or paying of wages.

> Let the union and workers' families understand that we are seeking a way to pay the wages for July and cooperate.

The union, however, responded not by withdrawing but by calling out the wives and children of its members to demonstrate in front of the company's office. For three days the families congregated, carrying placards and yelling demands for the wages. The company declared its intentions of paying the salaries on September 6, and so for several days the families did not appear, but when the 6th came and went without the wages being paid, the demonstrations began again. This time they were more vociferous, with several company men being pushed and hit as they tried to get into the office building. Some of the women were arrested. For two days the families marched, yelled, and demonstrated.

The demonstrations had, however, also broken the solidarity of the union. On the 6th, the last day of the demonstrations, 187 office workers and skilled operators published in the local newspapers their withdrawal from the union. They gave two reasons: for the sake of the country the workers had to complete contracts for twenty ships ordered by Taiwan; and, second, the union, they said, was a form of despotic leadership that their consciences could not follow. The defection of the white collar employees created dissension among the workers and split the union. The leader of the defecting group was a vice president of the union, himself a white collar employee. The union's executive committee, which heretofore had operated in solidarity, was now shattered with strife.

On September 18 the government stepped in. The strike was declared detrimental to national security and therefore illegal. The union president and eleven other officers were arrested and charged with violence, sabotage and incitement to riot. The lock-out ended. The workers went back to work. A wage increase of nearly 15 percent was granted.

The Chosun Kongsa case illustrates the government's philosophy of labor-management relations. The union and company were free to bargain and resolve their differences, but the government always retained the right to impose a settlement when it felt it was necessary to do so. Under this system, Korea experienced a rapid increase in the number of union members, a very low rate of work stoppages, and a rate of economic growth that was the envy of other poor nations of the world.

The re-structuring of unions along national-industrial lines, the practice of collective bargaining and the tolerance of some open conflict were on the whole positive contributions by the government of Pak Chung Hee in the 1960's. To some degree the struggles of labor in the 1970's and 80's have been an effort to return to those three fundamentals.

The Korean Worker

For the Korean worker in the 1960's the situation was grim. $80-$225 per capita national income equals misery for most everyone. Workers lived in overcrowded sections of town near the factory in which they worked. Houses were but shacks made of mud and straw, with perhaps two nine by nine rooms and a dingy, outside kitchen. Winding, narrow paths connected house to house and the neighborhood to the outside world. No roads. No playgrounds. Sewage and drainage were primitive. The average worker cared for a family of three or four children and perhaps a mother or father. While young women were hired by textile, plastics, or electronics industries, they lost their jobs once they married. The husbands were considered the bread winners, but desperation drove many a wife out to the market place to sell fruits, vegetables, shoes or other merchandise. The husband was away working in the factory most of the time. It was not unusual for him to work six or seven days a week, ten or twelve hours a day. By the time he finished work, shared a cup of *makkoli* (a cheap Korean rice wine) with his comrades and walked home, he had little energy left. He ate, slept, woke up and started over again.

At the job, life was no better. The supervisor was on his back constantly. The job was physical, even if he ran a machine. His body ached constantly. Safety provisions did not exist. Management, though often well intended, made many mistakes in the production process which were seldom admitted by those responsible. The workers bore the blame and the penalties. For the opportunity to labor and put up with all this, the average worker by 1969 received a monthly wage of $50–$70. If, however, he happened to be a temporary worker, as about twenty five percent of all employees were, that amount would be more like $35–$50 a month, enough only to keep one alive if no illness or emergency arrived. Most everyone was in debt to someone else. They had to borrow to meet emergencies or to send their children to school.

About thirty percent of employed work force in the 1960's (194,000 in 1963 and 466,000 in 1971) were young women, aged 14 to 24. They came from the countryside either by their own initiative or by the persuasion of company recruiters. They were housed in company dormitories where their every move was supervised, or they lived in small one room huts where they slept in shifts, night shift girls sleeping in the room during the day and day shift girls using it at night. In textiles, in plastics, pharmaceuticals or electronics their work was always demanding, and required long hours. Though some of the better places allowed one day off a week, most gave only two days off a month. The women suffered sexual harassment from their male supervisors, and the humiliation of "low talk" in every communication from management.

Towards the end of the decade foreign firms entered Korea. Many American and Japanese companies took advantage of the government's new policy of industrial estates and set up production in Korea. The low tax rates and the low cost of industrious labor made it well worth their while. Wages, of course, differed with different industries and firms, but they were all uniformly low, bordering on a subsistence level.

Negative Inheritances
The numbers of workers in mining and manufacturing increased from 689,000 in 1963 to about 1,400,000 by 1971. They were quite aware of the poverty and oppressiveness under which they lived, and they were often quite

bitter. Korean workers of the decade were persons with an elementary or middle school education, though many had finished high school. They were intelligent and well informed about their own society and about foreign places. They knew their productivity was soaring, but they saw little improvement either in their income or in the way management treated them. Workers saw a few members of society, namely high military people and company owners, driving large cars, living in luxurious mansions and sending their children abroad to school. Workers in Korean industry during the 1960's were keenly aware that a small minority was gaining exorbitant wealth while they were asked to sacrifice for the good of the nation. A story illustrates the point.

It is often the practice of company presidents to visit one of their factories, gather all the employees together and exhort them to make greater efforts. In one instance the company president had just returned from the United States where he had completed a deal to export some of the company's products to America. He spoke to the workers in this vein: "I was able to secure this contract with the American firm only because our products are cheap. And our products are cheap only because of your hard work and low wages. You are the true builders of our nation, the true patriots." Then he stepped down from the podium, got into a big black car and drove away. The response of one of the workers who was listening to the speech was, "You son of a dog. You and your car! I can't eat patriotism. "

Observation and discussion with workers over a decade would indicate that this one man's bitterness represents the emotions of a large number of Korea's industrial work force. As the years of economic progress wore on, the bitterness grew worse. An increasing tension between employer and employee along class lines was one of the negative legacies of the 1960's.

The other negatives of the period were inheritances from the Japanese that the 1960's passed unchanged on to the next generations. Compared with the 1970's or 1980's, police brutality was an uncommon occurrence. Yet the police still were retained as the chief agency regulating labor. They kept the accounts on unionists; they made regular trips to union halls; they coordinated their every act with the companies; and when the time came, they were there to arrest and inflict damage or to call "communist." These roles of witness, judge and executioner never seemed to be questioned.

A third negative that passed on into the seventies, and perhaps only now in the eighties is beginning to be changed, is the system of sampo. Sampo was the patriotic organization established by the Japanese back in the early forties. After liberation, the patriotic groups ceased to exist, but when it came time to organize unions, the pattern of those patriotic groups was resurrected. Four major ingredients characterize the system.

Union officers at local, regional, federation and confederation levels are paid by the company; union offices, furnitures and utilities are all provided by the company; management has easy access to and perhaps even membership in the union; and decision–making authority in the union is regularly exercised by the president of the union with little or no reference to the workers. The system originally was intended as a support for the company as it produced Japanese war goods. The Japanese, of course, have been removed, but the rest of the system remains.

Sampo provides a familiar vehicle for relating union to company and union to workers, but it is not a vehicle upon which collective bargaining between equals can be established. It is based on a class philosophy. In the industrial relationship employers assumed the role of the superior and the workers were forced to accept the role of the inferior. It was not uncommon to see employees enter the office of the company president on New Year's Day to pay him homage. Three times they would bow before him and wish him health and prosperity. This relationship put the worker at a psychological and moral disadvantage in the practice of collective bargaining.

This same mentality tended to define the internal operations of the union as well. The one elected as president of the local union, the national federation or the FKTU tended to think of himself as the superior and assume that those of lower rank were subordinate. Instead of solidarity, the result was factionalism.

The End of a Democracy

While conflict between democracy and authoritarianism never seems to end in South Korea, during the exciting days of the 1960's, it looked as though democracy and economic planning might actually work together. Such an alliance, if it had been allowed to grow, might have become strong enough to free Korea from its twentieth century legacy of authoritarianism. But such was not to be the case. New factors were inserted into the equation, chief of which was Pak Chung Hee's unwillingness to give up power. After two terms as president (1963–71), he had nowhere to go. In 1969, he forced through the national assembly, just as Syngman Rhee had done a decade before him, an amendment to the constitution allowing him to run again. His third campaign in 1971 was a disaster for him. His opponent, Kim Dae Jung, predicted Pak would become a military dictator like Chiang Kai Shek in Taiwan unless he were defeated in the elections. The people were persuaded. They wanted no dictator and had no desire to relive the later years of Syngman Rhee. Pak was forced to use chicanery, bribery and threats. He won the election by four percentage points, but he lost the respect of his people, a respect that he had built up slowly during his previous eight years. Towards the end of 1971, Pak decided he was done with democracy and its restrictions. He declared a fictitious national emergency and suspended the constitution. At gun point he set himself up as dictator for life. Once that was done, the police and the Korean Central Intelligence Agency (KCIA) were loosed on society. Unions became a chief target for red–baiters. In every dispute and conflict, the police reported the specter of communism. The democratic promises of the 1960's had been an unexpected gift from the military. Now they were taken back. The old authoritarianism, enforced by modern techniques, was re–instated.

The ideology of the economic developmentalists also worked toward the demise of democracy and labor unions. As Korea moved successfully through its first and second five year plans, increasingly demands were made for more control over all the variables. Every nerve was to be stretched to reach the export quotas, to expand investments, increase productivity and decrease costs. Criticisms from politicians, media and labor were identified as obstructions to development. According to the theoreticians and business interests, labor unions were obstacles to the accumulation of capital needed to speed up investment and development. During the 1960's the economic development ideologues were overruled by the military's flirting with democracy. When that flirtation came to an end, the developmentalists and the military found they had much in common.

Foreign Investors

Another factor that contributed to the re–instatement of authoritarianism was the behavior of foreign investors. Korea's economic plans depended on foreign financing. Towards the end of the decade, first American and then Japanese private capital began to flow into the country. Unfortunately the Korean government, the American Chamber of Commerce and Forbes magazine, among others, advertised Korea as a great place to do business because labor "cheerfully" worked 60 hours a week for very low pay. After 1971 a union–free climate was also included in the advertisements. When, however, the foreigner set up his business and began production, he would often find that though the workers were indeed energetic and productive, they tended not to be as docile as the foreigner would have liked. Korean workers, men and women alike, often protested grievances and personal affronts.

When this happened, the unsuspecting foreigner felt as if he had been misled, even betrayed. Petition and complaint were sent to the Korean government, even to the President himself. The complaints eventually paid off. On New Year's day, 1971, a new law was promulgated. It was called the "Special Law on Trade Union and Mediation of Labor Disputes in Enterprises Invested by Foreigners." The new law placed heavy restrictions on union organizing in foreign invested firms. Several foreign companies can claim credit for this law, but one small firm from the state of Illinois had a central role.

The OAK Electronetics Corporation operated in the Inchun area. It employed about 300 women, most of whom had recently come from the country. The average wage at Oak in 1968 was about seventeen dollars a week, low even by Korean standards. The American sent over to manage the plant apparently had little understanding of his workers, and he immediately established for himself the image of a tyrant. And as foreign companies frequently do, OAK put a Korean man in charge of personnel relations who followed the authoritarian pattern set by the American manager. The result was tension and bitterness among the employees. Into this situation came the Metal Workers' Union.

Under the leadership of several men and women inside the shop, a local of the Metal Workers' Unions was organized. The company refused to recognize the union. Instead it dismissed the man who had been elected as the union president, Kang Chang Il, charging that he had used fifty sheets of company paper, worth some twenty cents, for his own personal purposes. The union countered by registering a dispute with the government's Office of Labor Affairs, and waiting out the cooling off period as the law required. Three days before the end of the cooling off period, after the company manager refused all attempts at negotiations, the home office, located in northern Illinois, decided to send a troubleshooter named Bradshaw over to Korea.

The union meeting with Bradshaw took place in the morning of October 23. He apparently wanted a quick solution to the problem. He admitted past managerial mistakes and on the spot reinstated Kang, with back pay for time lost. The union had a strike deadline for the next day and so put on pressure for an immediate solution not only to Kang's problem but also the wage increase demand and the signing of a collective contract. Bradshaw pleaded that he needed more time. The proposed contract had not been translated into English. Bradshaw had shown good faith in reinstating Kang, and his attitude was one of friendly cooperation, so the union agreed to postpone the strike for a week. Nevertheless, there was much to do and negotiate, so the union suggested a meeting for the next day. Bradshaw not only agreed, but suggested that the meeting be held in the union's offices in Seoul. This may have been the first time in Korean history that an employer was willing to go to the union's offices for anything. The union men were encouraged.

By the next afternoon Bradshaw's attitude had changed. With cool curtness he announced that the company had decided to close up operations in Korea. Production costs, he said, were too high and under those conditions the company would invest no more. Bradshaw never sat down. He gave his brief homily and abruptly left. That was the last the union saw of him.

It was not, however, the last they heard from him. The company kept its word and pulled out. The obvious reason for the withdrawal was a case of bad management, but to cover its path, the company blamed the unions, claiming that the big reasons for its pullout were high wages and irresponsible unions. Several international publications quoted Bradshaw's attacks on the unions. Why Bradshaw had such an over-night change of mind and why he attacked the union has never been explained, but one thing for certain is that he and his company, in complete disregard of Korean law, had never entered into negotiations with the union. He could have controlled his labor costs by the very common method of negotiating them with the union.

The company's attacks weakened the government's biggest selling point to foreign capital, namely low wages and docile workers. The company's anti-union blasts had considerable influence on government policy. Within a few months the new law that strictly regulated the operation of unions in foreign invested firms were promulgated by the Korean government.

Foreign firms tend to have the same authoritarian attitude toward labor as do Korean businesses, but the foreigners are in a position to exert even greater political pressure because they control the capital and technology that Korea needs for its economic development. The human rights of the workers, as well as their legal rights to organize and act collectively, are crushed under the arrogance of foreign and domestic capital.

And so the 1960's which began with the overthrow of a dictator, ended by ushering in another. In between Koreans had a taste of democracy the memory of which the military rulers of the next decade and a half tried to erase but never quite succeeded.

CHAPTER NOTES

1. George McCune, <u>Korea Today</u>, Harvard Press, 1950, p. 327.

2. <u>Ibid.</u>, p. 322.

3. Ta Chen, "Labor Situation in Korea," <u>Monthly Labor Review</u>, XXXI (November, 1930), p. 33.

4. Ta Chen, <u>Monthly Labor Review</u>, XXXI, p .32.

5. Asagiri, "Korean Labor Movement," <u>The Labour Monthly</u>, XI, September, 1929, p. 568.

6. Ta Chen, <u>Monthly Labor Review</u>, XXXI, pp. 32-34.

7. <u>Trans-Pacific</u> (Tokyo), "300 Koreans Taken by Police in Raids," July 30, 1931, p. 7.

8. Bruce Cumings, <u>The Origins of the Korean War</u>, Princeton University Press, 1981, p. 127.

9. For further coverage see Henderson, Gregory, <u>Politics of the Vortex</u>, Harvard Press, 1968.

10. Stewart Meacham, <u>Korean Labor Report</u>, November, 1947, p. 2.

11. Stanley Earl, "Report on Korean Labor," Seoul, 1950, p. 4.

12. Richard E. Lauterbach, <u>Danger from the East</u>, Harper and Brothers, 1947, p. 238.

13. Commander-in-Chief United States Army Forces, Pacific, <u>Summation of U.S. Army Military Government Activities in Korea II</u>, 1976, No. 12, p. 12-14.

14. <u>Ibid.</u>, 40.

15. Stewart Meacham, "Korean Labor Report," Seoul, 1947, p. 34.

16. Lauterbach, <u>Danger From the East</u>, p. 239.

17. United States Army Military Government in Korea, <u>South Korean Interim Government Activities</u>, (4 Vols.; Seoul: National Economic Board, October, 1947-December, 1948), I. Nos. 25, p. 76. Hereafter this work will be referred to as <u>Interim Government</u>.

18. Interim Government, I, No. 26, p. 86.

19. United States Department of Labor, The Labor Situation in South Korea, p. 4.

20. Chung Hi Pak, Our Nation's Path, Donga Publishing Company, Seoul, 1962, p. 4.

21. Nodong Jo'ng (Office of Labor Affairs), Nodong Sao'b Onyu'n Kyeihweik, (Labor and the Five Year Plan, 1967–71), 1966, p. 68.

22. Ibid., p. 68.

23. "Nodong Siltae Kaeju'ng" (The Reform of Labor Conditions), Donga Ilbo, May 21, 1970, p. 3.

24. Office of Labor Affairs, Hyun Whang (Present Conditions), Seoul, 1970, p. 17.

25. Han'guk Nodong Chong Yu'nmaeng (Federation of Korean Trade Unions) Sao'b Bogoso' (Activities Report), 1969, p. 92.

II. ECONOMIC INNOVATORS

Within twenty-five short years Korea has been economically transformed. In 1961 the output of the nation stood at a poverty level of $2.1 billion, just about where it had been before the war in 1950. Twenty five years later that figure had become $95.1 billion, and in 1987 GNP surpassed the $100 billion mark. In the early 1960's 75 percent of the nation's households were still in rural settings. In 1989 all but twenty five percent had moved off the farms into the cities. Korea's industries now take great pride in their exports of ships, electronics, and automobiles. Twenty five years ago the major exports were textiles, plywood and wigs. It took an hour and a half to drive over bumpy, pitted roads from Seoul to Inchun. Today the same distance is traversed by comfortable rapid transit in thirty minutes. The speed of economic achievements of South Korea is perhaps without parallel in human history.

In 1963 that which was started by the Japanese was pushed full throttle. South Korea decided to go on the fast track toward "modernization," and compete with the big economic powers of U.S. and Europe. From dire poverty in 1960 it became the world's tenth largest economy by 1987.

How did such a wondrous thing occur? Part of it has to do with the nature of the people themselves. Koreans seem to be innately tough, energetic and intelligent. A personal experience is illustrative. In 1954 right after the war the author lived in Korea. At times I rode a bus from the city of Taejon to the little village of Kongju. The bus was put together from parts of discarded military vehicles and its body was forged from fifty-gallon fuel drums. The road took us through two rivers. The bridges had been blown out during the war. One day as the bus was lurching its way through the rocky bed of the river, I noticed there in the middle of one concrete slab of the ruined bridge sat a man cross-legged with a hammer and chisel. He was chiseling away at what was left of the bridge. Several weeks later when I passed by that way the slab was gone and a bee hive of people were clearing up the rest. A year later a new bridge took the place of the former debris.

The argument from national character aside, the success of Korea's march to modernization is best accounted for by five innovating actors. These five have complemented each other in such a way that in the twenty five years from 1963, to the present, the Korean economy has experienced an unbroken process of expansion. Five innovating factors are given credit for this success: a strong centralized government, a system of centralized economic planning, a generous supply of foreign investments, a model of export development and a small number of huge conglomerates called *chaebol*.

After his seizure of power in 1961, Pak Chung Hee gradually assembled this impressive caste of innovators. It was a success from the beginning and

29

regardless of the political twists and turns since then, the economy has continued to expand. The only real dispute about the innovators has been whether or not it was necessary to change the strong central government system of the 1960's into the oppressive military dictatorship of the 1970's. The system of the 1960's gave every indication of being able to carry the burden of both economic growth and democratic political-social participation. Pak, when he brushed the democratic political processes aside and established the dictatorship in 1971, could give no persuasive argument as to why it was necessary. He resorted to the old excuse of saving the country from communism, though there was no sign of any new communist threat. The forced interjection of the military dictatorship was a consequence of his own political ambitions and those of the military clique behind him, rather than any economic necessity.

However, the entire responsibility for setting up the dictatorship should not go to Pak Chung Hee alone. The ideology of the economic developmentalists which calls for a strong central government coincides very closely with the military thinking of Pak. In this ideology, a military dictator is just as acceptable as a strong democratic government. Under the subterfuge of "value free" economic development, the developmentalists were not disturbed when their political partner became a dictator. Those in the economic world like the *chaebol* who interpret life in terms of profits and anti-communism also welcomed the military. Nor were the foreign investors opposed to the dictator taking over. Their concern was with making a profit. If the military could make that more probable, then the military was to be accepted. The foreigners could justify their faithful cooperation with a dictator by quoting the old cliche about staying out of politics. So when Pak Chung Hee decided to throw out the strong central government of the 1960's and replace it with a military dictatorship, he found that he had many allies willing and ready to join him.

As the innovators accepted the military dictatorship, they unfortunately also accepted a military mentality. They set themselves up as generals arrayed in battle against their own people and especially against the workers in the factories who ultimately are the producers of wealth. In theory the innovators' system was well integrated; in results it was unsurpassed. But because it limited itself to a narrow, military mentality, it had to have an enemy to overcome. They identified the workers as that enemy. The innovators could never conceive of the workers as partners or equals. Thus were produced the tragedies that populate the history of South Korea from 1971 to the present day.

This chapter introduces the innovators and describes their chief characteristics and achievements. Chapter III follows with a discussion of the innovators' labor policy and the mechanisms used to enforce that policy.

30

MILITARY DICTATORSHIP

General Pak Chung Hee marched into Seoul on the night of May 16, 1961 with no opposition other than a few random shots that hit no one. People were frightened and anxious. Rumors about the new leader were rampant. Some thought he was a communist in disguise. Others figured he was a temporary military adventurist. Most everyone agreed that the military was not to be trusted. In Korean history, though there were examples of military seizure of power, professional military people were never high in social status, nor were they maintained for long in places of statesmanship.

Pak Chung Hee, however, proved at least in part, to be a different breed. He was a graduate of the Japanese Manchu Kuo Military Academy in 1940. He also served a decade or so under the American military. With such a background, it has been argued that Pak and a few of his comrades in arms, possessed the best management and administrative skills in the country. As a military commander, he gave orders and people obeyed. He knew how to analyze a military objective, seek out its weak points and marshall his resources to achieve his goals. He could use his lieutenants to delegate authority and yet hold them responsible for results.

All of these military skills had their counterparts in the civilian world of administering economic growth. The objective to overcome was poverty and a lack of resources. Immediately upon taking power, Pak gathered his command under the umbrella of the Economic Planning Board (EPB). He commanded his experts and business practitioners to take inventory and devise a plan. They did as ordered, and the result was one successful economic plan after another. Pak Chung Hee stayed around to see four of them completed. Though he delegated authority, he kept enough to make sure that the plan was carried out.

Economic planning under Pak involved a variety of people, but at the same time it was highly centralized. Major decisions were made at the Blue House (the president's mansion). A cadre of executive experts made the central decisions and then passed their work on to the EPB and its committees for fine tuning and execution. That ability to make quick decisions that carried authority was probably the most important single factor in successfully launching the economic-planning system.

Perhaps equally important, however, was the Pak government's capacity for seeing that decisions were followed by action. He was reputed to be a strict disciplinarian who would close down a business if it did not measure up, or if it tried to evade specifications set down by the government. To make sure that commands were heard and obeyed the whole way down to the plant floor, Pak had military comrades appointed as president or vice president of companies, as members of the board of directors, as heads of the personnel department and to other key positions. To complement the military presence in industry, about

38% of non-economic jobs in government also went to military appointees.[1] This permitted Pak a direct and personal supervision of the entire industrial and political complex. It also injected an intimidating factor into business, while at the same time nurturing a fraternity of interests across military and business lines.

His ability to command and lead the troops of planners, bankers and *chaebol* executives is recognized by many as the linchpin that kept the forces of innovation working together in harmony. Forbes magazine in 1979 said that without his "masterful management of the Korean economy, it is unlikely that Korea's economic miracle could have taken place."[2]

Unfortunately for everyone, and especially for Pak Chung Hee himself, he was not nearly as adroit at this political rule as he was at economic administration. During the 1960's he governed as a legitimate president. He stood for elections on two occasions and won by majority of the popular vote. There was a national assembly, a comparatively free press and unions were permitted to organize, bargain and act collectively. During that period it looked as though the military general might be the one who would introduce democracy to Korea's political body. For about seven years (1963-1970) rapid economic development was going on hand in hand with democratic political processes.

But alas, it was not to be. Pak Chung Hee was too much of a military man to be a democrat. He reneged on his earlier promises to step aside after two terms (1963-71). He threw out his own democratic constitution and set up a military dictatorship which he euphemistically called *Yushin*, meaning "restoration" or "making new." Pak liked to call it a "revitalizing reform."

Once the Yushin was set in place Pak's political legitimacy was invalidated. His "right" to rule was thereafter based on the amount of economic development he could deliver. That, however, did not prove to be adequate. Increasingly he resorted to physical force to keep himself in power.

The Central Intelligence Agency (KCIA) and the riot police joined with the armed forces to guarantee "political stability." In the 1960's this open use of physical power had not often been necessary. When the "consent of the governed" was gone, however, all Pak had left was the sword. So he ventured out to manage the entirety of society as he had the army. He failed, but in his efforts he brought senseless suffering to his people. Finally on October 26, 1979 he was assassinated by his closest friend.

Pak's systems of Yushin and economic development lived after him. By 1979 the process that Pak started in 1963 had gained its own momentum. The practices of planning and systematic execution of those plans were now well institutionalized in Korea's government and business community. After a year or so of stuttering in 1979 and 1980, following Pak's death, the economy took another great leap forward. Pak Chung Hee apparently had done his work well.

32

The economic growth process which he crafted was able to keep going on its own without further need of a general to command.

Pak's successor was a disaster. He had little of Pak's astuteness or ability to command loyalty. He, also, was a military general, but the tide of the people was beyond him. His only authority came from the barrel of a gun and that was not enough. Within a few years the political and labor arenas erupted in rebellion. Despite those eruptions, the economic system initiated by Pak Chung Hee continued to grow and expand in world markets.

THE PLANNERS

When the military took over the government in 1961, there was considerable apprehension among the Korean people and in the American embassy that General Pak Chung Hee was starting a communist takeover. The apprehension was heightened further when, as one of his first acts, he established at the center of his government an Economic Planning Board (EPB), and ordered it to produce within three months a five-year economic development plan. Five-year economic plans were thought to be the strategies of Soviet Russia.

The Red-fear, however, was quickly allayed. Pak had been converted to capitalism. His ideas had come not from Moscow, but from Harvard. American scholars of economic development, as early as 1952, had begun to develop data and to propose certain avenues for developing the Korean economy. The government, which Pak Chung Hee overthrew, had gone far in devising a five-year plan of its own. When the Pak initiative in planning was discovered to be of American vintage, the communist antennas were taken down, and full support was provided. American economists were engaged to help lead Korea toward free-market, laissez-faire capitalism. To achieve a self-sustaining capitalism, a plan was made to lead Korea's "undeveloped" economy step by step into mature capitalism. (Similarities between this theory and that of communist planning which is to culminate in "mature" communism, may not have been intended, but there they are.)

Robert Nathan who had been a primary author of the earlier plans in 1952 and 1960 commented that from the very beginning there was a consensus concerning the goals and methods of the planners. The goal was to create a free enterprise capitalist economy. The system would begin with "guided capitalism," where government, through the EPB, would guide, and private companies would follow. They would act like executing agencies of the government plans. Down the development path, gradually the guidance scaffolding would slough off and the missile of free capitalism would blast off on its own.

There was also a consensus on the development model to be used. With few natural resources to exploit, and no capital surplus, an export model financed by foreign capital was considered the best bet for Korea. Since everyone agreed on goal and model of development, it was possible to devise and implement the plan with efficiency.

The steps for doing economic planning are straightforward. First the EPB projects the production and investment plans for the five-year period. Targets to be reached in each sector are indicated; then the private sector makes its own plans as to how it will help the government reach EPB's targets; the government selects those firms that seem best qualified to achieve the targets and provides financing for them during the period; and finally the plans are put into action with the EPB having the authority to see that things are implemented as planned.

Before the plan reaches the implementation stage, however, it is always exposed to the critique of many others. Committees from industry go over it; bank officials evaluate it; experts from academia give advice; and a battery of foreign advisors chip in their opinions. In this way the plans have wide support before they are published. Since the plan is reviewed each year to judge its relevancy and achievements, all of these bodies have an on-going input into the plan's implementation.

The system has had amazing success. Despite the national political turmoil and the vagaries of international markets, the planners have adhered to their game plans. There have now been six five-year plans. Each has been successful in its own right and each has been built solidly on the foundations laid by the previous achievements.

The first plan of 1963-67 focused on development of electrical energy, increasing food production and development of infra-structures for industry. The second plan (1967-71) built carefully on the first. It aimed at expanded employment, self sufficiency in food production, and modernization of basic industries like textiles and chemicals. This second plan was an enormous success. GNP shot up at a rate of 12 percent per year.

The third plan (1972-76) ran head-on into the international oil crisis when the price of oil multiplied four fold. All of Korea's oil was imported and the major proportion of its industrial and agricultural achievements were built on an oil base. Rather than shrink back, however, the EPB plunged ahead. It increased its outside borrowing. It expanded exports with a frenzy, and it dispatched Hyundai Construction Company to the Mideast to earn foreign capital in the heart of the oil producing nations. These moves paid off. The plan had targeted an average growth of 8.6 percent. The actual figures showed a 10.9 percent increase. To make it even more remarkable, it was in this period that the planners decided on a major shift from light industry into the heavy industries of steel, ship-building, automobiles and machinery.

In the middle of the fourth plan (1977-81) President Pak Chung Hee was assassinated. For two years the economy faltered, but then regained its strength and ended the plan period with a 5.7 percent rate of expansion.

The fourth plan had primarily been an extension of the third. By 1982, however, a new challenge faced the economic planners. They had been so successful in their electronics, automobile, shipbuilding, and steel industries that they found themselves competing, and competing successfully, with Japan, the U.S. and Europe in these fields. Meanwhile, technological innovations were not slowing down. Indeed the pace was increasing. To continue to compete meant almost a quantum leap into the world of high technology. The men at EPB decided to take on the giants. The fifth and sixth economic plans have increased space for foreign investments, have expanded research and development and set ambitious goals for extension into the world of microchips and computers.

The ability of the planners to analyze the situation, identify the heart of the challenge and respond in an energetic and accurate way is one amazing dimension of South Korea's economic miracle.

FOREIGN CAPITAL

The Economic Planning Board's (EPB) first five-year plan was announced to the public in 1963. Prior to that date a large transfusion of military and economic grants from the U.S.A. ($12 billion from 1945-1965), plus considerable aid from the World Bank had kept South Korea afloat. As the economic planners began their work, they knew that those sources could not continue. U.S. grants were already being discontinued. In order to finance their first five-year plan, the planners turned to Japan. As part of an agreement to normalize relations between Korea and its former colonial master, the Japanese government provided a grant of $300 million and loans worth another $200 million. Private Japanese firms were persuaded to add another $300 million in investments. This $800 million along with continued aid from the U.S. assisted South Korea through the first five-year period.

The economic planning process that the government launched in 1963 required a systematic infusion of capital over an indefinite period of time. To meet the long-term needs for development capital the EPB opted for three strategies: first, it would continue to seek loans from foreign governments and international government agencies like the World Bank and the IMF; secondly, foreign commercial banks were encouraged to make investment loans in Korea and to also set up direct banking services within the country; the third method was to encourage foreign corporations to establish production facilities within Korea. All of these strategies have been highly successful, and all three have played key roles in helping Korea's economy reach the "take off" stage of development.

Loans from foreign governmental agencies are negotiated by the Korean government. Commercial bank loans are secured either by action of government or corporation. Regardless of the method of inducement all foreign capital is an integral part of the financing of the five-year plans. The third plan (1971-76), for example, was financed in part by $4.5 billion loans from foreign commercial and governmental sources. Direct foreign investments added another $488.1 million. During the time of the next plan (1977-81) foreign loans tripled to $13.1 billion and direct investments increased slightly to $531.8 million. The fifth plan (1982-86) saw a small decrease, but nevertheless a very high rate, of borrowing. The total was a little more than twelve billion dollars, and direct investment figures more than doubled up to $1.1 billion.[3]

There has always been a generous supply of foreign capital. In 1977 Business Week magazine commented, "...record numbers of foreign banks have been streaming into Korea. About forty foreign banks have branches or representative offices, triple the number three years ago, offering money at bargain rates undreamed of in the early 1970's."[4] As expansion has moved into ever more costly levels of economic growth, foreign capital has kept pace. Loans from commercial and governmental sources have been central to the Korean scheme, with direct investment playing a comparatively less important role. Loans, all of which make their way through the Bank of Korea, provide maximum freedom to distribute investment capital to those sectors which the planners want to emphasize. Loans also avoid the troublesome issue of foreign ownership. By accentuating loans and de-emphasizing direct investment the planners hope to avoid any suspicion that foreigners control the economy.

The strong influx of foreign loans has contributed heavily to the large foreign debt accrued over the last decade. In 1973 the debt amounted to only $4.3 billion. In 1985 that had multiplied ten times to a figure of $46.8 billion.[5] As Korea moves more and more into the atmospheres of high-tech and capital intensive industries, its need for foreign loans will expand, and if figures for the first half of the decade portend the future, the foreign financial world will be there to supply whatever is needed.

However, a fortunate thing has occurred. With the expansion of its economic base, today Korea is better able to service its debts. Domestic savings have increased phenomenally. In 1970 domestic savings stood at 17% of GNP. In 1985 they had burgeoned to 30%. Domestic savings in that year actually surpassed investment requirements.[6] In addition an international trade surplus over the last four years puts South Korea in the fortunate position of being able to increase its loans from abroad without adding to burdens of national debt. Indeed statistics show that the debt burden as a percentage of GNP decreased from eighteen percent in 1973 to fifteen percent in 1985.

The third strategy EPB used to secure foreign capital was to induce private firms to set up business in Korea. To encourage them in that direction a package of benefits was provided. Foreign firms were wholly or partly exempt for five years from a variety of taxes, including personal income taxes for foreign employees. Capital goods imported for processing and export were free from import tariffs. Infrastructures were developed and utilities made available at reasonable rates. The government established Free Export Zones and Industrial Estates where foreign firms could set up their businesses at minimum cost. In addition they were assured an ample supply of low-cost female workers who would not be distracted by labor union organizations.

Japanese and American firms have responded by rapidly moving into Korea. From 1962 to the end of 1987 2,412 foreign firms invested about $4,692,000,000 in South Korea. More than half of the investment dollars ($2.82 billion) have come in since 1982.[7] Following the path directed by the EPB, in the early seventies foreign investments came primarily in labor intensive, light industries such as textiles, electronics, plastics and clothing. As the planners switched emphasis in the late seventies and early eighties, the foreign investors began to make larger investments in capital-intensive sectors such as automobiles, steel, machinery, and chemicals. In recent years increased amounts of direct investment capital have been flowing into the country. During the seventies the yearly average stayed at just around $100 million. In 1984 investments jumped to $170 million. In '86 they increased to $477.5 million, and in 1987, a year of thunderous labor disputes and social upheaval, direct foreign investments registered $625 million.[8] The Korean government has ended some of the tax advantages granted to foreign investors, but on the other hand it has opened up almost the entire manufacturing sector to foreign investment where previously it had been quite restrictive. Foreign firms can now own one hundred percent of an undertaking. Formerly they were required to enter joint ownership agreements with Korean partners. Furthermore restrictions on profits that can be remitted to the corporate headquarters have been eliminated. These new inducements more than make up for the loss of benefits that had come from tax advantages.

The Japanese lead the list of foreign investors. They account for 64.8 percent (1,600) of the total number of foreign ventures, and 51.1 percent of the total value in dollars ($2.396 billion). The U.S. comes a far second with 20.9 percent of the total ventures and 28.3 percent of the foreign dollars invested in Korean industry.[9] Japanese investors have evenly divided their funds between manufacturing and service sectors. In the Masan Free Export Zone, for example, 90 of the 110 firms that employ 25,000 workers -- mostly women -- are Japanese firms. The Japanese also have invested heavily in tourism and the hotel industry in Korea. At the same time they have deep interests in the automobile, steel, heavy machinery and electronics industries.

Companies from the U.S. tend to concentrate in the manufacturing sectors, with 87 percent of their capital focused on the same types of heavy industries that attract Japanese attention: automobile, transportation equipment, heavy machinery, chemicals and electronics.

As noted above, direct–foreign investment is quite small as compared to the sums of money that come in through public and commercial loans. Direct investments by private concerns are important because they are the channels through which the technologies, labor skills and managerial know–how move into the Korean economy. They are the stimuli that get domestic businesses moving and competing. They become the model for entrepreneurship that Korean businessmen follow. Foreign firms are the catalysts that get things going. They are also important for creating employment in the critical growth sectors of the Korean economy. The amounts of direct private capital brought into Korea, for instance, from 1978 to 1983 represented only 1.87% of GNP, but that amount accounted for almost ten percent of total employment in manufacturing. Perhaps as high as 20 percent of total output of manufactured goods and 24 percent of all export goods were produced by foreign capital during that same period of time.[10]

In the last few years the Korean economy has become more open to the penetration of foreign capital. Since the planners are committed to ever more sophisticated levels of technology and industry, larger amounts of foreign capital will be needed in order to succeed. The investors are already demanding greater freedom to invest in any and all sectors of the economy. That, of course, is part of the price that Korea must pay for becoming a full–fledged member in the international economic system. It also probably means that its dependence on foreign capital in the manufacturing section will increase rather than decrease.

Foreign businesses are interested in continuing their investments and operations in Korea as long as profits show gains that cannot be achieved elsewhere. Over the years, investments in Korea have proved to be very lucrative. An aggregate figure published in 1986 by the U.S. Embassy in Seoul reflects the situation: remittances to American businesses from Korean operations amounted to $368 million or about forty five percent of total U.S. investments.[11] Foreign banks share in the high levels of profits. In fiscal year 1988, for example, the Bank of Korea reports that fourteen Japanese banks operating in Korea posted an after–tax increase of 57% over 1987. U.S. banks increased their profits by 24.5 percent during the same year.[12]

Korea has been, and in all likelihood will continue to be, a profitable place for international banks and corporations to invest. Despite the anxieties over two oil crises, proclaimed fears of communist invasion, the assassination of Pak Chung Hee and nation–wide labor revolts in 1987, foreign capital never wavered. It continued to flow in at greater rates than before.

38

THE EXPORT MODEL

The fourth component of Korea's economic dynamic is the export-model of development that the EPB has followed since 1963. All of the five-year plans have been export-centered. According to Robert Nathan, South Korea did not have enough capital, natural resources or primary commodities to permit it to go another direction. Its one advantage is its large supply of educated, productive, low-cost labor. The export-model followed by the EPB is based on that advantage. The concept is straightforward: first capital is borrowed from foreign sources. That capital is invested in those industries where cheap labor can best be used; the commodities produced are sold on international markets where, because of the low cost of the labor-component, they enjoy a competitive edge; the money earned is then returned to investment in the mother country and the cycle begins again. Because of the labor-cost advantage, each cycle will allow the home economy to expand incrementally, creating new jobs and new industries. In theory if this can be continued long enough, the entire economy will begin to function according to the capitalist market system. "Take-off" will have been achieved and everyone will be happier.

Korean labor has given its nation three forms of comparative advantage: low labor costs, high productivity and high levels of skill. During the 1960's and early 1970's the low cost, high productivity of women workers in textiles, clothing and pharmaceuticals allowed Korean commodities to successfully compete in world markets. Korean shirts, dresses, textile materials, footwear, etc., took over many of the retail markets in the U.S.A. Seventy percent of exports during the period were textiles and clothing. From the late 1970's, Korea's advantage in high skilled labor has come to the forefront. 70 percent of exports are now capital intensive or high-tech goods. Each year for almost two decades, Korean exports have expanded by about 40 percent, accounting in large part for the 8.6 percent average yearly advance in G.N.P. The expansion has been of remarkable proportions. In 1965, exports totalled $175 million. Eight years later they earned $3.27 billion. Ten years after that, the figure had shot up to almost $25 billion. 1986 recorded $34 billion and during the next two years of political and labor turmoil exports almost doubled to the level of $61 billion.[13]

A variety of tactics were used to stimulate exports. In 1964, the Korean Overseas Trading Promotion Association (KOTRA) was set up to develop international markets for Korean goods. A variety of inducements was given to any company that would export.

In 1970 the government decided to add another strategy to the export policy. It established Industrial Estates and Free Export Zones around over the country. Foreign entrepreneurs, usually small in scale, were invited to set up business in the Zones. Advantages to the businesses were many: no taxes on imports, low bank loans, exemption from corporate income tax, discounts on transportation and utility costs.

Direct retail contract with big companies in the U.S.A. and Japan was another channel through which Korean exports hit the world markets. Large name retailers like Sears and Roebuck, Penney's, and K-Mart bought textiles and clothing directly from producers, small and large, in Korea. Giants in sportswear like Nike and Reebok copied the same pattern.

The fourth and most significant of the export strategies was that of the General Trading Company (GTC) system which was initiated during the third economic plan when the pattern of production and exports was being changed from light manufactured goods to heavy and high tech products. In 1975, businesses over the nation were asked to take part in a gigantic competition. They were invited to export commodities throughout the world and if they reached the goal of exporting 2% of the total, they would be rewarded with prizes that could very well guarantee long term success and power. The successful companies would be designated as General Trading Companies (GTC). They would receive bank loans at about nine percentage points lower than non-GTC; cheaper import goods would be accessible; sources of foreign capital would be opened; and they would be included in the committees that advised the EPB.

The competition was made into a national, patriotic game. Meeting export targets became a matter of national honor. The yearly presentation of the Presidential Citations was accompanied by bands playing the "Export Promotion Song." Big floats proclaimed slogans such as "Nation Building Through Exports" and "Think Export First!" President Pak, surrounded by TV cameras and newsmen, made the presentations in person. The competition to receive a citation was fierce.

When the smoke of the contest settled, to no one's surprise, the winners were mostly subsidiaries of one or the other of Korea's large business groups called *chaebol*. Their success in the GTC arena gave them an advantage which they have never relinquished and from which they have come to dominate the Korean economy.

The GTC system, the switch to heavy industry and the giant leap forward by the *chaebol*, all went hand in hand.

Emerging protectionism in international markets and increasing competition from other low labor-cost countries cautioned the planners to vary the products available for export. By the 1980's products of light manufacturing were de-emphasized and more durable goods were promoted. A contrast between 1970 and 1983 is instructive of the change that has taken place.

In 1970 electronics accounted for 4% of exports while in 1983, 12 percent of exported goods were in that category. Exports of steel went from 2 percent to 11 percent. Exports of ships, from zero to 16 percent. On the other side, textiles which had dominated the scene in 1970 at 41 percent, declined to 25 percent in 1983. Wigs and plywood which had accounted for 9 and 11 percent respectively at the earlier date, were not among the exports of 1983. The exporters have been able to keep up with the demands of the planners. As the EPB has directed production to higher levels of technology, the exporters have adapted their techniques so as to continue the expansion of Korea's shares in world markets.

The planners and industrialists give no evidence of being willing to stop, or level off the development for fear that would freeze Korea into a satellite position vis-a-vis Japan or U.S.A. The goal, apparently, is a highly independent, industrial, high tech foundation that can deal from a position of strength with the rest of the world.

To achieve that goal, the continuing expansion of exports is an absolute necessity. Internal markets can in no way absorb what Korea is now able to produce. Competition in world markets of heavy industry and advanced technology is the only open road.

Korean companies have already penetrated some of the world's important markets. Samsung with its video-cassette recorders and Lucky-Goldstar with its color TVs are beginning to steal customers from Japan. The hottest personal computer in 1985 was reported to be the "Leading Edge Model D" made by Daewoo. It costs about one-half the comparable IBM PC. The top selling auto import in Canada is the Hyundai, overtaking Honda in only 18 months.[14]

South Korea's distinguished achievements in international markets are partly because of large risk-taking, effective marketing technique and systematic planning, but they are also made possible by the remarkable achievements in skill development and labor productivity. From 1965 to 1981 labor productivity expanded by 13 percent. Comparable figures for Japan and the U.S.A. are 9.1 and 2.3 percent respectively.

As the economic planners and exporters switched over to heavy industry and sophisticated technology, they also increased their demands that there be strict control of the workers, no union organization and only minimum wage increases.

THE *CHAEBOL*

The fifth, and crucial, dynamic for economic innovation in Korea's "guided" capitalism is the *chaebol*.

The Korean word *chaebol* is used to designate a group of companies that is usually owned or controlled by one person or family and administered from a central headquarters. It is the Korean version of the more popular Japanese word, *zaibatsu*.

41

The *chaebol* have been pivotal to Korea's economic expansion. There are about twenty firms that deserve the title of *chaebol*, and four could be considered as super–*chaebol*. About half of the twenty had their beginnings in very humble circumstances in the post liberation years of the late 1940's and '50's and have followed patterns of growth quite similar to one another. Since those early days, an unusual number of energetic and capable entrepreneurs have founded not only their own businesses, but have piloted those businesses in a short time into world–class corporations. In 1982, nine Korean firms were listed among Fortune's top 500 international companies. One example is Daewoo, one of the four super–*chaebol*. It was established in 1967. Within a space of 20 years, under its founder and director, Kim Woo Choong, it has grown from an initial investment of $18,000 to a yearly gross sales of $15 billion, placing it 39th on Fortune's top 500 non–American corporations.

A close partnership between government and business made this phenomenal growth possible. This close relationship can be understood by looking at history. For forty years (1905–45) Korea was a colony of Japan. At the end of World War II when Japan finally retreated to its own islands, all of its Korean properties, which included the factories, transportation and communication systems and much of the land, were taken over by the Korean government. For a time the government owned and operated most of the industry of the nation.

After the Korean War, however, the Syngman Rhee government set about divesting itself of Japanese properties selling them to private citizens, some of whom were entrepreneurs and some who were not. It sold them at low bargain rates, with little obligation to pay the government the actual worth. After the Rhee regime fell in 1960, these same citizens were accused of gaining illicit wealth by collusion with a corrupt government. Many were arrested. President Pak called some of them in to discuss the situation. Lee Pyung Chul, the founder and president of Samsung *chaebol* was the spokesman for the accused. Lee was a patriot who promised to make the businesses under his management prosper so as to benefit the nation. He and others asked permission from President Pak to seek foreign capital to invest in their companies to increase production and employment. Apparently Lee was persuasive. Nothing more was said about illicit wealth, and several of the future *chaebols* went out on the international markets to gain investment capital.

A second big event in the partnership between government and *chaebol* came about a decade later in 1972. Korean companies have always operated under a heavy load of debt. It is estimated that the average debt to equity ratio of the largest of the *chaebol* is around 400 to 1. In the early seventies, despite almost a decade of unparalleled economic profit, many of the nation's leading corporations were on the brink of disaster. Coincidentally, President Pak Chung

Hee was in the midst of a crisis of his own. In November, 1971 he had declared a national emergency, and usurped all government power into his own hands. The people did not take kindly to the destruction of democracy. Protests and demonstrations erupted. An economic collapse would have been disastrous for Pak personally. He could not afford to let any of the *chaebol* go under.

A meeting was held with the heads of the nation's corporations. Their request was simple: reduce the rates of interest on the debts owed the banks. The government decision came on August 3, 1972. The request of the business men was honored. Corporate tax rates as well as rates of interest on bank loans were lowered.

The "August (8/3) Decree" was received with great jubilation. One executive of a *chaebol* who was meeting with the company's board of directors, when President Pak's decision was announced, stated, "We had no other solution except to declare bankruptcy. Everyone was in despair. Suddenly we received news about the decree. Everyone screamed 'Hurrah! We are saved!' and we all cried with tears."[15]

Chung Ju Yong, president of Hyundai, saw the "8/3 Decree" as an epoch-making decision and called upon the government to coordinate all industrial and fiscal policies so as to revitalize the economy.[16] The government was all too glad to do that very thing. Indeed that was the exact intent of the "8/3 decree." Banks had already been nationalized. All loans from abroad had to be initiated by the EPB or gain its approval. Foreign investments were all channelled through the government out to selected Korean enterprises. This system, plus the proclivity to direct funds to firms, that had succeeded in the past helps account for the steady, but rapid expansion of a comparatively few firms to *chaebol* status. Chung Ju Yong's call for a more thorough coordination between business and government was right on line with government intent. Korea's *chaebol* were propelled into world-class status, however, by the establishment of the system of the General Trading Company (GTC), as referred to previously. In 1976 when the system was initiated, thirteen companies qualified. Subsequently that number was reduced to ten. The largest of the *chaebol* were to gain most. The qualifiers already were among the largest conglomerates in the country, but once they gained the GTC label they quickly outdistanced all other rivals. This was achieved by the simple device of channelling GTC financial advantages to all companies in the *chaebol* so that they could increase production, buy up other firms, invest in research and development and direct their commodities through the GTC to world markets. A good example is the Sun Kyong Group that at bargain-rates acquired the Korea Oil Company. It imports its own oil, converts it into secondary chemicals in its own refineries, turns them into polyesters in its own plants, manufactures garments and sells them abroad through its own trading

43

arm.[17]   The ten *chaebol* which won the designation of GTC now account for 60% of all exports and dominate every aspect of the Korean economy.

The *chaebol*'s effect on the nation has been enormous. Through their efforts and successes, the Korean economy has broken all records. Though it is certainly not their efforts alone, yet the *chaebol* can take a bow for the fact that per capita GNP is up from about $80 in 1961 to about $2,300 in 1986. The ingenuity and ability of men like Chung Ju Yong (Hyundai), Lee Pyung Chul (Samsung), Kim Woo Choong (Daewoo) and Koo Cha Kyung (Goldstar), has made it possible for Korean industry to meet the challenges of capricious international markets and has come out victorious.   From their Mideast construction initiatives to fishing in the South Seas, to ship building, steel producing and ventures in high technology, the *chaebol* of south Korea are competing with the best in Japan, U.S. and Europe.

The success of the entrepreneurs and their huge business conglomerates also confronts South Korea with a mammoth problem. They dominate most every facet of life. It is often said that "Koreans cannot live without the *chaebol*. As soon as we get up, we wash with soap and toothbrush made by Lucky *chaebol*, wear clothes made by Samsung *chaebol*, go to work by a bus made by Shinjun *chaebol*, work in an office built by Hyundai *chaebol* (but built with cement made by Ssangyang *chaebol*), take an elevator made by Lucky *chaebol*, use a telephone set made by Lucky *chaebol*, eat food made by Samsung *chaebol*, drink beer made by Doosan *chaebol*, etc., etc."[18]

There is a sense among the people that not only do the *chaebol* surround them at every step, but also that they (the people, the workers, the farmers and small business people) have been taken advantage of, that the nation's resources and their own labor have been drained into the coffers of a few families.

Political collusion between government and *chaebol* is a cause of deep concern. When Pak Chung Hee decided to become dictator in 1972, he had to seek his legitimacy in rapid economic development. Working through a few large industrial groups made it possible for him to control the development process, but it also made him dependent on the *chaebol*, and it gave their executives easy access to, and influence in, government circles. One company official saw himself and other business participants in the planning process as an "...equal policy–making body." "When we have a problem we call a meeting of government ministers," he said.[19]   The cooperative relationship was partly personal since the heads of government and the chief executive officers of the *chaebol* spend so much time together, but it is more than that. It is a systemic intertwining of government and business structures, functions and goals. The collusion between government and *chaebol* has become so entrenched that the government which once was the "guide" in the "Guided Capitalism" concept has become the "follow–along."   Capitalism has sloughed–off the guidance of government and has taken the leadership to itself. The capitalism in South Korea is a corporate capitalism specializing in monopoly. Capitalism of free competition among many contenders in free markets never had a chance. It was squeezed out when military dictatorship fell in love with the *chaebol*. The combined assets of the big four now represent 43.9% of the nation's GNP and they seem to be adding to it each year as they buy up shares of other companies by means of loans from banks which they control. Last year alone (1988) their assets soared by 21.1 percent.[20]

A dilemma facing South Korea as it moves into the future without its military dictatorship of two decades is, "What is to be done about the *chaebol*?"

SUMMARY

The land has been transformed -- for better or for worse is not always easy to decide. Nevertheless if one compares the standard of living in South Korea in 1989 with that which existed in 1961 when Pak Chung Hee first came to power, or in 1963 when the first 5-year plan was christened, it is clear that people are economically better off. Poverty has been attacked with considerable success. More people live well. Fewer live in abject poverty. A spirit of pride in the remarkable economic achievements of two decades is noticeable even in the attitudes of the most critical. The five innovating factors of centralized planning, foreign capital, the export development model, *chaebol* and a military dictator have forever changed Korea.

Paradoxically these very same innovators were committed to a labor policy of repression. Labor in abstract was extolled. Labor as person or collective, social entity was demeaned. To enforce that policy the innovators resorted to a subsystem of enforcement that was manipulative and oppressive.

CHAPTER NOTES

1. Chung–Kil Chung, "The Ideology of Economic Development," Seoul National University, 1987, p. 39.

2. Forbes, April 30, 1979, p. 56.

3. Major Statistics of the Korean Economy, Korea Foreign Trade Association, Seoul, 1988, p. 201.

4. Business Week, August 1, 1977, p. 36.

5. Korea's Economy, August, 1987. p. 23.

6. Korea's Economy, February, 1988, p. 5.

7. Figures taken from "Industrial Labor in Foreign Invested Firms in Korea," Young–ki Park, Sogang University, Seoul, Korea, November 1988, p. 4. His source was the Ministry of Finance.

8. Major Statistics on Korean Economy, Korean Foreign Trade Association, 1988, p. 201.

9. These figures taken from Young–ki Park, "Industrial Labor in Foreign Invested Firms in Korea," p. 4.

10. Directory of Statistics of International Investment and Production. New York University Press, 1987, p. 535.

11. Paper Subject: "Foreign Equity Investment in Korea," 1986, p. 4.

12. Korea Times, May 20, 1989.

13. Korea Times, July 13, 1989. Fifty percent of the 1988 figures was accounted for by electronics and textiles, where employees are almost exclusively women.

14. Newsweek, "The Koreans are Coming," December 23, 1985, p. 46.

15. Seok Ki Kim, "Business Concentration and Government Policy: A Study of the Phenomenon of Business Groups in Korea, 1945–85," Ph.D. Thesis, Howard University, 1987, p. 179.

16. Ibid., p. 179.

17. Far Eastern Economic Review, June 2, 1983, p. 63.

18. Seok Ki Kim, Ibid., p. 89.

19. Far Eastern Economic Review, June 2, 1983, p. 64.

20. Korea Times, June 6, 1989, p. 8.

III. LABOR POLICY AND LABOR CONTROL

Korea's economic transformation was so remarkable that few bothered to look at the underside of the "miracle." The economic planners, the engineers, the think-tank people, the foreign investors and the *chaebol* were perceived as heros for bringing prosperity to a once poverty-stricken land. Ironically and sadly, their great successes were built upon a labor policy that violated the human rights of workers, a labor policy that required pervasive, and often cruel suppression of the nation's working people.

A subsystem of labor control had existed in Korea since the introduction of the factory system by the Japanese around 1915. It existed in the 1960's under a fairly liberal regime. With Yushin it intensified and with the emergence of Chun Doo Hwan in 1980 it became a sub-system of blatant cruelty.

The five innovators recognized labor as the critical variable in South Korea's drive toward industrialization. Cheap, skilled, energetic labor was understood by all to be Korea's comparative advantage in world markets. Yet paradoxically they all feared and distrusted workers. Though labor as the crucial ingredient in economic planning and production was extolled in warm tones, the laborer as a person and unions as organizations of those persons were anathema. While seeking in good conscience to develop the nation and save it from poverty, the innovators exhibited a pervasive hostility against workers and workers' organizations. Each had its own reasons for fearing workers, but all were in agreement that they had to be controlled. Actively or passively the innovators gave their consent to a sub-system of worker control that inflicted humiliation upon the very people who produced the economic miracle.

THREE ASSUMPTIONS

The innovators' labor policies rested on three assumptions:

* low labor-costs were the only basis upon which economic advancement could be achieved;

* laboring people belonged to a lower class of society that should show deference to the higher class of society;

* collective action by workers was probably inspired by communists.

Only the first of these three was officially expressed. It provided the "scientific" rationale for behavior that originated primarily from the other two assumptions.

Low-cost Labor

The first assumption about labor is, of course, championed by the economic planners. For them labor is one of severable variables put into the computer to make projections of what should be done to achieve pre-determined ends. Labor as person or collective social organization does not fit into mathematical formulas. Indeed it is assumed that these two dimensions are contrary to economic growth. From the perspectives of those who set down the basic plans for economic development labor productivity must be pushed ever higher and costs ever lower. It is the margin between the two that is thought to propel the economy to greater heights of prosperity. Capital accumulation was given priority over wages, worker safety, pensions, job securities and all else. In theory, the cheaper the labor costs the higher the margin of profits. The higher the profits, the more capital is available for further investment. Investment creates jobs, brings in technologies, and turns out new products for the market. Through these few economic steps, it is argued, the entire society, including the workers, is lifted to higher levels of prosperity. According to the EPB planners everything depends upon keeping labor costs as low as possible. Each year during the 1970's the EPB would publish a maximum rate of wage increase to be permitted in the subsequent year. Employers could pay less, but were not to go above the EPB figure.

The export model of development as practiced in Korea reinforces the low-cost labor assumptions of the EPB. Exporters maintain that they can penetrate international markets primarily because of the differential between Korean wages and wages paid to workers in the U.S., Japan and Europe. In the 1960's and 1970's, it was the female workers in the nation's textile industry that gave Korea its advantages in American markets. Their wages and other costs were always kept minimal. The cheap and productive female labor was the factor that enticed many American and Japanese businesses to set up operations in one or the other of Korea's industrial estates or free export zones. In the Masan Free Export Zone, which has higher wages than most, the women were in 1981 making $175 a month.

Since the late 1970's when the nature of Korean exports shifted, capital-intensive and high tech industries have taken on a new importance. The export model for these commodities now demands not only cheap labor and productive labor but also highly skilled and intelligent labor. The demands are being put upon the male workers in the heavier industries of steel, automobiles, machines and ships. Under the forced march of the early 1980's while productivity of these highly sophisticated commodities shot up at a rate of about 24 percent per year, the real income of the workers rose less than 15 percent.[1] The exporters herald the difference as Korea's comparative advantage.

48

Foreign investors participate, of course, in the same assumptions about labor costs. They come to Korea for the very purpose of using Korea's chief resource -- low-cost, productive labor. American investors consider a well educated, inexpensive labor force to be "Korea's major asset. Korean workers are known to be highly productive and easy to train."[2]

Furthermore, the dogma of low-labor costs has a double advantage to the investors from abroad. By seeking their own profit they also help others. Like domestic entrepreneurs, the foreign firms make use of low cost labor for their benefit and in turn contribute to jobs, technology, management skills and markets. The "truths" of capitalism as seen by the foreign investors are paradoxical: you serve others best when you gain all you can for yourself. Thus it is both good business and virtuous to take advantage of Korea's cheap labor.

When, however, the workers of Korea protest the low wages and the shabby treatment they receive, the foreign investor is likely to become angry; and if the Korean employees dare to form a labor union, the anger grows to outrage. Workers, they complain, are violating economic laws and are thus interfering in Korea's development process. The OAK Company set the pattern in 1969 (p. 24).

The first assumption held by the innovators was that low labor-costs were a necessity, that economic development required a policy where wages and other labor costs would be minimized.

Authoritarianism

The second assumption girding up labor policy has its origins in traditions that pre-date any thought of industrial society. It is the inherited legacy of authoritarianism based on class distinction. The legacy permeates all of Korean society, but is best exemplified by the relationship between the *chaebol* and their employees.

The image most referred to when discussing the labor policy of the *chaebol* is that of the "father-son" relationship of Confucian ethics. The familial relationship is much heralded by *chaebol*, and owners in general, as the rightful framework within which industrial relations should be practiced. The company's owner and his representatives in management assume the role of father. The employees are cast in the role of son, or daughter. The ideology is that the father (employer) has the wisdom, virtue and compassion to know what is good for the children. The sons and daughters (employees) out of gratitude for being taken care of, and also because they accept their own inferiority, express loyalty to the employer by diligence and hard work.

This ideology as utilized by *chaebol*, government and some foreign businesses is, however, quite misleading. The father-son idea is but one unit of a more fundamental philosophy. Society, according to that philosophy, is built

49

on distinct lines of economic and moral class. Society is not egalitarian. People are not equal. Nature itself, the argument goes, structures two classes into society: the rulers and the ruled. Rulers are superior in social–economic power, but more importantly they are also morally superior to the lower class. Because the ruler accepts himself as morally superior, he then rightfully exercises authority over others. He rules by his moral example and persuasion. Confucius is said to have thought that the superior man moves others before him as the wind blows the grass -- not by force but by moral persuasion. Chung Ju Yong, president of Hyundai and Kim Woo Choong, President of Daewoo, both express similar philosophies. Kim's biographer writes that "Setting a personal example is the hallmark of his leadership. It compels subordinates to follow his lead. By his own example of austerity and sacrifice Kim contributes to easing the complaints of wives and families at home."[3]

The father–son relationship does not transfer intact across the economic social lines of employer–employee. True, the employer may take a paternalistic attitude toward an individual employee (a servant) but that individual employee–servant would never make the mistake of making a son's claim upon the employer. That would violate the moral relationship (superior to inferior) between them. The employer, who is the supposed father figure, may if he wishes, look kindly upon the employee, the son. The employee, however, always remains the servant, not a son, and if he displeases the employer, fatherly thoughts are quickly replaced by the punitive powers of the ruler.

The class concept of the "superior man" prevails in Korean industrial relations. The superior men, in this case the owners and the management, govern their "kingdoms" not by law nor by political consensus, but by virtue of their own assumed moral superiority. It is autonomous and absolute. It is thought to be the natural order of society.

When the *chaebol* formulate their labor policy in terms of a father–son relationship and plead for a cooperative or familial attitude from the employees, they are intending a relationship far different from what those two words seem to indicate on the surface. More accurately they are calling upon the workers to accept their social role as "the ruled," to willingly accept the superior wisdom and virtue of "the ruler." Decisions about wages and working conditions are to be left to the superior wisdom of the company. They are being told that the employees (the inferiors) have no rights and no qualifications to interfere in company affairs.

Furthermore, as the *chaebol* increasingly engage in the whirlwind of competitive international markets, they pay even less attention to the "father's" obligation that their version of Confucian ethics places upon them. Decisions made deep in the organization of conglomerates have little place for "fatherly" compassion or obligation. *Chaebol* make their decisions on the basis of production costs, markets and profits. The hierarchy of the *chaebol* make those decisions and they want no interference from employees. "Father–son" talk is used as a subterfuge. It invokes old class values to enforce a new style of authoritarianism.

Anti–communism

A third assumption of the labor policy embraced by the five innovators is that a communist underground foments every independent, collective action taken by workers. Collective action is in and of itself viewed with suspicion. Part of that is because of the spectacles of superiority worn by the ruling class, but there is also a proclivity on the part of government and employer to equate collective action by a union with a communist plot. Ever since the Japanese started the practice back in the thirties, government officials and company managers have assumed that communists are either in control of unions, or are somewhere in the background pulling unseen strings that manipulate them. When the Japanese were on their hunt for "Reds," they probably had good reason for doing so. Communists had joined the underground that opposed Japanese colonial rule. It was quite likely that there were communists among the workers. Certainly at the time of liberation in 1945, communists were very active all over the South. Chun Pyung, though not completely an instrument of the North, had communist leadership. Chun Pyung and its sister political organizations called Peoples' Committees were disbanded by the U. S. military and the Syngman Rhee regime. Neither Rhee nor subsequent governments, however, could believe that the communists were really gone. Over and over they fought the specter of Chun Pyung, assuming it was still alive, still lurking somewhere ready to strike again.

This fear of Chun Pyung's ghost was part of a wider political policy. Anti–communism was the primary pillar of the Rhee government and the primary course of study for generations of school children. Pak Chung Hee, when he needed a justification for destroying the democratic practices and setting up in their stead his Yushin dictatorship, turned quite naturally to anti–communism. The nation was informed that a new and even more dangerous plot from the North had been uncovered and to protect against it, a dictatorship was necessary.

Part of the anti–communist fervor of the government was perhaps the machinations of charlatans, but part of it was because they were true believers in the inevitability of a battle of Armageddon between the forces of communism and anti–communism.

A personal experience relates something of the passion these believers brought to their job. In 1974 I was arrested by the KCIA and interrogated for seventeen hours. I had spoken in public on behalf of eight men falsely accused

51

of being communists. They were all sentenced to die, despite the absence of any evidence. Hour after hour the interrogators tried to get me to admit to being a communist or to helping the communists. Around eleven o'clock at night I was taken to the office of Lee Yong Taek, chief in charge of the KCIA's 6th section.

"You have been in Korea a long time, Mr. Ogle, but obviously you still don't know much about Korea. And you know nothing about communism. You have violated our anti-communist law, but because you are a foreigner, we are going to be generous. I am going to prove to you that these eight men are indeed communists."

Lee then repeated to me the exact same accusations that had come out in the newspaper. The only piece of evidence that he showed me was what he said was a copy of a speech made by Kim Il Song, the Premier of North Korea. One of the eight condemned men, Ha Chae Won, had listened to the North Korean radio and copied down Kim's speech and then showed it to some other people. Otherwise, Lee Yong Taek appeared to have no support for his case against the accused.

Then an amazing transformation took place. Instead of a cool, calculating man reciting alleged "facts," Lee switched over into an emotional monologue.

"These men are our enemies," he screamed. "We have got to kill them. This is war. In war even Christians will pull the trigger and kill their enemies. If we don't kill them, they will kill us. We will kill them!"

"If our government does not kill these men, I will go to the national cemetery and confess before the grave of every dead soldier that our country has been sold out to the communists. I will go to the United States and visit the graves of Americans killed in Korea and I will confess how they have shed their lives in vain. We've got to kill them! We will kill them!"

What was going on? Lee was transformed in front of me. His eyes were afire. His face clenched with hate. He marched in small, tight circles. His emotional high was far beyond any evidence of guilt against the condemned men. Here was a man locked in mortal battle with Satan. The world depended on him. He would save his nation from communism even if it meant executing innocent people.

There was no let up in the drums of anti-communism under the Chun regime of 1980–87. One of his first acts was to "purify" the nation of labor leaders who were contaminated with "unclean philosophy" –– one of several euphemisms for communism. The few remaining independent unions were broken to "protect freedom." Religious bodies that had been doing education work among laborers since the sixties were attacked in a nationwide campaign that denounced them as front groups for a communist conspiracy. Despite all the rhetoric, all the energy at enforcing anti-communism, not once in the fifteen years, from Yushin's beginning to the end of Chun's regime in 1987, was there

52

any real communist plot ever uncovered or any genuine communist brought to light. Many suffered mercilessly because the "true believers" could not rid themselves of the specter of the past.

Labor policy of the innovators was based on these three assumptions. The three can, of course, be separated for purposes of analysis, but it is necessary to keep in mind that these three assumptions are all incubated in the same minds, emotions and values of the same people. The three assumptions are but three aspects of one mentality. The assumption that labor costs must be kept as low as possible in order to achieve economic development is itself a class, authoritarian assumption. It is heralded as though it were a universal law discovered recently by economic developmentalists and capitalists. In fact, of course, it is only one of several possible assumptions about labor and its costs. Workers could be considered as partners in development whose participation would add to productivity; workers could be accepted as the potential buyers for the commodities produced. Wages thus could be kept above the survival level and the commodities produced could be shaped to serve the domestic markets rather than the demands of foreign markets; it is also possible to see workers as moral agents who because of their central role in production, have a moral right to achieve an equal share of the profits.

The Korean innovators have rejected all options except the capitalist assumption that the worker is only labor, and labor is a factor of production that must be kept under control and paid as little as possible. Their view of labor is artificial and one dimensional. It coincides nicely with Korea's traditional class superiority and the inherent authoritarianism of foreign investors.

The innovators by enforcing the lowest possible labor–costs shoulder the development burdens onto the workers, while at the same time channelling the new wealth to themselves. Perhaps no where in recent experience has new wealth become concentrated under the control of so few people as it has in South Korea. Forty percent of GNP is produced by the four super–*chaebol* and fully 60% of the GNP is accounted for by only ten of the conglomerates. In Korea each *chaebol* is owned and operated by one family. Ten families have gained the lion's share of the newly produced wealth –– this at the same time that hours for workers have been the longest, injuries the most and wages among the lowest in the world.

SUBSYSTEM OF ENFORCEMENT

The labor policies of the five innovators are translated into action by those who manage labor at the place of work. One observer suggests that Korean management at the work place divides its employees into three groups: those with higher levels of humanity who can be managed by reward; those of least humanity who can be motivated and controlled only by the infliction of punishment; and those in the middle who need a little bit of both.[4] The task of labor management then has been to distinguish between these three types of employees and administer doses of reward and punishment as circumstances require. To help control workers in the second and third categories a six-layered sub-system of enforcement and punishment has been devised.

Legal System

The law governing labor unions is the first layer. Three times in the last fifteen years labor law has undergone radical change. In 1963, workers could apply to the Office of Labor Affairs to have their union registered. If approved, the union could commence negotiations with the company. Collective bargaining was closely circumscribed, but permitted. If agreement was not reached, then the union could enter into a cooling-off period of twenty days during which time, mediation and arbitration by Labor Committees were available. After the cooling off period, there were two options: the union might be allowed to call a strike or the government might declare that the national security was endangered and then impose a settlement.

The 1960's saw a considerable amount of union activity, and some legal work stoppages. Unions, however, were always under the control of the administrators who granted the union charter and the Labor Committees who could order settlement when they felt necessary.

When Pak Chung Hee turned to dictatorship in 1971, he made two drastic changes. First, he promulgated the Special Law on Labor in Foreign Invested Firms which made most union action in foreign firms illegal. Second, and most critical, he declared a State of Emergency under which all collective rights of labor were suspended. The State of Emergency lasted from 1972 until 1981. Workers were allowed to form unions, but were not allowed to strike. They were required to "cooperate" with the company. The State of Emergency made any disruption of the social order a punishable crime.

The third change in labor law came in 1981 after Chun Doo Hwan took over. He lifted the State of Emergency but to impede union activity and prevent strikes he manipulated the law in other directions. First, he required that at least thirty workers, or twenty percent of the work force petition for union recognition before the Office of Labor Affairs would register it. Previously, the number was not designated and therefore it was difficult for the employer to control the establishment of a union. This new requirement made control much easier.

Second, the Chun regime, with the strong support from the employers, made it illegal for any third party to interfere in collective bargaining. Furthermore, bargaining could take place only at the enterprise level between a local union and the management. Excluded from the bargaining process were church groups, students, lawyers and also the FKTU and the national industrial

54

federations. All collective bargaining was done locally. The local unions were isolated from all outside help.

Chun wanted obedience of the heart was well as conformity of behavior. As part of his "reforms" he opened up "Purification Camps." They were military–like compounds set up in remote mountains away from contact with the outside world. Two hundred some labor leaders from around the country were arrested and sent to these camps. Through intense physical exercise, spartan existence, self criticisms and moral exhortations, the inmates were to be converted, to see the error of opposing the government's "good will." A graduate of the camp tells of his experience:

> Right before supper we were beaten out of our minds and at suppertime we were given 3 spoonfuls of barley rice. Even though we offered thanksgiving for this, we were beaten again. For one laugh — 80 lashings. In the morning there is a marching song period which is called a screaming time but we were so hungry we couldn't shout and then they beat us with clubs until we screamed. One friend of mine, a Mr. Chai, could not scream because of a throat infection (TB) and therefore, he was beaten to death. Another person, a Mr. Lee, was also beaten to death. Two out of the eleven in our group were killed. They asked those who were experiencing pain to come forward for treatment and I went forward also, and they beat us again. I was so bruised that I had to receive treatment for 6 days in the infirmary.[5]

Korean labor law has seldom been an instrument for defending workers or for protecting their human or civic rights. Most commonly law is understood as an instrument of control used by the powerful to control the weak.

Management

Employers are the chief enforcers of labor policy. For most of Korea's industrial history the employer has had a free hand to treat his employees much as he has wanted. The American military authorities in 1946 promulgated a "Labor Standard's Act" that is still in effect. It sets down standards on hours, overtime, child labor, accidents, health care, etc., but the enforcement of the law has been very selective. Management has been free to bend and violate the law with little fear of penalty.

Management, moreover, has never seen labor relations as much of a priority. The personnel manager or person in charge of labor affairs was usually the one with the lowest status in management ranks. He needed no special training or experience. The reason was simple enough — labor could be managed by command. Top management would give orders about layoffs or

55

wages or safety or whatever and the plant manager would see that the commands were carried through. Day by day supervision of workers was left to the line supervisors and foreman who reigned with a free hand. It was always expected that the workers would obey. If for some reason, they did not, they were required to write an "apology." Three such "apologies" and a worker was out. Or, if the offense was considered large, or the worker considered a trouble-maker, he/she was dismissed without prior warning. Since a supply of unemployed people was usually available, recalcitrants were easily replaced.

As pressures for economic development began to build, however, signs of resistance began to be seen among the workers, and as the labor market became tighter, especially in the skilled sectors, it was not always expedient to solve the problem by dismissing the workers. Education programs became a popular recourse. One of Pak Chung Hee's early initiatives was called the "New Village Movement." It was an attempt to "modernize" Korea's villages by organizing work crews and lecturing them on the spirit and ideals of Pak's Yushin dictatorship. With the cooperation of the National Organization of Korean Management, the "New Village Movements's" education program was adapted to the industrial work place. The content of the education focused on a few central points: for the good of the nation the company must succeed; for the company to succeed, workers and management must cooperate and live in harmony; disruptions in production are a help to our enemies and a blow to national goals. Therefore cooperate, work hard and endure for the sake of the nation. For over a decade and a half the industrial workers of South Korea heard this message. Once a week or once a month they were gathered together for lectures and exercises intended to inculcate this "spirit" into their hearts.

The actual spirit of the New Village Movement was demonstrated elsewhere. In 1979, the government sponsored a Commerce and Industry Day to celebrate "the Movement." A newspaper reports that both industrialists and businessmen renewed their determination to raise productivity by intensifying cooperation between labor and management. They gave credit to the New Village Movement for fostering the spirit of cooperation and sacrifice for the motherland. Those present to hear these accolades to the "Movement" included the heads of the Korea Traders Association, the Korea Chamber of Commerce and Industry, the Korean Federation of Industries, the Korean Federation of Small Businesses and, of course, Prime Minister Choi Kyu-hah, head of the EPB. No mention is made of any labor or union presence at the meeting where cooperation and the spirit of harmony were being so heralded.[6]

Labor-Management Councils were used to command "cooperation." In the 1960's, they were established to facilitate collective bargaining. In the 70's and 80's, however, the Joint Councils came to be used as a substitute for collective bargaining. Each work place with one hundred or more employees was ordered to set up a Labor-Management Council. Ostensibly the two sides were to discuss and make decision on such matters as employee training, production problems, worker grievances and safety matters. In fact the two sides were always uneven. Votes on any issue required a two thirds majority. Workers at times would vote with the company, but seldom was that reciprocated by the company. The company maintained control and used the Councils primarily as a forum from which to direct the employees. Furthermore, the Joint Councils were structured independently from the labor union. The union was limited to bargaining only about wages. Everything else was to be handled by the Joint Council. The two, of course, came into conflict with each other. The resulting dissention only weakened the workers and provided the company with a convenient means of playing the workers off against each other.

Management preferred to use persuasion, layoffs, education and the "cooperation" of Joint Councils, but if its workers were discovered to be thinking union, different strategies were brought to play. Once it was reported that a worker, or group of workers, was unionists, the direct line supervisors would be instructed to keep careful records on the suspect's comings and goings and especially on the calibre of his/her work. If the person was indeed a unionist, careful records of misdeeds on the job could be used to either blackmail or dismiss the offender. Another frequently used method was to assign the suspect to the care of a low-level manager. He would be expected to bring the errant worker back to the fold. The approach would go something like this: If the unionist were a man, the sub-manager would invite him out for a drink. After many drinks, the worker was told how much he was valued by the company and that he had a good future ahead. It would be foolish of him to risk it all by getting "misunderstood" because of his relations with the union. If the worker were a woman, she would not be invited out for a drink, but the message would be the same. If these friendly warnings were not heeded, the union person could expect the reprisals to begin. First, his line supervisor would find fault with his/her work. He/she would be ordered to write "apologies" for some alleged misconduct on the job; an order for the offender to be transferred to another department or to an entirely different plant miles away might come down from "upstairs"; and friends would be called in by management and asked to help save the unionist from impending dismissal or perhaps even arrest. If all these measures failed to persuade, the unionist might receive yet another friendly call from the sub-manager. The previous speech would be repeated, but this time a fairly large sum of money might also be offered, with the promise of more to come later.

If Mr. or Ms. Union is stubborn enough to resist even this token of company good will, then things can get rough. If the union leader is a woman, her parents are likely to get letters from the company which accuse her of being "impure" and associating with "corrupt elements." Man or woman, he/she is quite likely to be fired and forbidden entrance into the plant. Blacklisting is a popular type of preemptive action by companies. Once fired for union activity, a person may never again get a job in that area or city. One woman fired from the Dongil Textile Company actually found employment in six other places, but in each place the police discovered her and, when notified, the companies dismissed her. By 1980, there was a nation-wide, computerized black-list that consisted of about one thousand names.[7]

Despite all these company efforts workers actually do persevere in their determination to form a union. If it comes to the actual organizing stage, the company's response might well move toward physical violence. Union people are kidnapped, locked into rooms for several days and/or beaten. These acts are administered at times by anti-union workers in the plant under management's direction. Often hoodlums from the outside are hired to do the job.

Somewhere in the higher echelons of management the word is given and someone at the lower level makes the contract and fingers the ones to be chastised. The hoodlums are given access to the plant and notified of worker gatherings. The hoodlums then, who are often trained in the manly art of taikwando, taunt, humiliate, beat and even kill. Kim Jin Soo made the mistake of talking back to one of the two goons that his company hired to discipline workers. He was stabbed in the chest by the fellow and then left to lie on the factory floor until he died. The killer was never reprimanded. The manager who hired him was transferred to another town and the company, of course, had no record of the hoodlum ever having been in the plant.

Some of the saddest stories one can ever hear come from inside Korea's factories, the very same factories that have lifted South Korea out of poverty into the status of a "Newly Industrialized Country." The very same people who gain accolades for being giants of industrialization are the ones who enforce their anti-union policy by hiring gangsters.

Union
The labor policy of the innovators is enforced by a multi-leveled sub-system. Legal strictures and company practices are but two methods used by the enforcement system.

A third instrument of labor policy enforcement is the union itself. Frequently the union's own structures and leadership have been used against workers and their efforts at forming legitimate unions.

Anti-worker union structures take three forms. One is the well known organization called a company union. In addition to the traditional interference and domination of the local union by the company, Korean companies frequently resort to a new type of trickery. When it becomes clear that the workers are determined to organize, management selects a few employees to quietly form a union and register it with the government's Office of Labor Affairs. When the legitimate unionists come to register their union, they find a union has already been recognized, and since there can only be one union in an enterprise, they are prohibited from organizing. The world famous Samsung Corporation is infamous for resorting to this type of tactic.

A more serious problem of traditional unions, however, is their financial dependence on the company. Union officials at the local levels, industrial federation levels and the FKTU level are all paid by their respective companies, not by the union. Union offices, furnishings and some of its program funds come from the company. This system has been maintained ever since it was initiated by the Japanese under their sampo system of World War II. Over and over again this system has subverted legitimate union action, but it still remains. The dependence of the union leaders on company money gives management an instrument of control that it uses liberally. It also maintains a psychology of dependence among union people.

The third form of anti-worker action by the union came through the KCIA control over the FKTU. Since 1971 KCIA has directly, or indirectly, appointed the leadership of FKTU and its member federations. Thus when workers at a local level insisted on organizing and demanding improvements in their working conditions, the FKTU would frequently be pressed by the KCIA into anti-worker action. The case of the women workers at Bando Songsa illustrates the pattern. The workers had organized against stiff company opposition and demanded a wage increase and improvements in treatment from their supervisors. The National Textile Workers Union (FKTU) first ordered the women to accept the company offer. When the women refused, the National then used its legal authority to disband the local. Once that was done the police entered the union office, which, of course, was on company land, and drove the union women out. The company then completed the task by dismissing the entire union leadership.[8]

Police
Under the Japanese, the only agents authorized to manage labor were the employer and the police. The latter were at the beckon call of the former, but were also free to investigate rumors and to prevent disturbances. Brutality was common place. Some of the most brutal of the police were themselves Korean. They kept the tradition of cruelty alive long after the Japanese went home. Stewart Meacham, an American official of the 1945-48 military government, observed how the Korean police used beatings, tortures and humiliations against the workers involved in the conflicts between Chun Pyung and No Chong. In

response the people of Taegu attacked and killed twenty three police during the general strike of 1946 (p. 11).

In subsequent history, police behavior has not improved. They still retain the job of keeping labor under surveillance. Each police precinct in an industrial area has an office in charge of labor. It works in close conjunction with the management of the companies. If management reports that there is a trouble maker among its employees, an investigation is begun. The worker, his family, friends, co-workers, neighbors, supervisor and co-unionists are visited, questions are asked and suggestions of impending catastrophe are scattered about. Police seldom work by themselves, however. In each jurisdiction, or in each case of conflict they enjoy full consultation with, and receive orders from, the labor department, the department of public order, the prosecutor's office and the KCIA. In the Free Export Zones, police have daily briefings with representatives of management in order to identify workers who might have pro-union inclinations.

On those occasions when strikes or labor demonstrations have broken out, the police role has been quite clear: either they act as an agent of the employer and administer beatings to the workers, or they stand by and watch others do the beating. Their reputation for brutality comes down unchanged from their Japanese mentors. In recent years that reputation has been made even worse by the addition of a Korean-style "swat-team," called baikgoldan (white skull squadron). It is made up of young men trained in the art of destroying an opponent in a brief amount of time. They wear padded clothing and white motorcycle helmets. Their very appearance heightens the intimidation and the violence.

KCIA

The Korean Central Intelligence Agency (under Chun Doo Hwan renamed Agency for National Security Planning [NSP]) has been mentioned before, but its role in enforcing the innovators' labor policy has been so pervasive that it deserves special comment. The KCIA was organized in 1961 by the military. During most of the 1960's it played little role in labor affairs, but as the dictatorship began to take hold after 1971, the KCIA became the major instrument of government enforcement. It dominated union and labor affairs from 1971 to 1987. Not only did it control the FKTU and the national federations as referred to above, its agents constantly made their presence known at union offices and at church or civic groups that might be in support of union efforts. The author worked in a Christian mission to labor and industry in the city of Inchun during the early seventies. All of a sudden beginning in 1971, we became aware that we were being followed. Phones were tapped. Unknown men who would not identify themselves would visit our office and demand to know what we were doing, and with whom we met. Gradually these agents closed down the labor education programs we sponsored by the simple means of gathering names, taking pictures and then threatening people with dire consequences if they did not stay away. The dire consequences might include a verbal warning, a beating, a loss of job, a "trip" to KCIA headquarters and/or the stigma of being called communist. Two of our staff were secretly taken off by the KCIA for a few months.

The same form of pervasive intimidation took place among union leaders at all levels. Even those who were hand picked by the KCIA were under constant surveillance. A black jeep with two men and a driver was enough to start one's heart beating faster. After one or two outspoken leaders disappeared and then returned very docile and quiet, the message and its fear spread wide and far. The KCIA was a master of inciting fear because it was a master of inflicting pain through torture. A "trip to South Mountain" (a euphemism for imprisonment at KCIA headquarters) by one union leader was enough to intimidate a host of others. Company management tried in various ways to manipulate workers and unions; the police were there to contribute to the brutality but it was the KCIA that injected fear into the stomachs of people.

Hoodlums

The last of the six levels of labor policy enforcement can be called "regression to gangsterism." Gangsters, or organizations of hoodlums, called *kangpae*, have a long and infamous history in Korean politics. As early as the 16th Century there are stories of how hoodlums were used by unscrupulous politicians to persuade or eliminate opposition. Their involvement in labor affairs goes back at least as far as the time of the American military government of 1945–48. Stewart Meacham, a labor advisor to the government, in his "Korean Labor Report" (1947) refers to two groups that were close allies of No Chong in its battle against Chun Pyung. One of these allies, the "Tai Han Min Chung" (The Great Korean Democratic Young Men's Association) was a terrorist organization, according to Meacham.

In April of 1947, Meacham reports that a leader of the Tai Han Min Chung phoned the headquarters of the printers union in Seoul. He told them he was coming to get them because they were Chun Pyung. He and his gang then proceeded to attack the union, severely beating twenty people who were there. They dragged two of them out on the street and continued to beat them. Police watched on, but did nothing. Sadly Korean history is full of similar examples.

In the 1970's at the Dongil Textile plant in Inchun, women workers elected a woman as the president of their local union for the first time. Male workers, supported by management, combined with a few local thugs, beat and humiliated them in order to force a decertification of their union.

By the 1980's, the companies had rationalized the system of violence. When disturbances arise from workers for wage increases, or for recognition of a union, the *kusadae* (Save Our Company Group) appear almost automatically. The kusadae are creations of employers. Most members are company employees, some of whom are hired because of their abilities at hand to hand combat. They undergo training and are often led by middle, or higher, management. Since all Korean men do three years of very harsh military training the kusadae usually takes on a military character. The leaders have often been officers in the military. Most kusadae members are anti–union, male employees of the company. Some are thugs hired from local gangs. One example will illustrate the process. At the Saeshin plant in the southern town of Changwon in early 1989 a labor dispute over wages lasted for 55 days. Finally an agreement was struck. Negotiations were to begin and back wages were to be paid. The next day, however, the workers found that the dormitory in which they had slept was surrounded by a squad of kusadae armed with iron pipes, gas guns and clubs. They wore helmets and acted in military fashion. The unionists were systematically beaten. The police, who were there observed the whole affair and then arrested several of the union leaders.

One spokesman for employers claims that the kusadae is merely a group of employees expressing their democratic right to oppose unions. In fact, what has taken place is a process of making thugs out of otherwise decent employees. Handsome benefits are given to those who volunteer for action. A simulation of war games is re–enacted on company property, setting employee against employee. There are many reports of companies hiring professional thugs to act as security guards or to do specific acts of terror, but the recent wide–spread use of kusadae suggests that some management has regressed to a state of gangsterism.

SUMMARY

The innovators behind Korea's economic miracle have never accepted the fact that labor, Korea's one advantage, comes "wrapped–up" in the body and person of human beings and those human beings live in communities and society. Labor, as productive power, is recognized; labor as person, as a collective, is feared. One observer has said that in Korea, labor management centers on how to efficiently suppress the human side of labor so that management can deal only with the productive side of it.[9]

To do that the innovators have increasingly resorted to some form of violence to subdue the workers. The three decades of the sixties, seventies and eighties can be seen as a pattern of worker control that began with traditional manipulation and built up to increasing use of violence. The pattern is not clear, nor is it discrete, but the dominant rhythms are there. In the 1960's, workers were exposed for the first time to a prolonged period when they were free to organize and bargain collectively. Their inexperience plus traditional authoritarian habits permitted the employer to manipulate the workers and their unions. Police were brought in at times and were often present for intimidation purposes, but their role was low key comparative to later decades.

In the 1970's, the KCIA was central to the relationships between management and worker. The very presence of the KCIA, with its reputation for torture, raised the psychological pressures against workers. A visit from an agent, a ride in a black jeep to South Mountain, a few people disappearing for a few days was enough to dissuade most people from "impure thoughts."

As the economic planners, the exporters and foreign investors pushed to secure greater levels of production, the levels of physical violence began to increase and become a greater part of the enforcement mechanisms. In the eighties, the use of physical force has been a regular practice. Legal manipulation, management intimidations and KCIA/NSP threats still continue, but they are now more frequently accompanied by some instruments of force.

From a different angle one might argue that police, company and KCIA/NSP violence has increased because of worker and union resistance to the less violent methods. While unions in the sixties were active and energetic in seeking to protect workers and get wage increases, most often they were out maneuvered by the company. Often union leadership was bought off or it succumbed under pressure. In the first half of the seventies, workers and the whole populace were cowed by the KCIA, but as we shall see in the next chapter, they never really gave in. Resistance was there and as the decade wore on, workers began more and more to actively oppose the control system. Women workers especially were apt to take action. As they did, police countered with force. In the 1970's, there were quite a few cases where police beat up women workers who were protesting mistreatment or demanding the right to organize.

Physical violence seems to have become the prevalent characteristic of the 1980's. New demands are being made by the innovators. They claim that the higher levels of heavy industry and technology demand even greater sacrifice by labor. Workers, however, have come to distrust these constant demands for sacrifice, and events in the eighties have set them on the path to demanding democracy. Chun Doo Hwan's only response to worker demands was to increase the violence. Before his impromptu exit in 1987 he had made physical force and torture fixed parts of the labor-control system.

During the last two years under a more democratic system of government there is still little evidence that the innovators have gained insight into the causes behind the labor explosions of 1987. Their responses so far have been dominated by talk of economic ruin brought on by high wages, by an appeal to law and order, and by exclamations about communist plots. These verbal stereotypes have been accompanied by a generous use of police, kusadae, and the military to keep the workers and their unions under control.

CHAPTER NOTES

1. *Han'guk Sahwei Nodongja Yu'ngu I* (Study of Korean Society and Workers) by Hankook Sawhei Yungoo So, Seoul, 1989, p. 125.

2. Suk H. Kim, "Financial Incentives for U.S. Private Investments in Korea," in Korea's Economy, February 2, 1988, p. 21.

3. *Kim Woo Choong*, by Kim Byong-Kuk, Bobmun Sa, Seoul, 1988, p. 21, 14.

4. *Han'guk Sahwei Nodong Tongjai* (Control of Labor in Korean Society) Korean Christian Study Center for Social Problems (Han'guk Kidokkyo Sahwei Yu'ngu Won) Seoul, 1987, p. 72-73.

5. Taken from an unpublished personal account.

6. Korea Herald, March 21, 1979, p. 3.

7. Control of Labor in Korean Society, p 50, 51.

8. Ibid., p. 58.

9. Ibid., p. 72-3.

IV. LABOR UNDER *YUSHIN*

Pak Chung Hee was elected in May, 1971 to a third term as president of the Republic of Korea. His victory, however, was an inglorious affair. He took millions of dollars from the Gulf Oil Company and several Japanese firms to buy the election. Even so his margin was by only four percentage points. For the first, and only time in Korean politics, the opposition parties joined behind a single candidate named Kim Dae Jung. Kim was an effective orator and drew large crowds to hear him denounce Pak. Kim predicted that if Pak won, within the year he would abolish democracy and establish a dictatorship.

SPIRIT OF RESISTANCE

His prophecy came true. On the fifteenth day of October, 1971, Pak Chung Hee declared a state emergency. The nation, he claimed, was in jeopardy of attack by communists. To protect against that attack and also to ensure Korea's continuing economic expansion, the democratic constitution as well as all civil rights had to be suspended. In their place Pak declared a new social order which he called *Yushin*.

Yushin is a word made of two Chinese characters meaning "restoration" or as Pak interpreted it "revitalizing reforms." Pak borrowed the term from Japanese history. The elevation of the house of Meiji to the status of imperial family in 1868 was known as *Yushin*. The term also signals the beginning of Japan's military and industrial expansionism. Given the decades of oppression at the hands of the Japanese, it is difficult to understand why Pak would think that he could rally his people under a symbol of Japanese origins.

The *Yushin* system established Pak as dictator. The national assembly became a rubber stamp; unions, schools, churches and media were put under surveillance by the KCIA (Korean Central Intelligence Agency); riot police controlled students, and public opinion was squelched by an army of spies. So much of this era is filled with irony and tragedy! Pak unflaggingly used his power to push his nation to higher heights of economic development, and at the same time showed disdain for his people. They bent under his attacks. They worked hard. They out-produced the world, but they never surrendered.

From the very beginning *Yushin* evoked thunderous opposition. Kim Dae Jung continued to denounce the dictatorship and took the lead in demanding the return to democracy. His courageous stance put his life in constant danger. Twice he was nearly assassinated. On one occasion, he stopped in Tokyo while returning from a trip to the United States where he had strongly denounced Pak Chung Hee and his *Yushin* order. The Korean CIA kidnapped Kim from his hotel room, put him on a small craft in the Japanese Sea, and apparently intended to dump him overboard. A chance appearance of a low flying helicopter saved

Kim from a watery grave. He lived through that episode. His captors let him free in the back alleys of Seoul, but for the most of the 1970's Kim Dae Jung spent his life either in prison or under arrest inside his own home.

Towards the end of 1973 a campaign led by 30 prominent citizens was initiated to secure a million signatures of people demanding a return to the democratic constitution. Pak, like everyone else, knew that many more than a million would willingly sign on to such a petition. To block it, he issued on January 8, 1974 his first emergency decree. It declared that criticism of *Yushin* was a crime punishable by up to 15 years in prison. Nine days later fifteen men stood up in public and read a statement demanding the restoration of the 1963 democratic constitution. They were arrested, tried by military courts and sentenced to fifteen years imprisonment. At the same time college students took to the streets in anti-*Yushin* demonstrations. Pak increased the pressure. In April, 1974 he made it punishable by death to demonstrate or oppose *Yushin* in any way. Military courts would make the decision as to guilt or innocence.

To explain to the world why it was necessary to rule by decree and military courts, Pak concocted a story about a communist conspiracy. Eight unknown men were accused of enlisting the support of a thousand prominent citizens, church leaders and students who were opposed to *Yushin*. The eight, it was charged, manipulated the thousand into taking part in a North Korea-inspired plot to take over the government. The whole case was a fabrication and the eight men were quite innocent. Yet they were condemned and executed. Throughout the 1970's, and especially following the U.S. departure from Vietnam, Pak's government manipulated the fear of communist aggression in an attempt to suppress opposition to *Yushin*.

So it went throughout the seventies. Always the government held the upper hand. It won every contest of strength. Yet always there were new volunteers to fill in the slots left empty by "martyrs" thrown in prison or tortured into inactivity.

The spirit of the Korean peoples' resistance to oppression is expressed in a poem written by Kim Chi Ha in 1975. Kim, himself had been arrested and sentenced to death by the military. While in prison, he happened upon the remains of a man named Ha Chae Won. Ha had been framed, tortured and forced to confess to being a communist. He was only a few days away from being hanged when Kim came upon him huddled in a dark corner of a prison cell. Kim wrote of that encounter:

> Out of the darkness
> someone calls me
> the cell on the far side of the bare
> rust-covered darkness the color of blood

crouched in the dark, wide open
two persistent eyes.

Ah--silence calls
gasps of breath, caught with phlegm,
calls me.

Low grey sky
drenching the day with constant
drizzle, ceaselessly
a voice calls:

Deny
Deny the lie.

That was the script of so much of the 1970's. The government demanding submission; the protestors resisting stubbornly even in death. Kim's words "Deny, deny the lie" catch the depth of commitment against Pak and his *Yushin* system.

TWO MEN

Two men who never met, whose lives were eons apart, symbolize the forces that produced the economic and social changes of the *Yushin* period.

The first man, Chung Ju Yong, represents genius and power. He is an entrepreneur who helped engineer Korea's economic miracle. He helped devise the innovators' labor policies and the sub-system of enforcement. Chung symbolizes Korea's formidable ruling class.

The second man, Chun Tae Il, was a worker in a miserable sweat shop. He represents all those production workers who receive their daily orders from men like Chung. He died before *Yushin*, but his self-sacrifice provided the spirit for the workers' resistance to *Yushin*.

Chung Ju Yong

In 1947, just two years after liberation from Japan, Chung Ju Yong, along with his brother, set up his first company. It was a small construction firm in Pusan that did contract work with the newly arrived American Army. Chung's brother spoke English. The company was named Hyundai.

Business was good, but when the war came in 1950, it became superlative. The demand for re-construction after the ravages of war quickly made Mr. Chung a very rich man, and being a very smart man he improved the skills of his workers and the technology of his equipment. He worked in close connection with the Korean government and the U.S. Army. When opportunity for doing business in Vietnam came, Hyundai was ready to move. It became one of the preferred contractors for the American and Korean armies during that war.

By 1972 the company had become a $64 million enterprise.[1] The construction company had spun off into other ventures so that a group, or *chaebol*, of six companies, all owned by Chung Ju Yong, had taken shape.

1972 was a pivotal year for the *chaebol*. Two big things happened. President Pak Chung Hee in his famous "August 3 Decree" (p. 43) reduced the rate of interest that Hyundai and the other *chaebol* were paying on their huge bank debts. The forgiven debt was like a blood transfusion. With extra cash on hand, Hyundai quickly diversified into still other lines of production.

The other big event of 1972 was that Hyundai went into the shipbuilding business. The story goes that someone informed President Pak Chung Hee that there was a great international demand for ships. Pak, is said to have importuned Chung Ju Yong until he reluctantly agreed to become a ship builder even though neither he nor anyone else in Korea had built a seafaring tanker or cargo ship. That mere lack of background, however, did not deter Korea's Andrew Carnegie. Chung persuaded a Greek shipowner to order two oil tankers of the 260,000 ton class on the promise that he would deliver them faster than any other shipbuilder. Chung failed to mention the fact that at the time not only did he not have experience, he did not even have a shipyard. With two orders in hand, he persuaded Barclay's Bank to lend him the capital. Next he had to learn how to do it. Sixty engineers were quickly dispatched to Scotland to learn the trade. Two years later, on time, the two ships were completed. Korea was in the shipbuilding business.

A decade later four Korean companies were building ships. Three of the four, Hyundai, Daewoo and Samsung were the largest of Korea's parade of *chaebol*. In 1983 they won orders for 179 vessels worth $3.03 billion. $2.85 billion worth was exported. 65,000 workers put those 179 ships together for wages amounting to one fifth of those of a European worker and one fourth the wages of a Japanese shipbuilder. The ingenuity of Chung and his engineers joined with the cheap wages of labor to give Korea an advantage on the international markets.[2]

Hyundai's success in building the two ships did not immediately catapult it into heaven. It faced near disaster in 1975 when a contract it held for three other tankers was suddenly cancelled. The ships were half finished. This time Pak Chung Hee returned the favor to Chung. He kindly brought Hyundai's plight to the attention of a government-owned corporation called the Korean Oil Corporation. Pak suggested that Korean Oil might want to lease the three tankers from Hyundai to transport oil from the Mideast. It was done. Hyundai was again on its feet.[3]

70

1976, however, may outweigh all the previous events in Hyundai's short life. In that year business again needed bolstering. The world was in the midst of an oil crises. Korea had no oil. It all had to be imported. To pay for it at the inflated prices, exports had to be increased. The government's political health was also in jeopardy. Ever since Pak took on his role as dictator in 1972, students, church leaders and civic leaders had raised up demonstrations against him. Demands for Pak's ouster began to be heard. An economic recession could have been politically disastrous to Pak.

In the nick of time someone, perhaps Pak Chung Hee himself, came up with the idea of the General Trading Company (GTC). Hyundai was one of the *chaebol* selected as a GTC, and therefore was granted special privileges, easy credit, and lower interest rates as long as it expanded its exports to foreign markets.

Since then, Hyundai's growth has been spectacular. Advantages won through being a GTC were quickly transferred to investments in a multiple of sectors. Today the Hyundai *chaebol* is a group of 28 very prosperous corporations that produce in addition to ships and cars, military weapons, textiles, machinery, oil rigs and electronics. Hyundai has offices in three foreign countries and raises much of its own capital on international financial markets.

The Hyundai story interconnects with many people and events, but central to it all is Chung Ju Yong. He is a "self-made man" in the classic style. With little education and little capital, but full of entrepreneurial ambition, he shaped Hyundai into the empire it now is. He is said to have remarked that he gave up religion and smoking early in life. Work became his religion. Sleeping only a few hours a day and seldom taking a day off, he haunted the companies of the Hyundai *chaebol* urging the staff to do the impossible as he himself had done in the case of the shipyards. He realized that labor and the workers' attitudes were keys to a successful business. Often he would gather his employees on the shop floor and exhort them to higher efforts. The company, he would say, depended on their doing their best and the nation depended upon the company doing its best. The objective of it all was to build a strong and independent nation.

Chung was reported to have said that the Western nations lost their advantage to Japan because Western workers do not have the proper attitude toward work. To keep his workers in the right attitude, Chung exhorts them as a father to a son. He promises good wages and secure employment.

In 1987 something went wrong. Most of Hyundai's 135,000 employees either walked out, or went on sit down strikes, or hit the streets in anti-Hyundai demonstrations. Workers at the shipyards, at Hyundai Motor, and Hyundai Precision demanded the right to organize a labor union. A new, unexpected variable had been injected into the scene and the *chaebol* for at least the moment was unsure of what to do.

71

Hyundai symbolizes the success of Korea's economy in the 1970's. Chung's close confidence with Pak Chung Hee facilitated the making of decisions that had to be done quickly and with authority. Chung and Pak saw the big picture. They gave the orders about what was to be done, and like all people with authority and visions they expected the lower echelons to carry out those orders.

Chun Tae Il

Hyundai Corporation and its president Chung Ju Yong symbolize the economic system created by the five innovators, Chun Tae Il and the *Chunggye Pibok* Union (Garment Makers Union) represent the workers who suffered under the innovators' subsystem of enforcement.

In a way it was appropriate that Chun Tae Il should die in 1970. The decade of the 1960's with its promises for democracy was closing down. Labor and the whole of society was on the threshold of seventeen long years of dictatorship. It was a good year for business. The second five year plan was already known to be a great success with an estimated yearly GNP growth of nearly 10 percent. 1970 was a juncture, from which businesses like Hyundai along with the military dictator would push the nation onto ever greater successes in economic expansion.

Chun Tae Il was a subsistence worker who achieved very little in life. He worked at Seoul's Peace Market making men's clothing. Aside from a meager salary all he received at work were humiliations and threats. His death was a protest against the system that on one hand could spawn industrial empires like Hyundai, and on the other show only enmity to the workers.

At the time, the Peace Market was a one-block long, four-story high maze of small cubicles inside of which workers produced garments for domestic consumption. Some of the cubicles had no more than four or five foot ceilings. Twenty thousand young women, and a few young men (aged 14–29), worked endless hours in these cubicles for a wage amounting to less than $30 a month (1970).

The new spirit of unionism and collective action that characterized the 1960's reached even into these dark shadows. Workers began to meet to talk over their miseries. One young man, Chun Tae Il, located a copy of the Labor Standards Act which guarantees minimal protection for workers on the job. Among other things the law said that workers were to labor no more than 48 hours a week. If their hours exceeded that, they were to be paid time and a half overtime. Children below the age of 14 were not to be employed, and women workers were to have a special monthly rest day to care for their health needs. None of this was applied at the Peace Market. Most workers did not know that such laws even existed. Chun Tae Il began to gather friends together to talk about discrepancies between the law and their working conditions.

They made appeal to the government's Office of Labor Affairs (OLA) charging that the law was not being adhered to by the employers at Peace Market. Perhaps earlier in the mid–sixties Chun and friends may have been given a hearing, but it was 1970, and the switch to authoritarianism was well on its way. When the young workers, ignored by the OLA, made a public demonstration in front of Peace Market, they were beaten and humiliated by the employers aided by the police. No one came to their rescue.

The next demonstration was ghastly. A second attempt to plead their case before the public was made. Again the police at the order of the owners attacked the young people. In the midst of the melee, Chun Tae Il poured gasoline over his body and set himself afire. A macabre specter of shooting flames! A young man's voice crying out from the flames: "Obey the Labor Standards Act! Don't mistreat young girls!" The flames were quenched. Too late. He died. And in a mysterious way this young man of twenty two years ignited a spiritual fire that has continued down through the subsequent years. His flaming body lit up the wretched Peace Market sweat shop and evoked a groan of anguish and protest from workers everywhere in the country. His act has become a symbol of resistance and rebellion ever since.

Chun Tae Il's mother was present at his death. His last words remind one of Jesus' last words on the cross. He said, "Mother! Now you are the mother of all the workers!"

For a week Lee So Sun (Chun Tae Il's mother) sat in the morgue with her son's remains. The police, fearful that his funeral would turn into an anti-government parade, forcefully took the body and buried it at state expense. Mrs. Lee responded by organizing a labor union among Chun Tae Il's co–workers. She was beaten for her efforts, but she did not back off. The union was established. A small room was secured on the roof of the Market. Under Mrs. Lee's guidance the young men and women of Peace Market used the room as a labor school. Basic education in reading and writing was complemented by classes on labor law and unionism.

Owners and police, however, were never comfortable with the union. Its one room office was under constant surveillance. It was closed time and again only to be re–opened by the stubborn resistance of the workers and Chun Tae Il's mother.

Not much changed at Peace Market during the 1970's. There were still twenty thousand young people jammed into close quarters working long hard hours for subsistence pay. In disgust Mrs. Lee denounced maltreatment of young workers, and made a public statement against the police for beating workers at a plant across town in Youngdong Po. In retaliation she was arrested and charged with being a communist spy. The union office was closed and put under police guard. Workers, however, attacked the police and a pitched battle ensued. One young man jumped from the third floor. The police retreated. The workers, mainly young women, sang and shouted inside the building. Finally the police proposed a compromise: Mrs. Lee would be freed in 10 days; the union could continue to use its office and no one would be prosecuted if the workers now quit the building and stopped the demonstrations.

The offer was accepted and almost immediately regretted. As the workers came out of the union office, they were seized and put in a police van. Taken to the station, they were all beaten. Eight were sent to jail for 15 days.

But the union office stayed open, and eventually Mrs. Lee was released. The workers issued a "Declaration of Desperation" that reflects their mood.

> For years and years we have been exploited by entrepreneurs who are protected by the public authorities. For years and years we have been beaten by the police. The six million laborers of this country have been deprived of their basic rights. In 1970 Chun Tae Il burned himself to death -- in vain.

> On July 10, 1977 when more than 300 workers led by our "Mother," Lee So Sun, marched in front of the Office of Labor Affairs, ten of us were severely beaten.

> On July 22, our "Mother" was arrested. For six years she had been helping us but she was charged with being a "spy." The prosecution demanded she be sent to prison for three years. That is an insult to the six million laborers in this country, and especially to the 20,000 workers of the Peace Market area.

> The police have occupied our labor school. We have been told we must get out. They say our school is a place used by communists.

> We cannot tolerate this oppression any longer. We have decided to fight to free "Mother" and to keep our school open. If necessary we will do what Chun Tae Il did -- sacrifice our lives. We have no other choice.

Four years later in 1981 still another chapter in a sorry history was written. Two years after the assassination of Pak Chung Hee, his successor, Chun Doo Hwan, intended to crush all opposition. The Peace Market union, though unable to substantially change anything, was identified by Chun as part of the opposition. He ordered the mayor of Seoul to disband the union and close the school. This time enough police were sent to make it stick. The union was closed down. The workers took their case to the offices of the National Textile Workers Union, but that august body was squarely under the control of the Korean CIA. The voices of the Peace Market youth were ignored. They picketed in front of the National Textile Union headquarters. They were beaten and arrested.

A few days later other members of the Peace Market union sought help from the Asian-American Free Labor Institute (AAFLI), an American branch of the AFL-CIO. The riot police were called. In desperation the workers took the AAFLI leader hostage in his own office. They threatened to kill themselves if the police broke in. The police came in and two of the young people leaped out the window, one breaking his back in the fall.

There is a small word in the Korean language that carries a big meaning. The word is *han*. That one sound expresses the accumulated suffering and anguish of a people, or a person. It is the groan of the human spirit demanding release from oppression.

The groan coming from the burning body of Chun Tae Il was the ultimate expression of han. It held within it the miseries of a generation past and a generation yet to come. It wrapped up together the groans of all the young women and men who work in the Peace Market. It calls with sure instinct into the souls of all working people as they have spent their lives for their nation. Han is personal, deep, to the quick, but it is also collective, embracing all who are victims into a spiritual solidarity.

Chun Tae Il's sacrifice was a burning demand for justice. In that, it joined a voice of nationalism from the ancient past and it incited a boldness that gave courage during the seventies and an explosion of action in the eighties. In 1987 the accumulated groans of workers could be repressed no longer. The workers' han exploded in places like Chung Ju Yong's Hyundai empire.

SUBSYSTEM OF CONTROL

The Chung Ju Yong's and Chun Tae Il's of Korea meet, as it were, at the workplace where production takes place. There it is that Chung's genius and moral authoritarianism get transposed into a subsystem that controls the lives of Korea's workers. During the 1970's that subsystem contained four components.

Management by Decree

The first component of the system was plant management. It had the task of keeping labor costs as low as possible. To do that, management had to hire workers and keep them productive at minimum wages.

75

Each year the EPB would indicate a maximum rate of increase above which wages should not go. The employer would use that rate to guide him in setting wage increases at his own company. If possible, the rate could be set lower than the EPB level, but if it went above, the employer might find that his financial credit at the bank had been reduced or withdrawn. Pressure from EPB was kept on the management to resist any excessive demands by the workers. Employers, however, participated in EPB's decision–making process and therefore actually helped set the rates of permissible increase. The system in practice had a lot of slippage. Government enforcement tended to be erratic. In most cases actual wage determinations were in the hands of the employer. If the employer were a *chaebol*, decisions on wages were made at corporate headquarters and then communicated down to the subsidiaries. It fell to the management of each plant to enforce the decisions made at higher echelons.

It worked. Throughout the decade of the seventies, wages were kept low. Workers' lives were humble indeed. Even by the end of the decade only ten percent of employees in manufacturing and mining were earning incomes equal to the government established minimal standard of living, and only half made as much as fifty percent of that standard.[4] Workers lived at subsistence, while out producing the rest of the world. Labor productivity always stood at levels considerably above the levels of worker income.[5]

Another way by which management kept labor costs low was to insist that workers remain on the job long after they finished the 48 hours set down by law. The extra hours were often not paid for or paid at a rate less than the time and a half prescribed by the Labor Standards Act. The *Tonga Ilbo* newspaper reported, for instance, that as recently as 1983 workers on average put in 33.5 hours a month without any compensation from the employer[6], and in addition in just six months of that year 230 firms were either delinquent in their payment of wages or paid none at all.[7] Such was the case throughout the 1970's. Korean employees worked more hours per week than workers of any other country in the world. The official figure was about 54 hours a week, but in actuality sixty hours would have been a more accurate figure. The popular American magazine, Fortune, looking in upon these long hours of labor interpreted them in these words:

> What positively delights American business men in Korea is the Confucian work ethic.... Work, as Koreans see it, is not a hardship. It is a heaven–sent opportunity to help family and nation. The fact that filial piety extends to the boss–worker relationship comes as a further surprise to Americans accustomed to labor wrangling back home.[8]

Fortune would have been more accurate if it had noted that a refusal to work those long hours would have resulted in dismissal, and that the hourly base wage was so low that without the long hours the workers and their families could not have survived.

Ignoring safety and health considerations was a third strategy used by management to keep labor costs down. Along with the long hours went one of the worst safety records in the world. In 1978, one year, 1397 workers were killed on the job, 13,013 were partially or totally disabled and 137,845 suffered serious injury. These are the statistics of only those incidents which were reported. The real figures could have been double that -- or more.[9] Seven years later, in 1985, these sorry figures were even worse.

Under *Yushin* management by decree was the front line of control over labor. Orders from above kept labor costs low.

Union Manipulation

The second component in the 1970's subsystem of worker control was the manipulation of unions. During the 1960's a provision in the nation's constitution protected the rights of workers to free association, to collective bargaining and collective action. Under *Yushin* those rights were at first suspended and then only the first two re-instated. An emergency decree in 1973 declared all work stoppages to be illegal. Unions, however, were permitted to organize and operate along lines similar to those practiced in the 1960's (p. 15). In fact most unions were organized on a "union shop" basis, so as Korea's industrial work force expanded so did its labor union membership. During the decade union membership grew from 473,256 to 1,093,679.[10]

The increase in numbers, however, signified very little. Following tradition built up since No Chong's victory over Chun Pyung in the mid-1940's, management always intervened in union affairs to assure who should or should not be chosen as union officers. Union decision-making power was controlled by management with only superficial input from workers. The ritual of collective bargaining was practiced each year in the spring. New contracts were signed. In 1978, as one example, 872,000 workers were reported to have been covered by 3,205 collective contracts.[11] What the figures do not disclose is that the content of the contracts was primarily a repetition of items already written in one of the labor laws. Wage increases were included as part of the contract agreement, but they were for the most part perfunctory and determined not by collective bargaining, but by joint decision of employers and EPB.

As management manipulated unions at the local level the KCIA performed the same function at the national level. It kept the Federation of Korean Trade Unions (FKTU) under its wing. Through the FKTU structures, the KCIA could control the seventeen member nation-wide industrial unions. The

77

industrials in turn exercised a decisive influence on the locals. This hierarchical system of control was cumbersome and at times was not as efficient as the KCIA would have preferred. It would have been easier for them if unions at all levels could just have been abolished, but as a "client" of U.S.A., the champion of democracy, Korea could not totally do away with labor unions. That would have appeared too undemocratic. The Korean government also maintained itself as an observer at the ILO, and FKTU is affiliated with the International Confederation of Free Trade Unions. Furthermore as mentioned above, the American AFL-CIO has a branch office, called the Asia American Federation of Free Labor Institute, in Seoul. Despite the fact that none of these Western bodies lifted a hand to restrain the oppressions of the seventies, still it would have been impolitic for the Korean government to have snuffed unions out all together. Therefore they had to use them. FKTU leadership was kept in the hands of the KCIA. The FKTU always agreed with government labor policy, even if the policies were counter to worker rights. When at the local level a serious dispute arose, the KCIA could send in an FKTU officer to persuade local leaders to obey the company. If that failed, FKTU would use its legal authority to disband the local and take direct control into its own hands.

From the perspective of the innovators, the control and manipulation of labor unions worked very well. Labor-management disputes were minimal and, with a few exceptions, actual work stoppages were seldom. The impact of organized labor on wages seemed to be well under control.

Propaganda
The third component in the subsystem of control in the seventies was propaganda. Workers were constantly bombarded by government and management propaganda intended to spur them on to greater heights of production. Appeals to patriotism and anti-communism were used to instill a sense of loyal urgency into the workers. Education programs, the "New Village Movement" and exhortations by owners, like Chung Ju Yong, were aimed at creating the image of a nation under siege whose very existence depended upon the loyal obedience of workers to their superiors.

At each plant a Joint Labor-Management Council was established so that the teachings about loyal cooperation could be put into practice. If workers recognized the great urgency to increase production, they would, it was thought, join management in overcoming all impediments and bottle-necks. The problem, however, was that neither management nor government knew how to cooperate. Traditional authoritarian patterns dominated the Councils. Worker representatives were selected, or approved, by the company, the agenda was set by management and the decisions made were usually quite insignificant. The Joint Councils were but part of the sub-system of worker control. They were part of a propaganda campaign to manipulate workers.

Fear

The fourth component of labor control under *Yushin* was that of fear. *Yushin* was tantamount to the militarization of the entire society. An endless variety of "law enforcement" agencies permeated all aspects of Korean life. There were the regular police and plainclothes policemen and women; there were riot police who were not police, but soldiers trained in controlling demonstrations; there was the army of invisible spies hired to penetrate the universities, the churches, unions, businesses and civic organizations; and there was the KCIA, most feared of all because it struck at night, condemned the victim to the stigma of "communist" and tortured him/her into compliance.

The factor of fear was central in the control of labor. The KCIA, and its informers, seemed to be ubiquitous. Any suggestion of opposition or criticism about wages, FKTU, education programs or anything else was sure to bring reprisal. That probability in and of itself tamed most workers and union officers. Those who were of a more hardy constitution received individual treatment. If a union leader were stubborn enough to persist in a dispute over wages, the consequent scenario might go like this: a black jeep with a driver and two KCIA agents would likely pick the unionist up early some morning. Four days or a week later he would be returned to his home and his job. He would be hesitant to talk about his experiences of the previous days, but he would let it be known that he no longer really opposed the company's position in the wage dispute. An agreement would be reached and signed by both sides. Not long afterwards, it would surprise no one if the union leader were to resign and leave the company, perhaps move to another city altogether.

SUCCESS AND RESISTANCE

How did the subsystem with its four components of control work out in practice? Apparently quite well from the innovators' perspective. Wages were always kept comfortably below productivity and this certainly contributed to Korea's increasing rates of domestic savings and investments which in turn strengthened its standing in international financial markets.

From another perspective, however, the answer is more equivocal. The innovators tried to impose two contradictory systems upon the nation's workers. On one hand they suppressed labor costs by manipulating unions, expanding hours, and disregarding safety; but at the very same time they demanded cooperation in order to expand productivity. The two are quite contradictory and in fact the innovators paid very little except lip service to the idea of cooperation. Their main energies were expended on the "suppress" side of the ledger. Given

79

the "superior class" mentality of the innovators that pattern was quite to be expected. Indeed it seems almost ludicrous to think of a Chung Ju Yong actually seeking cooperation from a Chun Tae Il -- obedience, yes; cooperation, hardly. Consequently, throughout the 1970's, as the working class expanded in numbers and increased in levels of education their sense of han, outrage and alienation, was also boiling at a more rapid rate.

Statistics from the Korean Development Bank suggest something of what was going on under the surface. For the first three years under the dictatorship productivity increases doubled those of wages. In the next four gradually the relationship was reversed. Real wages increased by a rate of 18.3 percent while productivity rose only 7.8 percent.[12]   Given the levels of control over unions and the efficiency of the EPB's system those statistics, if at all accurate, are surprising. One would have guessed the exact opposite. If union suppression would keep wages down, certainly the 1970's should have accomplished that. If government and company exhortations through Joint Councils and ceaseless education could push up productivity, then productivity should have gone sky high. Perhaps somewhere in the mid-seventies an inverse reaction set in. Suppression of personal and collective freedoms may have led to reduced efforts toward productivity. Perhaps the sham harmony of the Joint Councils bred resistance rather than cooperation. Throughout the 1970's, however, worker resistance was of the quiet, stubborn sort. Only women workers in textiles and electronics openly challenged the enforcement system nurtured by the innovators.

WOMEN WORKERS

Many credit the miracle of the Korean economic expansion to the sweat, blood and tears of young women who worked in the export industries during the 1960's and 1970's -- textiles, garments, electronics, chemicals. The textile industry which dates back to colonial days especially has been the central engine for creating exports, and exports have consistently expanded and earned the foreign currency needed for new investments. Eighty three percent of the employees in the textile industry are women. They are 16 to 25 years of age, and have come primarily from the countryside. As agriculture declined, according to EPB plans, both men and women were forced to leave home and seek employment in the cities. That process still goes on. Skills used in the textile industry can be learned quickly. Once the machines are in place a steady supply of cheap, diligent labor is all that is needed. The country girls provided that labor. In 1970 there were already 600,000 female employees in manufacturing. That was about 30% of the entire labor force. Most of those were in textiles. As the decade moved on, the numbers expanded. By 1980 there were about a million and a half female workers employed in mining and manufacturing. Percentage-wise women made up about forty percent of the employed work force in manufacturing.

Working Conditions

Patterns and attitudes set in place by the Japanese when they established the textile industry back in the 1920's still remained intact fifty years later. Recruiters would go to the countryside to hire workers. The employment contract was understood to be as much with the family as with the person who was actually employed. The family, as it were, stood responsible for its daughter's work and behavior at the factory. Once employed the young women were housed in a company dormitory that was usually located within the company wall. A house mother was provided to supervise the "girls." While the more affluent mills provided adequate dormitories, in the smaller shops they were often nothing more than rat traps.

Beginning in the sixties the dormitory system began to break down. Too many women were being recruited to supply housing for them all. Consequently, the new hands coming into the city were forced to find their own housing. Often this meant that the women were crowded into *hakabans* (shacks) jammed up against each other in the most dilapidated part of town. Four to six persons to an eight by eight room was not unusual. Frequently they would rent such quarters on a part time basis, sleeping in shifts according to the time they worked at the factory. Their meager earnings at the mill would permit nothing better. And though the textile industry, has become modernized and highly automated, changes in the living facilities for the female employees have not kept pace. Indeed the dormitories that still are being provided by some employers today are probably more crowded and less well kept than those of earlier days.

Conditions inside the shop are parallel to the meanness of the workers' housing. Though attitudes are changing, it must be remembered that Korean society is heavily male dominated. Women traditionally have had no intrinsic value. Their function was to reproduce and serve the male members of the family. Beatings were, and still are, administered when for some reason the man becomes irritated. An old Korean proverb says "Like a globe fish you have to beat a woman to make her soft." The author remembers coming upon an old cemetery in the mountains not far from the city of Inchun. Here and there a grave stone would merely have engraved on it Lee from the town of Andong, or Kim from Chunju, or the like. Upon enquiry I was told that in the old days when the woman died, her grave was marked only with the family name and the home town of that family. When Korea was forced into the so-called modern industrial age, this attitude and behavior was not automatically changed. It just became expressed through different channels.

In the factory setting women are usually supervised by men. The men expect traditional style obedience. They assume a traditional style superiority. They speak in commands of traditional "low talk" and when irritated, they may well respond with a traditional crack on the head or a slap to the face. Forced to meet demands for increased production, supervisors and foremen live lives of high tension. Their threshold of irritation tends to be low. Under the best of circumstances, factory life is a high-stress situation. Conflict and friction are unavoidable, every day events. When, however, the company and its supervisors persistently express a disdain for the worker, anger builds up. Even women used to traditional ways begin to think new thoughts and young women who are partly in the world of tradition and partly in the "modern" world of equality and democracy begin to react in an untraditional manner.

Pangrim

Women at Pangrim Textiles, one of Korea's largest firms, had taken more than enough abuse at the hands of male management. From docile, obedient farm girls they became self-assertive persons who formed a labor union. Following is a public statement they wrote in 1978.

Pangrim boasts about its 6,000 workers; its net profit in 1976 of 8,000,000,000 won (U.S. $16,000,000); and the fact that they were one of the pioneer spinning and weaving factories in Korea.

In the dark shadows of this pride and glory, we, women workers, have for too long worked too hard, and experienced too much pain. Our one reason for working is to help our poor parents. We want to wear a student's uniform, but instead we have left our home town in the country and have come to the strange surroundings of Seoul to work in a factory. We came to earn money, but it has been more difficult than we thought possible.

In our factory we work three 8 hour shifts, but from when to when we do not know. We are forced to come early and leave late. We must start 30-60 minutes early and work until the job is finished -- 1 or 2 hours -- it doesn't matter! If we are supposed to finish by 10 p.m. we often get home just before curfew at 12 p.m. If we live in the company dormitory we sometimes work until 1 a.m. or 2 a.m. If for some reason a worker comes at the scheduled starting time, then the foreman and lead girl worker give her a hard time. From that time on, the work for this girl is harder and the increasing pressure means that she eventually leaves. The contemptuous eyes of the foreman and lead worker are fixed upon her. Each worker does not want to be last to arrive and so tries to arrive before her friends. When work is finished no one wants to be the first to leave and so all stay longer. Those who work the longer hours are looked upon favorably and may receive wage increases in the future. Because we work for our daily food, we must work like this. Several years ago when the company started this policy of extra work it was justified in terms of the "saemaul" (New Village) movement. (This is a movement started by President Pak Chung Hee to supposedly increase the diligence and improve the spirit of the Korean people.)

We do not receive a weekly holiday. We work continuously throughout the year with only some of the public holidays off per year. When special public holidays come we want to visit or parents, but we must stay in Seoul and work by our machines. It is a crime that workers cannot fulfil their traditional filial duty to their parents. Animals have a rest time. Why must we work harder than the animals?

Because we have no holidays, night shift is too tiring and so our bodies are exhausted. Therefore we take "Timing," a medicine, to keep awake. Some of us have eaten too many and are now addicted to these pills. If we fall asleep we are reprimanded, beaten and shaken. There are many examples of this. Last night a worker was beaten by the supervisor. In our eyes this means that the company is in fact the one doing the beating. What work do we do? We make many different types of yarn and cloth. Because the machines run continuously we are so busy that we cannot have a meal break. If the machine needs fixing we must do it immediately or suffer the consequences of a reprimand. We are ashamed to say that sometimes we cannot go to the toilet and so must use the factory floor. The machines never stop!!

Such stories do not exaggerate the conditions under which females worked in the seventies -- and to a large degree continue to work in the eighties. One imaginative employer set up his wage system on a piece work basis. Each month the top five producers were given a bonus. The bottom five were fired. The women workers were forced into such a steam of competition and long hours that within a few months many collapsed from fatigue.

83

In the Masan Free Export Zone managers and police regularly meet together to exchange reports on the conduct of the workers, most of whom are women. In the case of Masan not only did all the conditions of Pangrim exist, in addition there was the nationalistic tensions added by the heavy concentration of Japanese employers. The long standing animosity between the two peoples was aggravated by the superior attitude of the Japanese supervisors and the use of the Japanese language in the shop. The Japanese, it is reported, seldom learn Korean. The very success of the Japanese owners in the Zone rubs salt in the wounded pride of the Korean workers who earn meager salaries and endure the usual insults.

Women workers, unlike their male counterparts, often responded to the harshness of the enforcement system by direct resistance. Most of the disputes registered in the decade were registered by women and the few cases of work stoppages were all by women. Earliest and most famous of the strikes was that which took place at the Dongil Textile Company in Inchun.

Dongil

The Dongil Company was originally a Japanese firm. Korean capital took over after liberation in 1945. At the time of the American military government Chun Pyung organized the workers at Dongil, but soon thereafter No Chong, with company support and money, was able to defeat Chun Pyung. From then on a union organization existed at Dongil, but it was always a "kept" union, always run by men, even though ninety percent of the workers were women. Working conditions at Dongil were no better than at Pangrim. Wages kept one alive as long as there was no emergency. The young worker could make it as long as she lived in a hakaban and wasted not her income on eating too much, or buying clothes. The young woman from the countryside also had to guard the treasury of her meager wages from the swarm of young men who cruised around the factory area for the purpose of detaching the women from their paychecks.

In 1972 about 1300 people were employed at Dongil. 1100 were women. A number of the women came to be associated with the Reverend Cho Wha Soon, a woman Methodist minister assigned to a church organization called Urban Industrial Mission (UIM). The young workers gathered for worship, recreation and talk. During the talk each person would relate her own story, tell of her background and share her hopes for the future. Gradually out of those discussions came a plan to take over the union at Dongil. It was decided that the only way the conditions of the work place could be resolved was to have a union led by women. Their work hours were long and unpredictable. Forced overtime without pay was common. The work was dangerous. Wages were miserably low and they were treated with contempt -- even beaten. The union as it then existed was useless. It was run by a few men who were in the pay of the company and cared nothing about the women, or how they had to live.

With the help of Reverend Cho the women from Dongil began a quiet campaign to capture control of the union. When elections for union officers took place in 1972, they were handled as usual by a few company men. The women, however, had planned well. Voting delegates to the meeting had been elected from each section of the plant floor. Without fanfare the workers had been persuaded to vote for delegates who would support a woman president for the union. When it came time to nominate, two names were put forth -- one man and for the first time, one woman, Miss Choo Kil Ja. The vote was taken by secret ballot. Lo and behold, Miss Choo was elected, the first woman in Korean history to become the president of a union. A second vote on an executive committee to share the task of running the union had a similar result. All those elected were women. The male domination of the union was ended.

The company was put into a difficult position. Legally, union officers had a tenure of three years. The company could not refuse to bargain about wages and other conditions of labor, but there was no law that made them like it. For three years they put up with the women, but it was a humiliation to have to bargain with young women, and from the outside pressures must have come to the company to get its house in order. Three years later, however, the same thing happened. The company used its influence to persuade, to transfer, to dismiss and to "buy" but to no avail. Miss Lee Yong Sook was elected and the executive committee was once more all women. The company now determined to end the matter. It had lasted too long. The union leaders and their small group were put under close surveillance inside the factory and outside. The leaders were threatened. Some were fired, and all the workers began to receive warnings that Reverend Cho Wha Soon might be a communist. Reverend Cho's arrest and imprisonment by the KCIA for several months gave the charge a ring of authenticity.

In 1976 new floor delegates were to be elected in April. The company had spread around money to force a vote of non-confidence in the newly elected president, Lee Yong Sook, but once more the company was out-smarted. The women delegates had indeed accepted the company's bribe money, but they brought it to the union meeting. When the motion for non-confidence was put on the floor, the women stood up and threw their money at the men, disclosing the sorry efforts of the company to bribe them and buy the union presidency. In the confusion that followed the union meeting was postponed until July. By then, the company had coordinated its plans with the police. The union president, Miss Lee, was arrested on charges of inciting to riot. The company candidate, a man named Ko Doo Yong, then managed to gather a majority of the floor delegates together and have himself elected as president of the union.

A demonstration resulted. The women workers gathered on company grounds and demanded the release of Miss Lee and the other eight who had been arrested with her. The next morning the police were sent in to clear the grounds. The women, tired and discouraged, lay down. As the police approached, taunting the women as they came, one of the women jumped up and took off her clothes and threw them at the advancing men. Others followed suit standing half naked before the men in defiance, thinking to shame them. It did no good, the men laughed, and swore and beat them with their clubs. Seventy two women were arrested. Fourteen were sent to the hospital.

The final scene of drama was yet to come. For nine months the struggle for control of the union went on. In April of 1977 there was finally a binding vote and for the third time a woman won -- but the end of these heroics was not far away. Both the company and the government had had enough of women's liberation.

February 21, 1978 was the date for election of new floor delegates. The union hall is on company property located right beside the factory gate. When the women went to prepare the hall for the meeting, they found that someone had preceded them. Everything was covered with human excrement. Men workers were in the hall breaking up the ballot boxes. As the women came in, the men began to throw the excrement at them and to rub it in their faces.

The company announced that 124 of the union women had been discharged for causing damage to company property. The National Textile Union (FKTU) then declared that the charter of the local union was rescinded and all officers of the local were dismissed. The officers were, of course, among the 124 who were fired and subsequently blackballed by union, government and employers.[13]

The battle had been waged for almost six years. It was unique. Women had struck a telling blow. They had not only come of age, they were the leaders of a movement that in another ten years would become nationwide. From the courage demonstrated by the women at Dongil other women workers in other plants took strength and acted to improve their own lot. Sygnetics, Bando Songsa, Pangrim, Hankook Mobang, Dongsu, Yanghaing, and Y. H. are names of a few companies where, in the 1970's, the women refused to accept the *Yushin* system of oppression. When in the mid-eighties the male workers began to take action of their own, they found that they were standing on the shoulders of women who had been struggling for justice for more than ten years.

URBAN INDUSTRIAL MISSION

Central to the Dongil conflict was Reverend Cho Wha Soon from the Urban Industrial Mission (UIM). She worked as a laborer in the mill and then as a pastor to the young women textile workers for the next twenty years.

Many of the struggles of workers in the 1970's are closely intertwined with Reverend Cho and the UIM.

Worker Priest

Urban Industrial Mission (UIM) took root among Korean workers back in the 1960's when a democratic air was in the ascendancy. In those days the excitement of democratic freedoms became intermixed in some Christian circles with the examples of the Worker Priests, in World War II France, who took up their ministry among the working classes. The Gospel of Christ was rediscovered in the midst of factory and dock workers. From the perspective of a priest working in a factory, biblical theology took on new meaning and new energy. In South Korea the Worker Priest discoveries were revisited by a small number of Methodist, Catholic, and Presbyterian clergy. For periods of time from six months to five years they labored in factories or on the docks. Through the pain and injuries of their bodies and spirits they re-examined society. Rev. Cho Sung Hyuk, the Director of UIM, and a colleague of Reverend Cho Wha Soon, worked in a plywood factory. He tells this story of how he was converted to a "new" Jesus. One day as he was helping unload a truck of plywood, he got into a fight with the truckman. The latter was on the top of the load lifting the wood down to other men below. Instead of taking his time and lowering it carefully, he threw the wood down as fast as he could with some force and cursed the guys when they missed. After getting his head jolted by a missile from above, out of pure anger Sung Hyuk yelled, "Do that one more time and I'll come up there and knock your teeth down your throat." The truckman cursed him soundly, but did as Sung Hyuk told him. Through that mundane experience, new worlds were opened to the spiritual eyes of Reverend Cho. It dawned on him that his comrades would live all their lives being dumped on by guys like that truckman. Religion and salvation were not a sermon or ritual, but a fight with a truckman to ease the pain of the man at the bottom. Justice for the worker became the key for understanding religion. Workers and those who struggle for justice were seen as reflecting the image of Jesus. Sung Hyuk's ministry with UIM was thereafter far different from that of other clergy who never stood up to a truckman. His life ever since has been involved in the lives of Korea's industrial workers, especially in their efforts to organize and gain respect from management and government. This has put him in the middle of many controversies, and on several occasions has also put him in jail.

Conversions similar to those of Cho Sung Hyuk's were experienced by other clergy who entered factories during the 1960's. The numbers were never great. Total figures probably did not exceed twenty five over the decade. In industrial areas of Inchun, Seoul, Chungju and Pusan UIM pastors set up their ministries. Those who worked in the mills gathered small groups of their fellow workers together after work either in someones' home or at a winehouse. A close comradery grew up among them as they would talk over their mutual problems in the plant. After they completed their factory work, UIM staff were assigned as "factory pastors." They visited unions and management offices; they made house calls on families of workers; and when accidents in the plant sent workers to the hospital a UIM person would be there to pray with them and their families.

At night workers gathered together to talk and sing and think about their legal and human rights. UIM offered courses in how to organize and run a union. In the 1960's that could be done. It could be done with the cooperation of the labor department of the city and national government. Workers were forming unions. UIM cooperated with them. As a staff member of the UIM, the author received, on several occasions, commendations from the government's labor department for his work with the unions of the Inchun area.

JOC

The UIM was primarily a Protestant operation. The Catholic Church had its own ministry among workers. It was called the JOC, or Young Christian Workers. Like UIM, the JOCs accept Jesus as the savior from the underside of society, i.e., Jesus of the poor. JOC was begun in Korea in 1958. The young workers, most of whom are women, are trained to act as individual apostolates to see, judge, and act within their places of employment. First look and see who is being hurt and why; then judge as to what can be done to remedy the hurt; and finally act to help bring about a change. In this way individual Christian laity are to give witness to Christ in the work place. In the atmosphere of Korea's *Yushin*, however, such action by an individual, or group of individuals, was considered subversive. One JOC experience is representative. Kim Myung Ja is a Catholic from the country-side who came to the town of Anyang in 1978. She was hired on at a textile mill. At the parish church, where she quickly attached herself, she met other girls who worked in the mills of Anyang. They were members of JOC so Myung Ja also joined and took orientation in the "see, judge, act" method. As part of the training, she had to relate the facts of her work place and share her judgments and actions with the others. From the very first day she saw that some of her co-workers were walking around in a daze and one woman actually fell into the machinery, injuring her shoulder and the side of her face. Myung Ja judged that the cause behind this behavior was lack of sleep. The work was too hard and the required overtime too long. Everyone was so fatigued they could hardly stay awake. The act that Myung Ja contemplated was to persuade several others to go with her to the supervisor to ask for more relief time.

Myung Ja never got to the third step. An informer reported to the police that Myung Ja was an "organizer" with the JOC. She was arrested. Her room was broken into and searched. She was fired. The police and company apparently thought such tactics would subdue the JOCs. The effects, however, were just the opposite. Anger at having a KCIA spy among them, and outrage at the treatment given to Myung Ja strengthened the JOC resolve. Her story spread through JOC groups everywhere. Instead of shrinking back they became more active. Along with UIM, JOC played a significant role throughout the 1970's in educating the female workers as to the goals and methods of unionism. They gave the women a religious motivation for their actions. It was this, the religious foundation, that the KCIA could never quite comprehend, but it was probably that religious dimension which accounts for much of the close community that has grown up among women workers of Korea.

So it happened that in dispute after dispute, the participants were found to be either UIM or JOC. The famous labor conflicts of the decade were mostly related in some way to these two movements -- Signetics, Dongil Textile, Hankook Mobang, Bangrim, Wonpoong, and Y. H. The conflicts were not initiated by UIM or JOC, but workers who had received education and communion with them frequently were in places of leadership and called upon UIM or JOC for succor when the company refused to bargain, or the police began to attack.

When in the mid-seventies, being related to UIM or JOC could cost a worker his/her job, UIM and JOC adjusted by going "underground" as it were. Workers would meet at irregular times and places, not in large numbers, not in the UIM offices, and usually late at night. The subjects studied were union organizing, labor law and scripture. Stories from the strikes of the women workers circulated throughout the groups. These combined with their own experiences and the courage that grows out of participation in secret and dangerous undertakings gradually changed the consciousness of many and helped set the scene for what was to become the democratic labor movement of the 1980's.

The women from Dongil introduced a different course of action. After their defeat, the dismissed workers continued to meet at the UIM offices under Cho Wha Soon's guidance. At first they met only to protect and heal each other, but later on they became an advisory group to women in other factories who were facing problems similar to the ones they had faced in Dongil. It became a pattern that continued on into the 1980's. Today, in 1989, groups of dismissed workers, many of whom have spent years in prison, have become major actors on the labor scene.

KCIA Attack

Attacks against UIM and JOC began immediately after Pak Chung Hee's declaration of emergency in 1971. KCIA agents suddenly became daily visitors. Staff were questioned as to what they were doing, who they were seeing. Education programs were interrupted or forbidden. In mid-1974 Cho Wha Soon was detained by the KCIA for three months. Cho Sung Hyuk and others were arrested. Workers related to UIM or JOC were threatened away. A barrage of propaganda was let loose on the public. Radio, T.V. dramas were used to warn the nation and especially the workers that UIM and JOC were "impure elements" (euphemism for communist) in religious clothing. One of the chief vehicles used by the KCIA in its attacks was the FKTU. A speech by the Chair of the Chemical Workers' Union to a gathering of the FKTU in 1978 illustrates the nature of the KCIA attack.

> Some rebellious elements have infiltrated into the labor unions under the cloak of religion and have stimulated separation and are fomenting social unrest. This is a great problem in the light of national security. From now on we have to fight against religion. The Vietnam war also ended in failure because of religion. I appeal for a resolution to be passed to sternly destroy those religious forces that have infiltrated our million members and intend to destroy our unions. Let's eliminate them from the roots!

After the chairman's motion was duly passed and he had finished his remarks to the assembled members of FKTU's "Committee for the Program to Improve the Working Environment," another gentleman arose to lecture the workers and union people on the dangers of outside forces. His topic was "What is UIM aiming at?" The content of his message was this: "The Christian movements involved in social issues are outgrowths of the international communist party. The UIM and JOC are red. You workers best beware of any organization whose name begins with 'Ki' (In Korea, Christianity is Ki-dok-kyo). They are dangerous things. This impure force has infected 75% of the textile unions and 70% of the chemical unions."[14]

The FKTU spent much energy, time and budget in its effort to stigmatize UIM and JOC. The KCIA and police haunted, hassled and even tortured people in futile attempts to destroy the two Christian groups. They failed because they were blinded by their own narrow vision. To them everyone who spoke or acted contrary to their commands were communists. To call them communist they thought would be the end of the matter. KCIA people never comprehended the absurdity of calling South Korean Christians communists. They had no mental framework within which they could understand that UIM and JOC were grounded in a theology that interprets history in terms of social justice and liberation for the poor. KCIA's efforts at suppression instead of stamping out JOC and UIM helped spread their theology to areas and people who had no direct contact with either.

After Pak Chung Hee's death and the seizure of government by another military dictator who committed as his first act a massacre of several hundred people in the city of Kwangju, the mood of the people changed. It was as though everyone began to say, "Enough is enough, and this is too much." Opposition to the Chun dictatorship that began in 1980 became more open, more brazen. The labor education groups sponsored by UIM underwent this same type of metamorphosis. They again began to meet in the open, but now the attitude was more aggressive. Anti–government slogans became part of the menu, and sentiments of anti–Americanism began for the first time to be expressed. Art, drama, music and dancing that related young workers to the past struggles of their nation became part of the educational content. History of the labor movement was opened for the young to see. Stories of Chun Pyung and the Peoples' Committees of 1945–47 were regained and compared favorably with the current FKTU and its captivity to the KCIA. Furthermore the new educators began to make connections between the oppressions against human rights and the division of the nation. Both North and South were military camps. Therefore democracy and human rights were always being violated in the name of national security. Demilitarization and reunification came to be seen as necessary roads toward a just society. From these roots a new and radically different analysis of the worker's plight began to take shape.

INTERNAL CONTRADICTIONS

The 1970's was primarily a time of change and metamorphosis. The economic achievements were monumental. At the same time changes were being wrought in the minds, attitudes and actions of the nation's working class. Increasingly they were being made conscious of their own subordinate and even oppressed situation in society. The innovators never seemed to be alert to any of these changes. Instead they kept applying greater and greater doses of manipulation–intimidation–violence. Not even President Pak, so astute in many other areas, gave any evidence of adjusting to the changes that were taking place in the nation's work force.

In a Liberation Day speech, August 16, 1979, President Pak Chung Hee said, "In time of hardships like this, entrepreneurs and employees are advised in sharing difficulties and rallying their resources to deepen their mutual trust in the realization of interdependence so as to overcome the current impasse. Only then, a family–like atmosphere of brotherhood can be created in management–

employee relations, generating a firm potential for further growth of enterprises capable of overcoming difficulties of any magnitude."[15]

Three months before Pak's exhortations about a "family-like" atmosphere, a corporation called Y. H. Trading Company had closed its gates because the company president had run off to the U.S.A. with all its assets. Five hundred women employees were thrown out of work. When they took over the plant in protest, police were sent against them. Two hundred of the young women were beaten mercilessly. Five were sent to the hospital for prolonged, intensive care. Five days before Pak's speech Y. H. women fled to the offices of the opposition political party for protection. Again police attacked. The women were again beaten by truncheons and dragged bodily out of the office into the street. One was killed.[16]

Pak included nothing about this little "family conflict" in his speech. Two days later three Y. H. women were arrested and charged with unlawful assembly -- a crime that carries a sentence of seven years imprisonment.

DEATH OF PAK

The violence against the Y. H. workers in Seoul incited riots as far away as Masan and Pusan. President Pak and his close friend Kim Jae Kyu, head of the KCIA, were discussing ways to handle the riots when Kim ended the discussion by shooting Pak in the head. Kim later claimed he did it to save the nation from a blood bath that Pak intended to rain down upon Masan and Pusan. Thus the eighteen years of rule under Pak Chung Hee ended abruptly on October 26, 1979. The *Yushin* system had established Pak as dictator for life. Not his enemies, but his friend, ended that life at the age of fifty four.

CHAPTER NOTES

1. Seok Ki Kim, "Business Concentration and Government Policy," Harvard, 1987, p. 172.

2. Harvard Business School Case Study "Hyundai Heavy Industries, March, 1986, p. 14, 15.

3. Outline of story comes from Leroy Jones and Il So Kang, Government, Business and Entrepreneurship in Economic Development, Harvard, 1980, p. 358.

4. min-ju no-jo South Korea's New Trade Unions, Asia Labour Monitor, Honkong, 1988, p. 7. Statistics taken from Korean Development Institute.

5. Young-ki Park, Labor and Industrial Relations in Korea: System and Practice, Sogang University, Seoul, 1979, p. 98.

6. Tonga-Ilbo, October 31, 1983.

7. Tonga-Ilbo, July 14, 1983.

8. Fortune, September, 1977, p. 171.

9. Young-ki Park, Ibid., p. 113.

10. Young-ki Park, Ibid., p. 44.

11. Annual Report, Federation of Korean Trade Unions, Seoul, 1978, p. 80.

12. Korean Development Bank, Financial Analysis 1972-1978, as found in Young-ki Park, Labor and Industrial Relations in Korea: System and Practice, Sogang University, Seoul, 1979, p. 98.

13. This account of the Dongil story was in part based upon a book by Cho Wha Soon, Let the Weak be Strong, Meyer and Stone, 1988.

14. Extracted from an FKTU document entitled, "The Program to Expel 'Outside Forces' from each Labor Union and Workshop," 1978.

15. Korea Herald, August 16, 1979, p. 5.

16. On Korean Laborers, a perspective and data base, Seoul, 1988, data 61.

Following the assassination of Pak Chung Hee, martial law was declared for most of the country, and Prime Minister Choi Kyu Ha became Acting President. There were no public uprisings and no demonstrations in the streets, but there was the widespread hope that the time had come for a transfer of political power to civilian hands. Surely the military, with their chief now dead, would return to their posts as defenders of their nation and give up their ambitions for political power. That, however, was not to be the case. Having experienced the benefits of governmental power, the military was not about to retire, and the citizens were not yet strong enough to force them back into their proper role.

MILITARY COUP

The military made the first move. On December 12, 1979 General Chun Doo Hwan used troops from the Demilitarized Zone to carry out a purge within the army. Forty top military officers, including the Martial Law Commander, were arrested. Chun elevated close friends into those positions.

At the same time, to ameliorate the burgeoning demands from the people for more freedom, Chun made a gesture toward democratization. On February 19 of 1980, he restored civil rights to leading political figures including Kim Dae Jung, the opposition leader who nearly defeated Pak Chung Hee in the 1971 presidential elections. Dismissed university professors were reinstated to their former positions, and expelled university students were allowed to resume their studies.

Chun's gesture was far from sufficient to satisfy those seeking democracy. University students revived their anti-government organizations and openly demanded that the KCIA be removed from the campuses and that martial law be ended. Professors, intellectuals and journalists rather than being pacified by the restoration of their civil rights once more became active demanding freedom of speech and the restoration of democratic processes. Kim Dae Jung went on a speaking tour. Crowds of fifty to a hundred thousand came to hear him denounce the military and make demands for a democratic government.

General Chun had no intention of leading the country into democracy. He was heading the other direction. He intended to see that the military dictatorship would stay in power. On March 11 (1980), he received support from an unexpected source. General John Wickham, Commander of U.S. Forces in Korea was quoted in the Asian Wall Street Journal as saying that the South Korean military's proper role includes "being watch dogs on political activity that could be de-stabilizing, and in a way making judgement about the eligibility and reliability of political candidates that may have some adverse influence on stability."

With this endorsement in pocket General Chun appointed himself as Acting Director of the KCIA. Already he held the posts of Defense Security Commander and Director of Martial Law Joint Investigation Department. His word to the Korean public was that the *Yushin* system would be preserved and that no criticism of the late President Pak Chung Hee would be allowed.[1]

Chun's "get-tough" policy, however, settled nothing. The people were not willing to meekly submit to his orders. By early May street demonstrations broke out all over the country. Some 200,000 students, 50,000 in Seoul alone, demanded a complete end to martial law, an end to military training on campus and the resignation of Chun Doo Hwan. Chun was not to be intimidated either. On May 17, he led a military coup d'etat, declaring a nation-wide state of full martial law, forbidding all political activity, closing universities, dissolving the national assembly and forbidding criticism of present and past national leaders. Hundreds of students, democratic leaders, and politicians, including Kim Dae Jung were arrested.

KWANGJU

Protests against Chun's coup began in the southern city of Kwangju. As in the Tonghak rebellion of the 1890's and uprisings of the Peoples' Committees in the 1940's, once more the Southwest became the center of political revolt.

The day after martial law was declared about 500 Kwangju students demonstrated, demanding an end to martial law and the resignation of Chun. In response soldiers and paratroopers surrounded the students and indiscriminately beat and bayoneted them leaving dozens dead. Shocked at the military brutality citizens joined the students. Charging paratroopers killed hundreds including children, women and old people. As word of paratrooper brutality spread, hundreds of thousands of citizens came out to demonstrate. Two radio stations were burned for falsifying the news. By May 21 angry Kwangju citizens seized arms from police stations and army stockpiles and commandeered vehicles. They drove the army out of the city. For five days citizens controlled Kwangju. By that time hospitals were full. Five hundred people were confirmed dead and 960 were reported missing.[2]

The citizens of Kwangju appealed to the U.S. government to help negotiate a solution, but the U.S. State Department declined saying, "We recognize that a situation of total disorder and disruption in a major city cannot be allowed to go on indefinitely."[3]

The peoples' committees were warned that at 4:00 A.M. on the morning of May 27, the 20th Division of the ROK army would enter Kwangju. They were instructed to give no opposition. At three o'clock, one hour before their announced time, the 20th Division invaded Kwangju, shooting as they came. Again scores of people were senselessly slaughtered.[4]

Thus Kwangju became an albatross around the neck of Chun Doo Hwan and a rallying point for opposition throughout the country. It also became the focus for anti-American sentiments that were beginning to be voiced among students. The 20th Division had been brought in from the front lines where it was under the command of General John Wickham, U.S. Army. It is widely believed that Wickham released the 20th Division to Chun knowing full well Chun's intentions to send it to Kwangju. When a few months later Wickham was quoted in the Los Angeles Times as saying that the U.S. would not object to Chun becoming president, the suspicions of America's involvement in the "Kwangju massacre" became more firmly believed.

How was the massacre to be explained? Korean troops randomly killing and maiming Korean civilians had to be explained! How could such a thing happen? Some likened the shock of Kwangju to the shock of having cataracts removed from one's eyes. Suddenly they saw clearly what they had known all along. For over a decade their government had been killing them in one way or another; and as General Wickham was seen to be behind the massacre in Kwangju so the United States was now understood to be behind the oppressions perpetuated by the Korean government. Had not the U.S. government and corporations propped up Pak Chung Hee? Was not the United States preventing democracy so that U.S. corporations could make big profits in Korea? All of a sudden the old ally became the suspected enemy.

THE CHUN REGIME

Three months after the Kwangju massacre as provided in the *Yushin* constitution, an electorial college designated Chun Doo Hwan president of the Republic of Korea. Before he took office he was already an enemy of the people. An immediate visit to the United States as President Reagan's first foreign visitor was intended to shore up his authority among the Korean populace. Instead it brought scorn upon both parties as it further fed the fuel of anti-Americanism and the suspicions of the U.S. involvement in Kwangju.

Politically, Chun was "dead on arrival," as they say. The time of the military had passed. A new mood was beginning to emerge in the country. People were tired of the senseless cruelty that had been perpetuated against them for a decade. They wanted to share a little more in the great economic miracle which they saw emerge all around them and above all, they wanted to taste those ideals called democracy and freedom. They wanted to elect their own government, to participate and criticize. Even without Kwangju, it is unlikely that Chun would ever have gained the sympathies of the people. With Kwangju, his departure was only a matter of time.

King Rehoboam

Chun, moreover, lacked wisdom. He had no insight into the mind of his people. His attempt to rule by force recalls an old Biblical tale. King Solomon had enriched Israel, built the temple, and created an economic abundance, but to do so, he had enslaved half the population. When Solomon died, his successor, Rehoboam, met with the spokesman of the opposition, a man named Jereboam. Jereboam is reported to have addressed the new king in this manner: "We have worked for Solomon and the glory of our nation, but he did us wrong. He enslaved and abused us. Only if you will now promise to lighten our load, shall we continue to serve you as King."

Rehoboam, however, had a hard head. He responded, "My little finger shall be thicker than my father's loins. My father (King Solomon) made your yoke heavy, and I will add to your yoke; my father chastised you with whips, but I will chastise you with scorpions." (I Kings 12)

Once that was said, the only road left open to Rehoboam was military force. From that day on there was civil strife in Israel. Rehoboam did not prevail. Chun Doo Hwan responded to his people in a manner like unto that of King Rehoboam, with the same results.

Immediately upon his elevation to the presidency, Chun initiated a series of disastrous policies. He rigged the so-called national assembly in the same way that Pak Chung Hee had done. That body then passed a new constitution which was the old *Yushin* in thin disguise. A new Presidential Election Law secured Chun in power. Edicts of the martial law command humbled the media into even deeper censorship, and the newly formed "Social Purification Committee" announced that persons of "impure" thought or character would undergo purification education. If after the initial education, an internee still persisted in his impurity, he or she would be "secluded" from society for up to ten years. To wrap things up into a neat legal package, Chun had the Anti-Communist and National Security laws combined. This would catch any "impurity" that might slip through other laws.

Kim Dae Jung

These were only a few of the Rehoboam-like measures that Chun Doo Hwan undertook. In one way, he outdid Rehoboam. He created a martyr figure to go along with the martyred city, Kwangju. Kim Dae Jung had been an enemy of Pak Chung Hee since the elections of 1971. Chun Doo Hwan inherited Kim as an enemy. As soon as he came to power, he moved to rid himself of this Jereboam. Kim, a native of the Southwestern section of the country, where Kwangju is located, was charged with masterminding the Kwangju rebellion (as the government called it). He was put through the charade of a military court and sentenced to die. Pressures inside and outside of Korea, however, were too great.   Chun backed off.   Kim's death sentence was commuted to life imprisonment. Two years later, on December 23, 1982, Kim and his wife were exiled to the United States. Kim Dae Jung became the hero figure to go along with Kwangju.

Student Opposition

The opposition to Chun included just about everyone -- politicians, students, and church groups. He had little support among the citizenry to offset these enemies. Students, as is usual in Korea, took the lead. Despite the fact that Chun had officially disbanded all student groups except his own Student Defense Corps, the students became even more adept at organizing and at out-thinking the authorities.   Rhetoric became more inflammatory, more anti-American. An example of the fired-up rhetoric came from a speech by one Seoul National University student: "The Chun regime is anti-nation, anti-democratic, and anti-people. It is fascist. It must be overthrown by the struggle of the people. The fascists, while dependent on foreign capital, enslave workers in low wages, and farmers in low prices and loss of land. It protects only the privileged class. The economic and political systems are but two sides of the same coin."[5] Demonstrations popped up like popcorn, out of control. Tons of tear gas were poured upon them, but to no avail. The demand for tear gas was so great that it stimulated a new industry in Korea. In 1987, it was reported that Mrs. Han Youn Jao, president of Sam Yang Chemical Company, earned more money than any other individual in Korea. Her business had been multiplied by two hundred times since 1979. Mrs. Han paid $3.4 million in taxes on a gross income of $7.3 million. On a daily basis, she made $20,000. Her company's one product was tear gas.

In addition to street demonstrations, increased numbers of dedicated students left college and found jobs in factories. Their mission was to conjoin the strength of students and workers to bring down the house of Chun. They were also accused of injecting anti-American rhetoric into the slogans of labor. When discovered, they were dismissed for giving false information on their applications for employment.   The government followed through by either drafting them into the army or sending them to prison for a couple years on other charges. Sending dissidents to prison is, of course, in the long run self-defeating. They come out more determined, better trained than when they went in. Neither Pak nor Chun seemed to understand that fact of life.   Each year they kept a ready supply of "graduates" coming out of prison to return to the task of bringing the government down. The numbers of college students who became factory workers may have reached three thousand or more. In one year alone, 1985-86, the police claim to have apprehended 671 such "agitators."

99

In 1986 a woman student named Kwon In Sook was discovered working in a factory near Inchun. She was arrested and put in the local jail. Her male captors unfortunately showed their disdain for Miss Kwon by assaulting her sexually and then torturing her with electric shock. When she gained consciousness, her humiliation was so great she tried to commit suicide. Other women prisoners prevented the deed. The attempt at suicide must have been cathartic, however, for when Miss Kwon was finally freed on bail she did a quite unprecedented thing: she made her story public and brought legal suit against the culprits and the chief of the police station. Kwon In Sook's story hit the nation like a slap in the face. It was one more sin that was piled up against Chun Doo Hwan and his regime. She was taken to court, found guilty of lying on her employment application, and sentenced to a year and a half in prison. At first, government prosecutors refused to indict the policeman directly involved in the case. Finally, after two appeals and much public protest, he was found guilty and was fired from his job.

Opposition Politics

Under the impetus of Kwangju even the opposition political parties joined ranks. From the days of Syngman Rhee the opposition politicians have always been factious, fighting against each other rather than providing the people with a credible option. In 1984 the two leading opposition political parties joined together. Kim Dae Jung led one party from exile in the U.S.A. Kim Yong Sam led the other one from inside Korea. Together they decided to dethrone Chun Doo Hwan.

On the third anniversary of Kwangju (May 1983), Kim Yong Sam began a hunger strike, demanding the return of democracy. Kim fasted for 26 days. To keep him from dying, the authorities took him to a hospital and force-fed him. They did not want another martyr. It was too late. Kim did not die, but his actions precipitated hunger strikes and anti-Chun rallies across the country. Policemen breaking into churches and attacking worshippers as they prayed and fasted for democracy further fueled the movement.

Then in August of 1983, Chun Doo Hwan gave the opposition the opening it needed, a cause and a date upon which it could focus its energy. Chun announced that he would step aside when his first term as president was over in 1987. However, the *Yushin*'s indirect system of presidential elections would be continued. There would be no direct elections to choose his successor.

From then on, the battle cry of the opposition became "direct free elections in '87." The tide became irresistible. Little by little Chun was backed into a corner. An end to military rule was in sight. Kim Dae Jung was permitted to return to Korea in early 1985. He joined Kim Yong Sam in attacking Chun on the issue of direct elections.

100

In the midst of these domestic eruptions, the American State Department managed to throw another log on the fire. Secretary of State George Schultz made a visit to Korea. He embraced Chun Doo Hwan, praising him for making progress toward democracy. It was a ludicrous posture for the Secretary of State, and it provided more evidence that the dictator Chun was being propped up by the U.S. government. Shultz's remark further enforced the suspicion that the U.S. had been behind the Kwangju massacre.

On April 13, 1987, Chun Doo Hwan ordered all discussion of direct elections and constitutional revision to be discontinued until after the 1988 Olympics. By then he hoped to have his hand-picked successor in place. Religious leaders strongly denounced Chun's order with fasting and prayer and led a nationwide campaign of resistance. Intellectuals, writers, lawyers and university professors issued statements demanding constitutional change and direct elections. Chun responded by stepping up the oppression. Opposition legislators were jailed; anti-government politicians and church leaders were threatened or arrested; and student demonstrators were beaten down with increased harshness. When a tear gas canister struck a Yunsei University student, Lee Han Yol, in the chest and killed him, the battle between government and people heated to a fury.

The next day (June 10) Chun's ruling party held its national convention and nominated another general, Roh Tae Woo, as its candidate for the presidency. U.S. Ambassador James Lilley was an honored guest at the convention to hear Noh's acceptance speech.

The demonstrations aggravated by the death of Lee Han Yol, however, did not abet. They grew into chaos. For nineteen days in thirty seven cities people lashed out at the government demanding direct elections. "People power" became a front page story. The viability of the Olympics and the government itself came under increasing attack.

In this context, candidate Roh Tae Woo, on June 29, made a surprise announcement. He said that he, and the ruling party, supported direct elections. Furthermore he promised that there would be release of political prisoners; restoration of civil rights -- even to Kim Dae Jung; freedom of the press; and an end to human rights abuses.

Throughout the nation, "people power" was celebrated. Everyone was sure that in the December elections the democratic opposition would win ending the decades of military dictatorship.

Then in one of those ironies that seem to populate so much of Korean history, Kim Yong Sam and Kim Dae Jung split. They had worked, suffered, and bled for the return of democracy, but when the opportunity arrived, the thirst for power and the drag of traditional factionalism was too much. Neither would defer to the other despite public pledges to do so. Both ran for president.

Neither won. Chun Doo Hwan's protegee got the victory. Some say that it was because of corruption and the use of force that Roh Tae Woo won. Perhaps. But psychologically and morally, the Kims had disqualified themselves. The hopes of the people had once more been betrayed.

CHUN'S ATTACK ON LABOR

Chun's policy toward labor was also taken from the pages of King Rehoboam. He intended to increase the already heavy weight of dictatorship on the backs of workers. A week before he was designated President (August 21, 1980), he, as general in charge of martial law, had promulgated "Guidelines for Purification of Labor Unions." Eleven of the seventeen national industrial union presidents were forced to resign. One hundred and six regional leaders and almost two hundred local officers were forcefully evicted from their unions. Others more friendly to the Chun Doo Hwan regime were put in their stead. Even after a full decade of *Yushin* interference with union leadership, Chun still could not trust the unions to do his bidding.

Despite all the precautions of the KCIA, legitimate unionists kept infiltrating the union structures. Some came from UIM or JOC, others were members of student groups, many were connected with organizations of former union leaders who had spent time in prison, and still others were rank and file workers seeking a solution to workers' problems. Indeed in 1980, there were still a half dozen local unions that maintained a modicum of independence from the KCIA. Chun's purification guidelines were aimed at eliminating all of these groups.

Chun was also quite aware of the connection between the Y. H. incident and the death of his mentor, Pak Chung Hee. He intended to take a little revenge and at the same time prevent the same thing happening to him. Not only were union leaders purged, any who talked back or failed to show adequate repentance for past sins were picked up and sent to the "purification camps" run by the military (p. 55).

The second stage in the offensive against organized labor came shortly after Chun became President. A new set of labor laws was decreed. Local unions were still required to belong to an industrial federation and the FKTU. In this way, the downward method of controlling unions would be continued. The other part of the strategy was to isolate the local from the Industrials or FKTU in regards to bargaining. Each local, at each company, would be on its own. Bargaining would be carried on only between the company and the plant union. There would be no help given from the outside. So called "third party interventions" were strictly prohibited. Church groups like UIM or JOC were the original objects of this law, but it was extended to include both industrial federations and the FKTU. They were forbidden to take any role in local union action.

The result was to make collective bargaining even more of a sham than it had been under Pak. Control over the union by company and police was enhanced. At the other end of the union spectrum, the FKTU captivity was made even more complete. It was chartered to conduct education programs and to act as liaison with various international labor organizations. Otherwise, there was little left for it to do.

To make sure the dismemberment and captivity of the unions did not go awry, Chun beefed up the KCIA. First he changed its name to National Security Planning (NSP), and then he established a special agency to deal with labor: "The Committee to Counteract Labor Insurgency." By using that imaginative title, all labor conflict became matters of "insurgency," a euphemism for communist activity. Any actions against labor, therefore, became justified. The NSP quickly gained a reputation for tortures that exceeded even that of its infamous predecessor, the KCIA.

Peace Market Union Disbanded

The NSP's first assignment against labor was to get rid of the few remaining unions that had not capitulated to the KCIA. The first attack, appropriately enough, came against the Chonggye Garment Workers' Union, the union formed in the wake of Chun Tae Il's death in 1970 at the Peace Market. Despite many efforts to close it down, the union had always survived. The mystique created by Chun's death was still strong and his mothers' presence among the young people seemed to constantly renew their resolve. The 1980 revision of the labor law had made regional and district unions illegal. Since Chonggye Garment was a union of workers employed in the Peace Market area and across many different employers, it was declared to be a district organization and therefore illegal. A squad of police enforced the decision.

In desperation, twenty-one of the young leaders went to the Asian-American Free Labor Institute (AAFLI), an arm of the AFL-CIO that had been in Korea since 1971, and from which the workers at Peace Market had received financial support for their labor school. Apparently they expected the Americans to see the justice of their position and render protection. When these expectations were not met, the workers took over the AAFLI office and staged a sit-in demonstration. The AAFLI director was temporarily held hostage. Barricades were set up to prevent police entrance. A demand for the reinstatement of the union was issued, and the workers waited for the inevitable. About midnight, the police broke through. Chun Tae Il's brother and another younger man jumped from the 4th floor window. Chun Tae Sam was caught by a net and uninjured. The other man was not so lucky. Shin Kwan Young, vice president of the union, broke his back. The others were taken to prison.

The Chonggye Garment Union was outlawed. The labor school was shut. But moral outrage was building up. Once more the image of the burning body of Chun Tae Il was being recalled by workers throughout the land. The union of workers at the Peace Market would not go away. Three years later (1984) six hundred Peace Market workers held a vigil at Myongdong Cathedral in downtown Seoul calling for the reinstatement of their union. A few days after the vigil, 3,000 students and workers demonstrated in front of the Peace Market demanding the right of workers to organize. The Chonggye Garment Union would not go away.

Union Defeat at Control Data

Following the defeat of the union at Peace Market, attention was centered on an American Company. Control Data had been in Korea for over fifteen years. Early on, a union had been formed and each year a contract that covered wages and working conditions was signed. Looking through high powered microscopes, the women produced tiny microchips for export. Matters of eye care and factory ventilation, in addition to wages, were always of concern in negotiations.

When contract renewal came up in 1982, almost from the beginning there was a stalemate. Ostensibly, the bind was over a pay raise and health issues, but there was more than that involved. Chun Doo Hwan had demanded that each company establish a "Purification Committee" that would root out "troublemakers" among the workers. In the midst of the stalled negotiations, Control Data's Purification Committee decided that six of the women workers had to be dismissed because they were agitating other workers against the company. Management teams were dispersed to the homes of the six. Their parents, were told of their daughters' dismissal, informed that their names had gone to the NSP, and were offered termination pay. It was hoped that the six would leave quietly and that there would be no disturbance. This, of course, did not happen. When the other workers heard what had been done, they immediately sat down inside the factory and pledged to stay there until the six comrades were re-instated.

The company at first resisted offers by the police to break up the demonstration. It continued to supply food to the workers in the plant. Negotiations were re-opened. The wage dispute was quickly brought to solution, with both parties agreeing to a 19.5 percent raise. Originally the union had demanded 20% and the company had offered 12.9 percent. The remaining issue was the six dismissed workers. The Purification Committee, as directed by the government's Office of Labor Affairs, would not hear to their re-instatement.

Into this dilemma walked two "trouble shooters" from the corporate headquarters in Minnesota. In retrospect, one can judge that it was a mistake to send those uninitiated to hot Korean conflict into such a caldron as Control Data had become. Nevertheless, the two men met with the workers to seek solution. One of them suggested that Control Data might pull out of Korea in any case. This was seen as a threat. The new anti-American emotions flared up. According to an account in Forbes magazine, eighty "screaming, shouting, fainting, and crying" women poured into the conference room demanding to know company intentions and declaring that the two Americans would not get out of there until the six were re-instated. After several hours of confusion, one of the captive Americans had an urgent call of nature. He was allowed to both relieve himself and make a phone call. He called his home office in Minneapolis, informing them of his quandary. Forbes reported that Control Data then called Senator Durenburg; the Senator called the State Department; and the State Department managed to get the Korean government to get the police into action.[6] In fact, the police were already outside the gate waiting their time. Finally they moved in, beat up several people, sending five girls to the hospital with serious injury.

Subsequently, Control Data closed down its plant in Korea saying that progress in technologies no longer made the operation there feasible. This action added another log to the fire of anti-Americanism that was igniting both in the political and the labor arenas, and eliminated one more of the democratic unions of Korea.

Union Broken at Wonpoong

The next independent union to go was the one at Wonpoong Textile Company. The union at Wonpoong had a proud and honorable history. Back in 1973 when the owners of the company absconded with company money and workers' wages, it was the union which had taken the initiative to cooperate with a bank appointed management team to get the company back on its feet. To help workers make ends meet, the union set up a credit union, a scholarship fund, a barber shop and a beauty parlor. Rank and file took active part and officers were always elected by the members, not appointed by the company, nor KCIA.

Chun Doo Hwan decided to bring the Wonpoong Union to bay. He arrested the union president, Bang Yong Suk, on charges of helping Kim Dae Jung instigate the Kwangju rebellion. The charge was a fabrication based on the fact that Bang and his union members had taken up a collection of money to send for relief to the people of Kwangju after the massacre had occurred. The National Textile Federation, at government direction, expelled Bang from the union. On the same day, the company consummated the three-way attack by firing both Bang and the union vice president. Within a few days, forty-nine union people were in prison. Others in places of leadership were made to resign. Four men were sent to purification camps. For a time, women paratroopers were lodged inside the women's dormitory to keep order and ferret out suspicious actors.

One might think that this forced removal of leadership might have cowed the workers, but as in Dongil, Y. H. and Control Data, such was not the case. New leadership came forward. The union continued to demand that the Wonpoong Company bargain in good faith and reach an agreement, especially on wages. For over a year, the company delayed decision while at the same time reducing wages and bonuses, and contracting work out to other companies. The number of employees was decreased. The president of the firm allegedly justified the reduction in forces by saying that he had every right to get rid of "garbage."

The final battle in the sordid affair took place in September, 1982. On the 13th of the month, the new union president, Ms. Kim Sung Koo, and a foreman on the floor (also union) were beaten and then fired for dereliction of duty. Two weeks later, a group of men, some of whom were from management, and some others who were hired thugs, took over the union hall and kidnapped the newly elected replacement for Kim Sung Koo. Her name was Chung Son Soon. The thugs kept her for seventeen hours. They beat her, threatened her, humiliated her and then threw her out of a car somewhere in the outskirts of town. Barefooted and bleeding, she walked back to the factory.

In the factory, Chung Son Soon's friends were conducting a sit-in. There was much jubilation when she returned, but the final defeat was just about to occur. Police, management men and thugs joined together to literally drag the workers out of the plant and throw them into the street. Union members were arrested. Supporting students were picked up and inducted into the army, and a prayer vigil attended by 2,000 people was broken up by the police.

In their final statement that was circulated throughout the country, the women at Wonpoong accused the government's labor department of being a "puppet of vicious industries." They set their own suffering in the context of the sufferings of the nation for democracy:

> When the true facts of the unjust treatment
> we have suffered become known nation-wide,
> the democratic consciousness of our people
> will become raised to greater height, and
> we believe that this we will hasten the day
> when democracy can find its roots in our land.

A MOVEMENT IS BORN

Chun Doo Hwan's seizure of power and his attack on labor created not a ripple among the innovators who were directing Korea's economic miracle. There were a few months of uncertainty after Pak's death, but composure was quickly regained. Business went on as usual. The processes of economic progress continued to make spectacular gains. At the very time that Chun was "purifying" labor, the economic indices were reaching new records. Exports continued their expansion. Automobiles, electronics, chemicals and textiles were being sent over the world in multiplying numbers. Foreign capital continued to flow freely into Korea's industries. By 1982, the gross national product had arrived at a figure of $66 billion, and the per capita average was at the impressive level of $1,500.

At the same time, pressures on the workers were increasing. The problems of hours and safety had not been addressed. In fact they had gotten worse. Labor productivity between 1975 and 1983 had shot up 147 points but wages had been increased by only 98. Consumer cost of living more than tripled the index of wage increases.[7] Inflation, low wages, and long, unsafe hours of work made every day's existence problematic. At the same time, the goods the workers were producing created a social-economic context of conspicuous wealth and rising expectations. Slowly, these pressures were creating the circumstances and attitudes from which a new movement was to be born.

A New Mentality

Along with the growing pressures and changed attitudes came a new style and philosophy of worker leadership. UIM and JOC education throughout the 1970's was based upon a theology of liberation. That theology begins from the economic-political situation in which the poor of society find themselves. The key for understanding scripture and society is the oppressive condition under which the weak must live. As in the experience of Reverend Cho Sung Hyuk in the plywood factory (p. 87), religion begins from the perspective of the one being dumped upon. From there, social analysis is done and actions for reform are taken. This philosophy and its methodology was embraced by women workers who became aware of their own miseries and organized to change their future at Dongil, Y.H., Control Data, and Wonpoong. The mystique of these women who suffered so greatly became the roots from which much of the democratic action sprang. The prophecy of the women at Wonpoong was fulfilled.

University students had also been "educating" factory workers for about a decade. First there was the Hakwon (night school) movement. Small group schools were set up in industrial areas where the basics of "reading, writing, and arithmetic" were intermixed with analysis of capitalism and political thought.

107

After a short life, this movement, as one might expect, was closed down by the authorities. That, however, did not close down the students. They became factory workers. Inside the factories they continued teaching about the need to organize and make society democratic.

New leadership was also being streamed into the union movement through "prison graduates." The periodic purges of labor union leadership over a period of fifteen years had created a substantial number of men and women dedicated to the improvement of the labor movement. Being of fertile imagination and considerable physical courage, these "graduates" of previous labor wars began to organize together in various configurations, some locally, others regionally. A few even ventured to set up national associations. None of these could be called labor unions as such because labor law specified there could only be one union in a shop or industry and that union had to be registered with the Office of Labor Affairs. There were no laws, however, forbidding the organization of citizens for ill-defined personal purposes. So a variety of quasi-labor organizations began to weave themselves around and through the official structures of unionism.

These various streams, filtered through the shock of Kwangju, brought forth a social philosophy that has captured everyone's attention -- though not everyone's approval. The Kwangju massacre forced people to recognize the unjust, repressive system that had committed the deed. In analyzing the causes behind the oppression, the answers came out in layers: the soldiers did the dirty work; behind them was the Korean military; behind the Korean military was the American; the military of both nations are but lackeys of corporate capitalism; and Korean *chaebol* are but puppets at the end of American capitalistic strings.

Such a system, the argument goes, can not be reformed. It must be overthrown. Chun Doo Hwan (and subsequently Roh Tae Woo) must also be overthrown. American troops and American capital must be withdrawn and South Korea must start down a new path of independence.

Obviously this type of thought resembles communism and has, along with other events, initiated a whole new debate about communism in South Korea. After Kwangju, this new "Marxian-like" interpretation of history began to gather an increasing number of adherents among students and industrial workers. Coupled with the "liberation theology" advocated by the church groups it engendered a new philosophy among workers: while oppressions are caused by the capitalists and militarists, workers themselves have the power to overthrow the oppressors. To succeed the workers need only a broad-based working class solidarity.

This revolutionary message spread quickly from worksite to worksite. Industrial structures created by the EPB and the *chaebol* facilitated the process. In their thirst for efficiency they had devised schemes of concentrating the largest number of workers in the smallest amount of space. The city of Ulsan is a good example. Twenty years ago it was a small fishing village. Today it has a highly concentrated population of 500,000 most of whom are directly or indirectly dependent upon the Hyundai *chaebol*. The crowded conditions and proximity of a large number of workers creates a natural conduit for the exchange of grievances and the sharing of new ideas. The new industrial cities like Ulsan provided a new potential for solidarity and large-scale organizing among the workers.

A comparable situation was created in the industrial estates and free export zones like Kurodong near Seoul and Masan on the southern coast. Tens of thousands of young women are employed within the walls of these large estates. Employers are most often small scale operators employing a hundred to three hundred workers. Often, the employer is a foreign concern producing for export. Not infrequently, the working conditions, the pay, and the employers' attitude toward the "girls" are embarrassingly mean. The crowded conditions of work, and the concentration of worker housing facilities inside or outside the estate's walls are all conducive to the spreading of ideas like the new ones coming out of Kwangju. In 1987, both the new cities and the industrial estates experienced sharp, extended worker revolts.

By the mid-1980's, the pressures created by the political dictator and the economic expansions were accelerating. At the same time, workers with new attitudes and new understandings of their own predicament were beginning to find one another. All that was needed was a drama around which the ideas and emotions could coalesce. That drama was provided in a timely fashion by two companies belonging to one of Korea's largest *chaebol*.

Skirmish at Daewoo Motors

Daewoo is one of Korea's top four *chaebol*. It, along with Hyundai, Samsung and Goldstar, is considered a super star. Daewoo had sales in 1983 of $4.3 billion, and was listed as 39th in Fortune's listing of the 500 largest non-American firms. By 1988, it had climbed to number 30, with sales of $17.3 billion. Like the other super *chaebol*, Daewoo produces most everything. In 1981, at government direction, it took over the Saehan Company's half of a joint venture with General Motors. At first, the plant was an assembly line for American made vehicles. Since 1986, however, it has produced the "Le Mans" and a variety of other popular automobiles, trucks and buses.

Daewoo Motors, as the new joint venture was called, inherited a labor union in the deal. The union, however, was not troublesome. Saehan had subdued it to a mild company-dominated union. Its leadership stayed in the hands of one man from 1976 to 1985, an unusually long time by Korean standards. Collective bargaining and the signing of contracts were perfunctorily performed each year. Wage increases followed the EPB guidelines of 3–5 percent per year, even as inflation doubled and tripled. A bonus increase had been agreed upon, but never paid. In the 1983 negotiations, the floor delegates had instructed the union officers to demand a 15.7 percent increase, but the union president agreed to 4.9 percent and quietly dropped the demand about the unpaid bonuses. Membership did not have the right to ratify the agreement, so it stood.

This self-evident manipulation of the union by the company flew against the changing ideas and attitudes of the workers. It also aggravated a situation where many of the workers felt their working conditions had become worse under Daewoo. The Daewoo line of command was much more demanding. Reprimands came easier, and disciplines were more arbitrary. When the time for negotiations came around in 1985, the tide of worker emotions had changed, though neither the company nor the union realized it right then.

Twenty-four new union floor delegates were elected in 1984. When they met to give the bargaining team instructions, they demanded that there be at least an 18.7 percent wage increase. The union president, however, repeated his performance of earlier years by reporting out that the company was only capable of paying a 5 percent increase and that the union could expect no more. This time worker expectations were not to be denied. Anger reached the point where union leadership was repudiated. A group of about 300 workers effectively took over the union. They selected three men to act as negotiators. On April 16, 1985, the new team began negotiations, 300 of their colleagues went on strike. They occupied the factory and threatened to destroy a computer bank if the police attacked. The next day, more than two thousand workers expressed support by demonstrating in the factory yards and in the cafeteria. Eight thousand police surrounded the plant. Food and water were cut off from the three hundred inside.

Then a most unorthodox thing occurred. Kim Woo Choong, the president of the whole Daewoo group, showed up at the plant and became part of the company team that negotiated with the three worker representatives. After a few days, he and the chief spokesman for the workers, Hong Yong Pyo, entered into private discussions and an agreement was reached: Basic wages were to be increased 10 percent and when the several other benefit increases were added, the total came close to the 18.7 percent demanded by the workers in the first place.

For the workers at Daewoo, a new consciousness was born. They had achieved by their own action the goal they had started out to achieve. They had done it despite the old company-dominated union. Strong, determined leadership supported in solidarity by the workers had done the trick. This lesson was not to be forgotten.

The 1985 negotiations and the strike were both illegal. Technically, both Kim Woo Choong and Hong Yong Pyo had broken the law. In one company, there can only be one union. Hong's group of 300 and his team of three did not represent the official union and therefore the agreement signed with Kim Woo Choong was null and void. To get around that, the company held meetings with the union president and signed an even better agreement with him to make it legal and to save his face. The other illegal item was the strike. According to law, a union had to notify the Office of Labor Affairs ahead of time and wait twenty days before entering a strike. Neither of these requirements had been followed. As Kim Woo Choong and Hong Yong Pyo signed their agreement, the police entered and arrested all three of the worker representatives. They were sentenced to a year's imprisonment. Kim Woo Choong, of course, was not detained even though his actions could be seen as equally illegal. Whether Kim Woo Choong had connived with police in the affair is not clear. The company says no, but the suspicion lingers. In any case, the events of 1985 became the emotional roots for a bigger show-down in 1987.

Several new features characterized the Daewoo Motor conflict. First, and perhaps most importantly, it signalled the reappearance of male workers on to the scene of union activity. This was the first time since the Chosun Kongsa case back in 1971 that male workers had taken the offensive in a major labor-management confrontation. Secondly, the action at Daewoo was against a big *chaebol*. Previously, the *chaebol* had seemed immune to collective action and were imaged as the "good" places to work. Thirdly, the appearance of Kim Woo Choong as a direct participant in negotiations illustrated that the *chaebol* were vulnerable. Daewoo must have been very anxious about the situation for the head of the entire group to have bent to meeting with a labor leader. Kim Woo Choong's role also left him open to suspicions of duplicity. Whether intended or not, the fact that Hong Yong Pyo was arrested after Kim had reached agreement with him was widely interpreted as company-police connivance.

A final new characteristic of the 1985 Daewoo Motor strike was the fact that a sizeable group of workers broke away from the official union and took its own action. The new organization called itself "minju nojo" (democratic union). The official union, related to FKTU, was labelled as "o'yong" (company unions).[8] Daewoo Motors was the first round of an internecine battle within labor. Young, more militant workers spurned the old company union and organized "minju nojo" to fit their demands for democracy.

These new characteristics of labor action at Daewoo were already latent in plants around the country. Within two years, they were to become the majority voice for Korean labor.

Solidarity at Kurodong

The second drama that helped ignite the new directions for Korean labor also took place in a Daewoo factory. Among Daewoo's many acquisitions was a small firm in the Kurodong Industrial Estate near Seoul. Kurodong consists of three large estate areas that cover several square miles of walled-in small work places. The size of the operations vary from a dozen or so employees to several hundred. All together, there are about 58,000 employees in the three estates. 38,000 of them are young women who live in crowded dormitories within the confines of their own company or in over rented apartments called "chicken houses." Daewoo Apparel is one of the small firms. It employs about one hundred people to turn out a variety of women's garments.

Ten days of work stoppage and turmoil within Daewoo Apparel in mid-June, 1985 would probably have gone unrecorded except for the fact that the conflict burst out beyond the walls of the company. The dispute began in mid-May when the union held a one day strike in support of its demand for a wage increase. The company had responded positively, and in a few days an agreement was reached. At the same time, however, the company quietly brought suit charging the union with an illegal strike. Consequently the union president and two others were arrested. The president was sentenced to two years in prison.

Union members took the arrest of their leaders as a breach of good faith on the part of the company. A month earlier negotiations had gone on in a positive atmosphere. There had been no further conflict. Why after that, had the company pushed a legal case against the union? Workers again struck and demanded that the union leaders be released. The company locked some of the strikers in a second floor room and fired some of the others. The police added their usual menu of beatings, insults and arrests. After ten days, the workers were so exhausted and beaten up and so many of their numbers had been fired that they had to give in. That part of the Kurodong drama was unspectacular because it was so common.

As in the Daewoo Motor case, however, there were a few unique items that subsequently were seen as harbingers of the future. No sooner had the Daewoo Apparel workers started demonstrating on behalf of their three imprisoned leaders than workers in nine other companies in the Kurodong estates took up their banner and staged sympathy strikes at their own places of work. A thousand workers stayed in solidarity throughout the whole ordeal and suffered the same arrests, beatings and dismissals, as did the workers at Daewoo Apparel.

In addition, no less than twenty-six support groups from various sectors of society gave both moral and physical encouragement. Student groups offered their support as did a variety of Christian organizations. The most prominent support group was the Minju Tongil Minjung Undong Yu'nhap (The United

People's Movement for Democracy and Unification), an umbrella organization for the many political dissidents of Korea. The Peoples' Buddhist Association stood with the union, and visible to everyone was the contingent from Chonggye Garment Union of Peace Market origins. At the time, it was legally disbanded. Yet it was one of the first to show solidarity. Its members took part in the actions until the end. The ghost of Chun Tae Il would not let go. He had been twenty-two when he died. Now a decade and a half later, his spirit still inspired the young.

The Kurodong experience portended the democratic labor movement that was to explode on to the scene in just two more years. At the center of that movement, was a deep alienation from the FKTU. During the Kurodong struggles, representatives from FKTU visited Daewoo Apparel. Their words were not ones of solidarity and support, but words that repeated the warnings coming from the company and police. Once more, FKTU demonstrated its subordination to the company.

The importance of Kurodong is that it brought solidarity to workers across lines that previously had divided them. It introduced labor to a whole array of non-labor supportive groups, and it demonstrated the need to act outside legal structures and to assert independence from the official union leadership. The revolts of 1987 inherited these critical legacies from Kurodong.

CHAPTER NOTES

1. "Korea, May 1980, Peoples' Uprising in Kwangju," Pacific–Asia Resources Center, September 1980, p. 21.

2. "Reports from Kwangju," North American Coalition for Human Rights in Korea, Washington, DC, September, 1980, p. 21.

3. Ibid.

4. Korea May, 1980: Peoples Uprising in Kwangju, Pacific–Asia Resource Center, 1980, pp. 17–18.

5. Korea Scope, September, 1982, pp. 17–18.

6. Forbes, October 11, 1982, p. 192.

7. *Han'guk Sahwei Nodongja Yu'ngu I,* Han'guk Sahwei Yu'nguso, Seoul, 1989, p. 35.

8. The word *O'yong* comes from two Chinese characters: *O'*, meaning "King" and *Yong* meaning "Being used by."

VI. THE DEMOCRATIC LABOR
MOVEMENT, 1987–1989

When Roh Tae Woo made public the platform on which he would run for president, it sounded more progressive and democratic than either of his opponents, Kim Dae Jung or Kim Yong Sam. Not only did he promise direct presidential elections and local autonomy, but he declared that, if elected, he and his government would guarantee the basic rights of all citizens. He would allow all sectors of society to practice self–regulation, ending strict government control over many aspects of life.

WORKERS REVOLT

The date of this statement, June 29, 1987, has become a pivotal date in the history of Korean labor. Noh's speech was like a match set to timber waiting to be kindled. It provided the opportunity for unionism to explode out of the confines in which it had been shackled. Decades of pent up humiliations were let loose resulting in wave after wave of worker demonstrations and union-organizing. The post June 29 period is reminiscent of the 1945 post–liberation period when workers and their allies, released from prison, organized thousands of industrial and agricultural workers in only a few weeks. Within four months after Noh's declaration, no less than 3400 labor disputes erupted throughout Korea. Within a year after June 29, 2799 new local unions were formed. 586,167 new members were added to union roles, an increase in total membership of almost 63 percent.[1]

To the consternation of many, the new wave of labor militancy was accompanied by a re–emergence of progressive and socialist thought. This also recalls the post–liberation period of 1945 when socialist thought was so much a part of the struggle. After Chun Pyung was eliminated (1947), any political thought other than conservative capitalism or authoritarianism became taboo. For four decades, any serious consideration even of progressive liberalism was forbidden. One who even mentioned the words socialism or communism would risk arrest.

Since 1947 Korean labor had been pent up within the confines of what has been termed economic unionism. Workers were told that the only legitimate function of a union was to improve wages and working conditions. Unions were not to become involved in politics. At the same time, every effort of the unions to improve working conditions was opposed by government and employer. Organizing unions and standing tall for wage increases were quite likely to be labelled as communist. Obviously a deception was being perpetrated, but there was little effort by union leaders of the 1970's to analyze its nature.

Kwangju changed all that. Under the stark reality that the powers in control were willing to kill their own citizens rather than allow democratization, students, workers, and other dissidents began to see Korean society in terms of class struggle. The *chaebol* and the military dictators were identified as the ruling class. Propping up that class were foreign capital and foreign troops. Workers, the poor and even the middle class, were seen as the oppressed and manipulated. In a word, Korean society was analyzed in terms of class struggle. From this analysis comes the obvious conclusion that the function of a labor union is not only to persuade the employer to give a few extra cents an hour for the workers' labor, but to also politically and socially confront the power structures so as to democratize society. A participatory society of equals must replace the oppressive class society that precipitated the massacre at Kwangju.

This form of class analysis spread through the underground circles of students, workers, and political dissidents. When the dam broke with Roh Tae Woo's declaration of June 29, 1987, the ideology of class struggle had already been widely accepted by those who became part of the minju labor movement.

The similarity of this class struggle ideology with that of Marxism and North Korea is obvious and therefore frightens much of the population which is still steeped in bitter anti-communism. Others, however, declare that only the phrases are similar. Actually, the class analysis reflects a Korean nationalism come of age. Korea is tired of being subservient in a world of big nations like the U.S.A., Japan, and the Soviet Union. It is now time to exert its independence by cutting loose from its old dependencies -- which primarily means the U.S.A. Likewise, it is time for the people to exert themselves against a ruling class that has too long kept them as second class citizens, and in the case of workers, even as serfs.

The widespread 1987 labor revolt significantly hit the larger corporations, the *chaebol*, the hardest. Some 69 percent of firms that hired a thousand or more workers were confronted with work stoppages. 38.5 percent of those hiring less than a thousand had the same experience.[2] The waves began in the South in the big industrial concentrations of Ulsan (dominated by Hyundai), Kojedo (dominated by Daewoo and Samsung) and Changwon (dominated by Goldstar and Hyundai) and spread north. The *chaebol* were organized first and then soon after, businesses of all sizes were rapidly organized. The enthusiasm spread outside the boundaries of the "blue collar" industrial workers, and into the "white collar" service sectors of health care, research at government agencies, education institutions, and insurance companies, opening up an entirely new dimension for Korean unionism.

The remainder of this chapter will focus on representative struggles that have taken place in each of the three sectors: the *chaebol*, small-medium industry and the "white collar" service industries.

THE *CHAEBOL*

The Korean economy is dominated by the four super-*chaebol*. They produce about 45% of total GNP. The success of the five-year economic plans and therefore the nation's economic development depends on them. Likewise, they set the patterns in labor-management relations. All four of them were hard hit by the initial shock of union action in 1987. Each of them reacted out of its own tradition and philosophy to end up two years later, in postures very distinct from one another. In this chapter, each of the four will be examined and comparisons noted.

Hyundai

The Hyundai Group, as noted in Chapters II and IV, is the epitome of Korean industrial success. Within three brief decades, it has grown from a small construction business into one of the foremost corporations of the world. Many of the production facilities for the Hyundai empire are located in the city of Ulsan, originally a small fishing village on the southeastern coast. Twenty years ago, Hyundai transformed it into an industrial camp of 500,000 people. There are twelve Hyundai companies in Ulsan employing 80,000 workers. Thus, directly or indirectly Hyundai provides the livelihood of most of Ulsan's population. Hyundai Motors, which exports the popular Hyundai cars to U.S. and Canada, has its plants there and employs about 20,000 workers. Hyundai's famous shipyards have another 20,000 or so on the payroll.

The Hyundai *chaebol* was founded by Chung Ju Yong in 1947. Some refer to him as Korea's Andrew Carnegie. He had little formal education, but was born with an innate genius. That along with inside connections with Pak Chung Hee propelled him into the leadership of Korean industrialists. He works, does not play and apparently seldom sleeps. His example, like the wind, he thought, would in good Confucian fashion bend the workers before him. They would model their lives after him and dedicate every nerve to the growth of the company. Chung's self-image and his evaluation of his moral persuasiveness, however, had little in common with the employees' image of him or the workers' concept of their relationship to the company. Chung was seen as a hard-nosed slave driver who had little compassion for those who worked under him. His sense of high calling and his break-neck habits of work when translated down the company chain of command came out to factory or shipyard worker not as moral persuasions but as harsh dictates. Workers were humiliated by front line management. Conditions were often unsafe. Many died during the construction of the Hyundai plants in Ulsan. Injuries are still common. Supervisors act arbitrarily dispensing discipline as they wish, reducing pay, slapping workers on the head or abusing them with curses and low talk. Guards at the gates detain workers and cut their hair or search them according to their own whims.

117

These practices of management grated on the spirits of the workers, most of whom were high school graduates. As the success of the company grew and the wealth it created became more conspicuous, the workers' sense of oppression deepened. Fairly high wages compared to smaller companies and other industries did not compensate for the accumulated grievances.

The Daewoo Motor Company strike of 1985 had shown that a big *chaebol* could be challenged. Roh Tae Woo's statement of June 29 presented the occasion. On July 6, 1987, Kwon Yong Mok and other leaders at Hyundai Engine decided that the union's time had come. Together with 120 fellow workers they organized a union and quickly registered it with the Office of Labor Affairs. Membership swelled immediately to over 1400. The union called upon the company to begin negotiations for a contract. It was the first union ever organized at a Hyundai plant. The union action at Hyundai Engine quickly provoked similar movement at other companies in the Hyundai Group, including Hyundai Motors and Hyundai Shipyards. Before workers at these plants could prepare the necessary registration documents, however, the company quickly sent their own men to the Office of Labor Affairs and registered a union in the name of its workers. When the bonafide union men came later, their registration documents were rejected. At an earlier time, the company's machinations might have been quietly endured by the workers, but not in 1987. Led by unionists at Hyundai Motors and Hyundai Heavy Industries, workers demonstrated and struck throughout the month of July, demanding that the company registered unions be withdrawn. Chung Ju Yong refused to give in and vowed there would never be a union at Hyundai.

The union offensive, however, was not to be denied. Representatives from the twelve Hyundai firms in Ulsan gathered together early in August and formed an Association of Unions at Hyundai. They intended to coordinate their efforts against the *chaebol*. Solidarity across company lines within the *chaebol* was thought to be important if the union was to develop any bargaining leverage. Kwon Yong Mok, of Hyundai Engine, was elected as chair.

Their solidarity was soon tested. On August 17, six Hyundai companies announced a lockout saying they feared sabotage from the new unions which they stigmatized as "radical" and "impure elements". Response was immediate. Forty thousand workers in gray work uniforms set off toward the city led by trucks, fork lifts, heavy vehicles of all kinds. Accompanied by drums, gongs, and flutes, the crowd sang newly learned songs, interspersed with chants of "down with Chung Ju Yong!" The parade stretched for a mile. Mothers, wives and children, over a thousand strong, marched along with the workers.

The crowd thronged into the Ulsan Sports Stadium. For hours they listened to speeches, sang and chanted. About ten o'clock in the evening a surprise guest was introduced -- the Vice Minister of Labor whose message to the crowd was even more surprising.

He announced that he had been in secrete negotiations with Hyundai and union representatives and that Hyundai was now ready to accept unions at eight of the twelve companies. The agreement, he said, included a promise to negotiate over wages and working conditions and, most importantly, to recognize the new democratic unions in place of the unions registered by company men. The forty thousand people in the stadium cheered wildly thinking they had won a great victory.

It turned out to be a victory, but of considerably less proportions than first thought. A company spokesman in Seoul initially said that the pact had been made between the government and union. Hyundai, he said, was not party to it.[3] Later at government insistence Chung Ju Yong consented to have his picture taken drinking a toast to peace with Lee Jae Shik, the union representative, but Chung was not one to give in after only one battle.

For another two weeks, havoc reigned. Six of the Hyundai firms in Ulsan were closed down completely. A partial break through came on the first day of September. Contracts were signed at three places: the Mipo Shipyards, Hyundai Heavy Electric and Hyundai Pipe Company. At other sites, however, negotiations made no headway. The *chaebol* clung to the old unions and refused to recognize the democratic leaders elected by the workers complaining that, contrary to law, "outsiders" had taken part in union affairs, and therefore the election of democratic officers were invalid. It appealed to the Office of Labor Affairs to invalidate the results of the union elections.

On September 2, twenty thousand workers again took to the streets. They marched toward Ulsan City Hall. Drums and gongs kept the cadence as workers shouted and chanted their demands. They were met by riot police, who waded in with clubs swinging, hoping to break the marchers into small bands and thus dissipate their strength. It did not work. One group of about three hundred stormed into the City Hall, smashing windows and breaking up furniture. Another group of about three thousand people got turned around toward the shipyards. They smashed into the company offices, scattering documents and setting fire to the furniture. The police stood by and watched. They were no match for the fury of the workers.

After two days, the police took the initiative. Special investigative teams were brought in from Seoul to ferret out "communist" involvement in the events of September 2. A dawn attack on a dormitory and a few homes netted thirty suspects. In all, 508 were arrested. Once more the workers took to the streets, 8,000 strong. This time, however, the police were prepared. Tear gas and water hoses cut the workers' lines, and they were dispersed.

119

At this juncture, the Office of Labor Affairs again made an appearance. It upheld the *chaebol*'s contention that "third parties" had interfered in the union elections and therefore the results of the elections were null and void. Who were the third parties? Primarily, they were union leaders from various companies within the Hyundai Group. The Association of Unions at Hyundai was declared contrary to law. Unions could not organize across company lines, and participation by the Union's Association in affairs of any one company was illegal. Twenty leaders including Kwon Yong Mok were sentenced to jail for their roles in organizing the Association.

Thus, the first phase of the struggle at Hyundai came to a close. It had lasted only a few months. The truce was uneasy and would not last long. The union movement had accomplished much. A sense of solidarity was much in evidence; a strong core of capable leaders had emerged; and both management and government had been forced to give begrudging recognition. On the other hand, the company had fired the final shot. By having union leaders sent to jail, it proved it could control the action and by paying some of its employees to oppose the union, it could disrupt worker solidarity. Hyundai resorted to intimidation and violence in an attempt to defeat the union movement. At Hyundai the "kusadae" (save the company group) made its first appearance. It is a group of anti-union employees, sometimes joined by hoodlums from the street who are paid by the company to prevent union activity. Intimidation, kidnapping and beatings are standard procedures used against union people. At Hyundai the kusadae was comprised of former marines who worked at Ulsan. Chung Ju Yong spoke at their "kick off" dinner. He declared that the labor unions were part of a planned communist aggression against the company and nation. He appealed to the Marines to once more come to the defense of the motherland by defeating the labor union at Hyundai.[4]

Not satisfied, however, with the protection of only the kusadae and the police, Hyundai added another level of violence against its workers. It recruited members of the Anti-Communist Youth League to serve as security guards at its Ulsan plants. The Anti-Communist Youth League is an association of right wing political toughs that dates back to the post- Liberation days of 1945-48. It joined the Syngman Rhee faction to help destroy the Chun Pyung labor union.[5] The use of violence against the union by the kusadae and hired hoodlums became a regular practice by management in its attempt to regain its traditional control.

The second stage of the union's battle to gain recognition at Hyundai started up in early 1988. Kwon Yong Mok was released from prison on February 4. His return to the union invigorated the workers and stirred up action. A party was given in his honor the night of his release. Part of his speech that night included the following words:

We formed a labor union because we believe the land wants to be democratic. Our lives are attached to the land we love. But they call us leftists and pro-communists. I speak plainly, our task is an inescapable task of history. It is born from our necessity. Though it is a dangerous road, let us not fall back. We reject the common place. Let us go forward with the strength and voice of the people who are now awake.[6]

Kwon's speech was an elegant statement of what many had come to sense and articulate: History was changing. The old authoritarianism must give way to the demands of the people.

Hyundai Engine was quite aware of the importance of Kwon to the union movement. The day after his release from prison, they fired him. Neither Kwon nor his fellow unionists, however, accepted the dismissal. They headed toward the union offices which were inside the company walls. Police and kusadae blocked the entrance through the front gate, but with aid of a thousand workers from Heavy Industry, Kwon and his men forced their way in through a back gate. The company conceded and said Kwon would be allowed entrance to the union hall, but no where else in the plant. The company still considered him to be disemployed.

The union at Hyundai Engine established a new direct-election system and proceeded to hold elections for a new slate of officers. Kwon Yong Mok was elected president by an overwhelming margin -- ninety percent of the votes. The company protested vehemently and refused to recognize the newly elected slate of officers. Kwon, they said, was no longer an employee of the company and therefore could not represent the workers.

The union leadership then decided to take an "heroic" action, trusting that somehow the suffering of the few would break through the hard and unjust hearts of the powerful. Kwon Yong Mok and a thousand of his comrades occupied the fifth floor of the office building at Hyundai Engine. They barricaded themselves in. Their intentions were to stay there until the company was willing to negotiate with the union officers elected by the workers. By declaring their own willingness to suffer, they hoped to morally persuade the company to negotiate. Their heroics gained immediate support from workers in all sectors of the Hyundai group. Statements were made; telegrams of support were sent; delegations came to the city to urge them on. The leaders on the fifth floor, however, had not planned well. The leadership left below was not instructed about how to use the support groups to bring sustained pressure on the company. After a few days the shouting and chanting melted away. The workers on the fifth floor were left to themselves.

The company, unimpressed with the heroics, sent in the police and the *baikgoldan* (a police unit especially trained in taikwando and other martial arts) to disperse the crowds and beat up on those who resisted. They gradually surrounded the building, closing off all access to the men on the fifth floor. They became prisoners. The company then whittled away at the prisoners' morale. Fake telegrams with notices of deaths in the family were sent, urging workers to return home; the fire alarm was sounded in the middle of the night, and a loud speaker declared the building was on fire and everyone must evacuate; family members were brought to the building to plead to the men to give up. Within a couple of weeks, the number of men in the building dropped to 300. Then the company played its trump card. They announced that unless the workers come down immediately, their exemption from military service would be withdrawn. Over two hundred of the remaining workers were affected. It would have meant not only loss of job and three years in the military, but financial ruin for most of their families.

Ninety remained. When the company requested negotiations, Kwon and four others went down to begin talks. Instead of talks, they were seized by the kusadae, thrown in a van and taken prisoner to another building. Word of Kwon's captivity spread instantly around the various plants. A large number of protesters surrounded the building where he was being kept. They demanded his freedom. He was freed temporarily but on March 27, 1988, he was again arrested.

For a time, the "fifth floor" incident caused much fury. Hyundai Electric workers voted to strike in sympathy. Wildcat strikes broke out in other plants. Once more, however, union leadership was in jail or in hiding. The fury of the demonstrations dissipated with little concrete results. The second year of uproar ended about where the first had: A union existed and workers were behind it; but the company refused to accept worker-elected leadership fighting them with the kusadae and police.

A third saga began in December 1988. For six months, the union at Hyundai Shipyards had been trying to negotiate a collective contract. Negotiations failed, and 20,000 workers went out on strike. Once more the whole complex of Hyundai companies was thrown into a turmoil. At about this time, the *chaebol*'s president, Chung Ju Yong, went to Moscow on business. Before he left, he gathered his chief executives together and ordered them to normalize the operations at Hyundai as quickly as possible.[7]

After Chung Ju Yong's departure, his son, who was president of Hyundai Heavy Industry, impressed upon his senior executives the need to end the strike and normalize production before his father's return. At this juncture a piece of intelligence came to one of the executives, Han Yu Dong. He learned that nineteen union chiefs from several Hyundai companies were planning to meet outside of town in a small resort village on January 8, 1989, at 3:30 a.m. The agenda was to develop plans for coordinated action during the coming year.

Armed with this information, Han decided to take action that he thought would resolve the labor crisis at Hyundai. First he made contact with James Lee, an American of Korean descent who assumes the role of a union–buster. Han instructed Lee to "discipline those hard line labor leaders by physical means."[8] The second thing Han did was to contact the superintendent of police on Lee's behalf. The superintendent agreed to cooperate.

James Lee then proceeded to plan a commando raid against the early morning union meeting. He enlisted a hundred company men to go with him. He commandeered three company buses, walkie talkies and a supply of iron pipes and wooden clubs. As Lee's commandos approached their destination, they were stopped by a police road block. The sergeant in charge would not let them pass, but a phone call to the police superintendent straightened him out. The vans were allowed to proceed. The union men were caught quite by surprise. Lee and cohorts beat them badly, broke Kwan Yong Mok's leg, and warned the unionists that they should give up their communist ways. The commandos then returned to the city where they broke into the offices of the "Association of Dismissed Hyundai Employees" and destroyed whatever could be destroyed.

The entire raid by the Lee commandos was to have been kept secret. The police were to cover their side. The company, of course, would officially know nothing of what actually happened. The presence of a foreigner, James Lee, however, was leaked out. Even Korea's censored press could not pass up a story like that. The whole episode was exposed.

When Hyundai president Chung Ju Yong returned from Moscow, he declared, "I do not believe such terrorist acts would help resolve our labor–management disputes. It is nonsense. I am sorry that our employees caused such trouble to the citizens."[9]

Once more Ulsan was thrown into a commotion. The workers hit the streets. Ten thousand marched one day and twenty thousand the next. The company denied responsibility and refused to apologize in any way for Lee's actions. Workers burned Chung Ju Yong in effigy. Chung's response was to engage more police. 562 workers were arrested, and again "crack detectives" were brought in to round up union leaders who might be hiding.

The union reacted with continuing strikes and demonstrations. Unionists from over the country came into the city to express solidarity. Students gathered and shouted slogans, and around the country they staged hit and run attacks on outlets for Hyundai products. Stones and fire bombs were thrown; placards with signs like "We denounce the business monopoly of the Hyundai tycoon" were hung on Hyundai buildings.

For 104 days, work at the giant Hyundai complex at Ulsan came to stop. It was a stand-off. Unions insisted that the company apologize for the James Lee incident, that it negotiate with the union leadership chosen by the workers and that it not interfere in union affairs. The company reply was, "Stop the strike; get back to work and then we will talk." To emphasize the point, they fired fifty-five union leaders on charges of violating company rules and destroying property.

Finally, on March 30, the police sent an attack force of 10,000 policemen into the Hyundai complex. They attacked by land, sea and air -- a coordinated military attack. Workers learned of the attack before it started and disappeared out through the many gates. By the time the military operation took over Hyundai grounds, they were empty. Another scene in the as-of-yet-unended drama was over.

A few days later, workers began to reappear at their work places. Directors and managers warmly greeted them at the plant entrances saying, "Let's get to work, united in heart and will."[10] Some top managers went directly to the homes of strike leaders and appealed to them to return to work so that things could be normalized.

At the same time, 300 plainclothesmen and about 2000 riot police were kept stationed around the premises.

The James Lee incident and its aftermath revealed much about labor-management relations in Hyundai. The line of command in labor affairs was, and is, clear. Chung Ju Yong gives ill-defined general orders. Chief executives under him repeat the command to their subordinates, but also with little instruction as to clear goals or methods. The underlings get the word to "solve the problem, and do it soon". It is significant that in the Hyundai case, both Mr. Han and Mr. Lee assumed that their plans to beat-up the union leaders were in keeping with the intentions of the highest management echelons which initiated the orders. Indeed, in all probability, Han's superiors knew about the plans and made no effort to stop them. There seemed to be a non-verbalized understanding that the violence committed by the commandos was within the acceptable parameters of Chung's initial instructions.

The Hyundai case can be generalized to some degree to other *chaebol* as well. Labor management policy is made at high, centralized levels. Their policies are made only in general terms. Therefore, the top men can, if they wish, always claim detachment from what actually results. Violence is often assumed by the whole line of command to be one of the options open. Chung Ju Yong never apologized, nor eschewed violence. He distanced himself by saying he did not think it would solve the problem, and he apologized to the citizens because our employees caused a disturbance. He did not apologize to the union or to the men who were beaten. The option for violence against the union leaders still stands, and everyone knows it. The process illustrated so well by Hyundai is not at all unusual. It helps explain the subsystem of policy enforcement discussed in Chapter III. This Hyundai method never allows for the growth of long-term mutual respect necessary to democratic labor relations. The company assumes that it has the right to inflict punishment on its employees to return things to what it calls "normalcy." The word "normalcy" is not spelled out, but assumes the traditional class relationship where employer is the superior; the workers are the inferior. The employer is "father"; the employee is "son." The "father" has the right to chastise the "son."

There is one other point that the James Lee affair illustrates: the close, coordinated ties between company and police. Police are actually subordinate to the company in doing its bidding. Managing Director, Han Yu Dong, confided the commando-like scheme to the Superintendent of Police, the second highest police supervisor in the area. Superintendent Kwon cooperated with Han and Lee even though it violated the law. Company and police commonly coordinate actions. In the particular James Lee case, the collusion was exposed. Han and Lee were imprisoned for a short time. A police superintendent under Kwon, who was also involved, was arrested. Such punishment, however, came about only because of the high level of publicity given the case. The pattern and practice of company-police collusion has not changed.

Hyundai has been forced to recognize unions in some of its plants. Even so, it adamantly fights the union and asserts its right to interfere in internal union affairs. Unless the union officers are acceptable to the company, the company refuses to negotiate. There is no evidence that Hyundai intends to normalize labor-management relations around a concept of equality and mutual trust. It is still very much wedded to a philosophy of authoritarianism.

Even so the union has burst on to the scene with genuine power. Leadership is strong and committed. Solidarity of the workers is periodically demonstrated. The frequent arrest of leaders and interference by the company, however, has not yet allowed workers and leaders to jell into a sustained or stable movement. Under the pressures, leadership and workers often are divided. The kusadae, though organized and paid for by the company, inserts a painful cleavage among workers. The union at Hyundai is not likely to go away, but it is constantly subject to the interference of the company and the threat of the kusadae. It will require years of persistent struggle before Hyundai will accept it as a legitimate partner.

Samsung

Perhaps the *chaebol* with the philosophy closest to Hyundai is Samsung. The two share a disdain for unionists and a dedication to a union-free workplace. In their efforts to achieve that goal, however, the two have differed considerably. Chung Ju Yong can be likened to the street fighter who takes on the opponent in open battle. Lee Byung Chul, founder, and until his death in 1986, the head of the Samsung *chaebol*, depended more on the quiet finesse of a CIA. Hyundai, with its straight out attacks against unions, has on several occasions been beaten. It has had to accept unions, even though it still interferes in their internal affairs. Samsung, however, has never been beaten. There were no unions prior to 1987 and none after 1987.[11]

Lee Byung Chul was known as a "Japanese gentleman." His wife was Japanese. His house was of Japanese style and furnishings. He patterned his own industrial empire after the Japanese *zaibstsu*, as all the *chaebol* eventually did. His employees follow the Japanese patterns of early morning exercises on the company grounds and "retreating" for periods of spiritual training. The Japanese Samurai code of "busido" which teaches loyalty to one's "master" is said to be the heart of the spiritual training. When the company was founded in the 1940's employees often lived in barracks, and the company town ambience commanded the relationship between employer and employees. All of these, says Professor Gregory Henderson, were taken straight from the Japanese patterns of 1935–1945.[12]

After Samsung was given new life by Pak Chung Hee in 1972 (p. 42), it quickly grew into one of Korea's most successful business groups. Today, it is a world–class corporation by any measure. There are thirty–six companies tied together in the Samsung group. Collectively they employ around 150,000 people. Their products range from refined sugar to ships, from heavy machinery to the smallest, most advanced computers. They operate in several countries and their exports reach all over the world.

The Group's anti–unionism stems from a saying often repeated by Lee Byung Chul: "I will have earth cover my eyes before a union is permitted at Samsung." The earth has indeed covered Lee's eyes, but his anti–unionism lives on. In recent years the anti–union stand has been absorbed into a wider company philosophy that sees history moving toward increasing individualism. Within five years or so, Samsung contends, Korean workers will be so grounded in the values of individualism that they, like their American counterparts, will prefer working in a non–union atmosphere. Industrialization, they think, moves inexorably toward individualism. So, if Samsung can stay non–unionized for another five years, it will have saved itself a lot of trouble and have the jump on the other *chaebol* as they try to adjust to the individualism of the future.

Samsung was well prepared to fend off union initiatives. Its spiritual education courses were effective in indoctrinating loyalty to the company, and its system of supervision quickly isolated and then expelled any who were disloyal. All employees were subject to a special series of education led by none other than James Lee, the "commando" who made the night strike against the union at Hyundai. According to employees, Lee liked to clothe himself in the mystique of the CIA and the Korean Security Command. His education was reduced to a simple formula: allowing a union in your plant is like opening the door to a thief, except in the case of a union, the thief is a communist. The communist theme was wrapped up in stories of subversion and treason. Thus before the union initiatives of 1987–89 began, Samsung employees were already steeped in a fear of unionism. As for those who were not persuaded by the education or who persisted in talking about a union, they were quickly expelled before they could contaminate others. Two examples illustrate. A young woman in the Samsung textile mill was overheard by her foreman talking about a labor union. She got a free ride home. A company car came to her room. One of her supervisors forced her to get in the car. She was then driven to the rural area from which she had come. Her parents were told that she was being returned because she was disloyal and into "impure affairs." Her wages and severance pay were handed over, and the car returned to the company without the former employee. Such treatment is not at all unusual. A young man at another Samsung plant was discovered to have talked to several of his fellow workers about forming a union. He was forcefully held in a room and interrogated in a manner similar to a KCIA interrogation. He was not allowed to contact friend or family. He was forced to go for a trip to the countryside accompanied by company managers. When he did not show up for work, he was dismissed. Dismissed employees say that when a "dissident" of any kind is identified, immediately two or three managers are appointed to isolate and finally to get rid of him or her.

Thoroughness is a key word at Samsung. Each action is thoroughly coordinated with the appropriate government agency and the police. Samsung, in most cases, exercises enough political persuasion that its proposals and information are readily received by the authorities. To make sure that the company is not embarrassed by press or T.V., a special public relations committee keeps the media informed about everything. For example, in one plant, five men entered the office of the company president and proceeded to conduct a sit-in on behalf of dismissed fellow workers. The kusadae came and inflicted a merciless beating on the demonstrators. In the foray, a few windows were broken. That night on T.V., the news showed one picture of the men sitting on the floor and one of the broken windows. That is all. The commentator said nothing about the reason for the sit-in and nothing about the kusadae.

Though the practices of loyalty education and worker surveillance protected Samsung from most of the union offenses of 1987–89, on a few occasions the union did penetrate its defenses. When it looked like a union might take root, the company utilized three strategies.

Samsung has the distinction of having invented a new word in union history, "yuryong johap," (ghost union). In several Samsung companies workers actually went to the offices of the Labor Department to register a union. In each case, much to their surprise, they found that a labor union already existed in their plant. Pro-company men had preceded the unionists and had registered a union. A special Samsung twist was that the pro-company men would then vote to receive no more members into the "ghost union."

A second anti-union strategy used by Samsung is the "sauhwei" (Company Friends Committee). In a few places where the union gained some strength, the company proposed the establishment of a Company Friends Committee where company and workers would have equal representation, and where wages and conditions of work could be negotiated. Company managers contended that they did not oppose a union, but they did not want interference from the outside sources that ordinary unionism brought. The Company Friends Committee would give all the benefits of a union without its draw backs. It is significant that Samsung would come up with such an idea. The Company Friends Committee is reminiscent of the old World War II Japanese patriotic club that was called sampo.

The third Samsung strategy to combat unionism is the "kusadae." Samsung has developed the kusadae to a science. One of its subsidiaries is called the "Korea Security System." This firm trains kusadae in large numbers and apparently dispatches them to locations as designated by corporate headquarters. Not only does Samsung train its own security guards, it provides squads of kusadae to its member companies.[13]

One story will illustrate the various methods that the *chaebol* employed to defeat worker attempts at unionizing. One company in the Samsung Group is called the Heavy Industries Company. It has plants in the city of Changwon and also shipyards on the island of Kojedo. On August 11, 1987 workers at the plant in Changwon went to the local Labor Office to register the union that they had recently organized. Their registration forms were rejected on grounds that a union had been registered for their plant just the day before. Only one union is allowed to a company. Ten anti-union men had their names on the Labor Department's union registration book. In protest the unionists occupied the offices of the city's Vice-Mayor and demanded their right to register a union. It was to no avail. The law was the law, they were told, and could not be changed. After several hours, the Vice-Mayor offered the union men a bus ride back to their plant. They accepted. As they neared the factory's front gate, the bus was stopped by a squad of kusadae. After a sound thrashing, the unionists were divided into small groups and taken away to nearby towns for "education". The president of the union was locked up in a hotel room for five days where he was visited by the plant manager. The manager is reported to have said, "If you form a union, you'll ruin the company. Forget the union and we'll let you go."[14] On the sixth day the union leaders were taken to the company training center, lectured and released. When eight of them still persisted in their efforts to form a union, they were arrested on charges of violence and interfering in the work place. While in jail, managers visited them saying that if they resigned, charges would be dropped and each would get severance pay and a stipend to meet living expenses. If they did not resign, they would be prosecuted and paid nothing. The men all resigned.[15]

In April of the next year (1988) workers at Samsung's Shipyards on Koje Island organized a union only to find that the company had pulled the same trick on them as it had on the workers at Changwon. A pro-company group had already registered a union. The shipyard workers went on strike, and 1500 demonstrated in protest. The company closed down the shipyards and sent in the kusadae. Heavy fighting lasted several days. On April 25, the company proposed a compromise. Instead of a regular labor union which would mean interference by outsiders into the Samsung family, the company proposed an in-house "Company Friends Committee" (sauhwei) that would perform all the functions of a union but have no outside ties. The proposal split the workers. Many wanted to give it a try. Others saw it as a subterfuge. Worker representatives were selected and a full time staff of three people was provided at company expense. The Company Friends Committee was formally initiated on June 1, 1988. Nine days later seven hundred workers went on a one day strike demanding a democratic union. Leaders of the democratic union group decided to take their cause to corporate headquarters in Seoul. Of the fifty men who started on the trip to Seoul, only seven made it. The others were picked up by Samsung's security forces somewhere along the line. The seven who did finally demonstrate in front of corporate headquarters were whisked away within twenty minutes by security officers.[16]

Disputes over the Company Friends Committee continued to divide the workers. Toward the end of October the company paid a productivity bonus of 50,000 won (about $75) and reported that it came as result of bargaining in the Company Friends Committee. The workers protested the small amount of the bonus and took a vote to dissolve the Committee. A large number of employees did not vote, but a majority of those voting voted to dissolve.[17] The situation was left in limbo. The Company Friends Committee still occupies its offices, but with little credibility. There is no union, though a good proportion of the workers would like one.

The Samsung approach to unionism has been quite successful in imposing the old authoritarian structures. By adapting the policies of colonial Japan to the situation of the modern *chaebol*, Samsung is showing the way on how to beat unions even in the midst of a strong trend in the other direction. The old class structures and class consciousness are no where seen more clearly than in Samsung.

Daewoo

Daewoo is the youngest of the four super *chaebol*. It was founded in 1967 by Kim Woo Choong. With $18,000 in borrowed money, he started a small trading company. Within twenty years, his company ranked 39th among the 500 largest corporations outside the U.S.A. Kim built his empire by taking over, at low cost, companies that were near bankruptcy. Close support and financial encouragement from the government aided the growth of the corporation. Kim was able to put together management teams primarily with his college-mates who could take over declining companies and make a go of them. Daewoo now produces everything from textiles, leather goods and home appliances to computers, automobiles and off-shore oil rigs.

The company boasts the largest textile mill and the largest shipyards in the world. 100,000 people are employed in the 25 companies of the Daewoo group. In 1987, they produced articles sold in domestic and foreign markets worth $15 billion. Many of the items bought by Americans at K-mart, Penny's, Sears, and Montgomery Ward, Caterpillar, and General Motors have been produced at a Daewoo plant. Daewoo is Korea's largest exporter.

The man who started all this and who is still chief in charge, has three points in common with Hyundai's Chung Ju Yong. Though Kim is a college graduate and described as a soft spoken gentleman, like Chung he eschews pleasure or relaxation. Work is his religion. "In my years as a business man, I have never taken a vacation nor rested at home during holidays," he says of himself.[18] Also like Chung, at least until 1987, he had great faith that his full-time dedication to the company would act as a moral example to everyone else. His moral force, he thought, would bend his employers into faithful followers who would work as hard as he does. The third and most fundamental of characteristics held in common with Chung Ju Yong is that they are both traditional authoritarians. Economic classism is the mental framework within which both men function. History, says Kim, proceeds from a creative minority which sacrifices for others, enlightens and guides the multitude of people. The upper class must sacrifice for the lower. The lower class must be elevated, but there is a "limitation in how far and how quickly the lower-class can be elevated to a higher stratum."[19] Kim's authoritarianism may be softened in practice by his own personality, but the mental framework is there.

Labor policy at Daewoo is centralized. An office at corporate headquarters sets the basic guidelines and the various companies in the group follow those lines, adapting them to their individual situations. Education in the "Daewoo Spirit" is apparently one program held by all the group members. The

130

three principles of the company as set up by Kim are "creativity, challenge, and self–sacrifice." These are characteristics of Kim Woo Choong himself. All new workers take a three week course in these three principles to gain the mental strength to follow Kim's ceaseless zeal. Managers take a refresher course once each year. Kim proudly claims that "Our employees work harder than most. They are ready to make sacrifices for society and the future."[20]

The flood of union organizing in 1987 swamped Daewoo as it did the rest of Korean industry. Daewoo had had a forewarning at Daewoo Motors in 1985. Following that debacle, management thinned the union's ranks by dismissal, transfer and forced resignation of about 250 of the minju union's stoutest defenders. The dismissed workers, however, did as dismissed workers over the entire nation had begun to do. They formed their own organization and continued to involve themselves in the affairs of the company. Through comrades still in the plant, the dismissed union leaders maintained their influence among the workers. The name of their organization was "Daewoo Motor Workers' Task Force to Reinstate Dismissed Workers." It met in a nearby "Worker's Church" started by the UIM. Needless to say, the mixture of dismissed workers, some of whom were college students with the UIM, was not happy news for the authorities.

The 1985 conflict had inserted into traditional union–management relations a new group of workers determined to reform the union and improve conditions at Daewoo Motors. The new group called itself the "minju nojo" (democratic union). It labelled the old union organization, which was part of the FKTU system, as "o'yong" (company dominated). The minju nojo's chief demand was that the o'yong union declare its independence from the·company and honestly represent the demands of the workers. The Daewoo Motor Company contends that it has been caught in the middle of an internal union squabble. That contention, however, is a bit of a subterfuge since management has always interfered in internal union affairs. In any case, the 1985 conflict ended without resolution of the fundamental issue of union independence.

At lunch time on August 10, 1987 members of the minju group took over the company cafeteria and read a statement with four demands: the o'yong organization should be disbanded; wages should be increased by $43 a month; minju workers dismissed in 1985 and after should be reinstated; and the contract with the General Motors Corporation of America should be discontinued. The union claimed that though G.M. owned only fifty percent of the company, it was extracting far more that fifty percent of the profits. Consequently Daewoo management was always under pressure to keep labor costs down.

The demands were read to the assembled workers who then sang songs and shouted slogans about democratic unionism. The three hundred minju supporters moved out of the cafeteria and into each section of the plant where they read the demands and led the workers in chanting slogans. With worker grievances high and a mood created by the democratic movement at Hyundai and elsewhere, an estimated 4000 workers took part in the demonstrations at Daewoo that day.

The company closed the plant down for two weeks, during which time it labelled the minju union members "outside agitators" and "impure factions" (communist) who did not represent the majority of the workers. Managers visited workers at their homes. Bearing gifts of peaches and grapes, they tried mightily to dissuade the workers from following the lead of the minju nojo. The minju people were radicals,the company men explained, who were out to destroy Daewoo and create chaos.

A week into the plant closing, the president of the o'yong union tried to rally support to his side claiming that because the company trusted him he could negotiate a better wage and bonus package than could the minju faction. He called on the company to reopen the plant and begin to negotiate with him. The company accepted the offer and reopened the plant on the 25th. The next day negotiations began, but they did not get far. No agreement was reached and the president of the o'yong group was left with only embarrassment.

The minju people immediately rose in protest. Four hundred or so marched on the plant's administration building. They seized the president and vice president of Daewoo Motors and forced them to bow down in front of them.

After this humiliation, Daewoo Motors became like a war zone. Police and armed guards were every where inside and outside the company grounds. Sit-down strikes and street demonstrations occurred daily. Police tried to control the situation by a liberal use of tear gas and arrests. One hundred and fifty were thrown in jail at one time when they tried to hold an all night vigil outside the company gates.

In the midst of the turmoil the president of the o'yong union announced his resignation. Elections to replace him were set for September 24. The minju nojo had been working for this moment, but now that it was upon them, they found themselves in a dilemma. The work place was an armed camp; worker anxiety over their jobs was high and the leaders of the minju were once again in prison. Under the circumstances, the minju unionists decided to accept a compromise candidate agreeable to both the o'yong and themselves. Though the candidate was elected overwhelmingly, almost immediately the compromise started to come apart. The philosophy and practices of the two wings were too different. The second round of the struggle for democratic unionism at Daewoo Motors ended inconclusively.

About two hundred miles south of Bupyong, where Daewoo Motors is located, the Daewoo *chaebol* was also having labor problems in its Okpo shipyards. Among the takeovers achieved by Daewoo was that of the nation's largest ship building facilities. Originally begun as a government corporation, it was equipped to construct not only ships, but also oil rigs for ocean exploration and "pre-fabricated" factories. The yards are located on a beautiful bay on the island of Koje, off the southern coast. The area is called Okpo and was the site, four hundred years ago, of Admiral Lee Soon Shin's famous victory over the Japanese navy. Admiral Lee had invented a metal covered, turtle shaped ship that single-handedly turned back a large Japanese armada.

The shipyards at Okpo have placed modern Korea in stiff competition with Japan to see which will become the world's largest shipbuilding nation. National pride, including the desire to match or overcome the Japanese, inserts a considerable amount of emotion in labor-management relations at Okpo.

Like Ulsan on the southeast, Okpo has been transformed into a large industrial town. A few short years ago, it was still a small fishing village. Today, it has a population of about 200,000 people. Fifteen thousand of those are employed at Daewoo.

Despite its historical significance, the Okpo shipyard has been a thorn in the flesh for Daewoo ever since President Pak Chung Hee ordered Daewoo to take it over in 1978. By then the shipyard was already saddled with a billion dollar debt. Pak had assisted in several of the other Daewoo takeovers and apparently had great faith in Kim Woo Choong's ability to bring order out of chaos. In this case, however, Kim has not been able to live up to expectations. Using his considerable persuasions as a salesman, Kim won world contracts that led the company to two profitable years. Profits of $7.5 million were reported for 1983 and $6.8 million in 1984, but these amounts were but a drop in the proverbial bucket. Even to achieve that small success wages had been frozen for five years, from 1983 to 1987. When the union uprisings of 1987 hit, the Daewoo shipyard was in a very vulnerable position.

As might be expected under such intensive financial pressures, the yards were not exactly a happy place to work. One worker described the plant floor where he worked as more like an animal farm than a human society. Workers were buffeted here and there by contradictory rumors and orders. A strong sense of employer distrust was engraved in the workers' minds. The company kept written records on each employee. Workers claimed that these records included material on their private lives, even the length of their hair. Workers could be arbitrarily dismissed or their wages reduced.

The fire was ready to be ignited when on August 8, 1987, Lee Song Yong climbed to the highest point on one of the huge cranes he helped to operate. From that vantage point, using a portable loud speaker, he began to shout, "Let's form a democratic union! We need a union! Let's join hands and form a democratic union!" In a short time, most of the workers in the yards had gathered around the crane. Lee's partners on the ground picked up the chants

133

and added a couple more: "Increase our wages! Abolish the Human Affairs Department!" (the department that kept records on everyone). Lee Song Yong, the man on the crane, was elected on the spot as president, and an executive committee was selected to organize a struggle. Lee, however, lasted as president for only two days. Many thought him too radical. A more moderate man, Yang Dong Saing, was elected in his place for a three year term. The strike was on. It could not have come at a worse time for the company. There was already a back log of 31 ships and eight oil rigs. Penalties for delay had to be paid. Bills piled up and income came to a stop. By 1988, it was reported that the total indebtedness had grown to $2.1 billion.

Unfortunately, relations, never very good between management and labor, had been left to deteriorate. There was little room for mutual trust, let alone compromise. The government tried to break the strike by force. It sent in the police and its special division called the *baikgoldan*. 1500 police and baikgoldan surrounded the shipyard and then attacked. They were impartial. They beat up on everyone, workers and onlookers, men and women. Tear gas was so heavy in the air that it condensed like rain. Demonstrations and counter demonstrations went on for many days. On August 22, 1987, a tear gas canister hit Lee Suk Kyu squarely on the chest and killed him. The death of Lee sobered everyone for a while, and the demonstrations subsided. However, no agreement was reached between company and union until April of the following year. Then a pay raise of 24 percent, the first increase in five years, was granted.

All sides took a six month breather. The union position was strong. The workers were in solidarity behind the leadership of Yang Dong Saing. The company, however, could not decide whether or not to provide the capital needed to stabilize the operations. The government for its part played two roles. As usual it dispatched the police to "keep the peace" and beat up on people when the occasion arose; but the government through the Reconstruction Bank, was also the financier behind Daewoo. The bank was irresolute about providing further investments.

Government, company, union knew they were in the same boat together and that the boat was on its way down. Each made public promises to help save the situation. Government spokesmen promised new capital. Daewoo spokesmen promised to sell five other subsidiaries and transfer those funds to Okpo. Union spokesmen said the workers would refrain from further wage demands for a period of time. All three made their statement, but none of them followed through with what they said.

Either the government or the company needed to take the initiative to break the stalemate. Only through decisive action on their part could new capital be raised, debts be paid and production stimulated. Neither party acted. The

134

company floundered. Decision was finally forced upon them by an outside and unexpected influence.

Daewoo Shipyards share the Okpo bay with another shipyard, one owned by the rival *chaebol*, Samsung. To forestall union organization in its yards, Samsung gave its workers a thirty five percent increase in wages. That put the income of Samsung workers considerably above that of their counterparts in Daewoo. Almost immediately pressures began to build among Daewoo workers. Their wages had been on hold for several years prior to 1987 and now they were in an inferior position compared to Samsung. Furthermore, they saw their *chaebol* avoiding the decisive action needed to protect their jobs.

Spring in Korea is the time for "wage offensives." When Spring of 1989 came on and the Daewoo Company seemed no closer to finding a solution to its debt crisis than it had been a year earlier, a wage offensive broke things wide open. The union demanded an increase of fifty three percent. Daewoo's chief executive, Kim Woo Choong, was flabbergasted, but responded temperately. A wage increase in 1989, he said , was out of the question. There was no money to grant any increase at all. However, if things went well, in January of 1990 Daewoo would give a wage increase retroactive to January of 1989. It would raise wages by $260 a month and pay a special bonus of $2000 per worker. The government for its part reacted to the union demand with indignation. It would not invest another cent until the union and company reached some agreement on wages.

The stakes were high. If the company went under, so might the Daewoo *chaebol*, and so might several commercial banks that hold about $1.15 billion of the debt. Even the Korea Development Bank was in peril. By itself it held over $750 million of the outstanding debt. International trade would be seriously effected, and the chance of overcoming the Japanese lead in the ship building industry would also be lost. The calamity to local business and the town of Okpo was nothing compared to the broader impact that a shut down could cause.

Then once again acts of unusual heroism and sacrifice interrupted events. Two workers at the Daewoo Shipyards, following the example of Chun Tae Il, burned themselves to death. Lee Song Mo set himself afire and jumped from the roof of a four story building before the eyes of his stunned comrades. Another worker, Pak Shin Suk, had committed immolation just twelve hours before. Their message in death was to the company: "Stop oppressing the workers!" "Increase their wages!" "Be democratic!" The wake for the two men was held outside in front of the hospital where the bodies lay. Throughout a long, heavy night thousands sang and shouted slogans and heard speeches. The elderly father of Lee Song Mo urged the workers to stay their course. " We are workers," he said, "who build up our nation. They call us communists and treat us like serfs.

My son sacrificed himself in protest against this injustice. He sacrificed himself to give others courage to fight for freedom."

The next morning it rained. It rained in a steady down pour as though the heavens were weeping. The funeral procession, accompanied by drums and gongs and the moaning of funeral dirges, wound in and out of each section of the vast shipyards, stopping momentarily at the place where the men had died. Afterwards their bodies were transported to Kwangju. Lee Song Mo and Pak Shin Suk were laid to rest beside the martyrs of the Kwangju massacre.

The union called for a general strike to begin June 22. The company repeated its offer. The government reiterated its unwillingness to invest but added to the intensity of the situation by threatening a full scale, land, sea and air attack on the union if it went into a general strike.

On the 22nd, at the last moment, a deal was struck. Wage increases of about $121 per month would be paid retroactive to March of 1989. The increase, however, would be paid in January of 1990. In addition, the work-week would be reduced to 44 hours from the previous standard of 48. Everyone breathed easy for the first time in months, but it was premature. Union representatives had to ratify the agreement. They turned it down by a vote of 28 to 26. The government mustered an assault team of 15,000 police. The company said it had had enough. It would close down. The union announced a general strike, but said it would open up negotiations as soon as dismissed union members were reinstated. With everyone looking down the abyss, the union was the one that gave in. After police arrested five of the more militant leaders, the union executive committee decided that the entire union membership should vote on the company proposal of June 22. So it came about that on the last Tuesday in June, 8,456 union members made the final decision. Fifty-eight percent voted to accept the wage agreement. A shut-down was avoided.

The fundamental dilemma, however, still remained. The debt was not likely to go away quickly even under the best of management. It remains to be seen just how far either government or Daewoo are willing to go to re-capitalize a concern that has made a profit only twice in ten years. Rumor has it that Kim Woo Choong wants out. His competition with the other big *chaebol* is hindered by the drain at Okpo. The government seems to be on the horns of the proverbial dilemma. A close down threatens calamity; continuing means yearly subsidies of millions of dollars.

Labor poses another yet unsettled side to the equation. There is general suspicion that throughout the whole ordeal, company and government conspired against the union and that the final outcome, though not all that bad in monetary terms, came in such a manner to leave a bitter taste in the mouth of workers. Early in 1990, there will be elections for a new slate of officers. The probabilities are good that the new union administration will be more aggressive than the present one.

For three years (1987–89) workers at Daewoo Motors and Daewoo Shipyards have been attempting to establish minju unions. It has been a long, hard struggle for both workers and managers. Little has been resolved. The peace that presently exists (November 1989) is but temporary. A final solution has yet to be created in either place. Unfortunately Daewoo management gives little indication of having learned much about labor relations or the minju movement. When asked what the self-immolation of the two workers at Okpo had taught Daewoo about labor–management relations, a vice–president in charge of such affairs responded that those two men were communists. They had been indoctrinated at secret brainwashing sessions and had committed suicide in obedience to communist command. The old crutch of communism is used once more to avoid reality. Workers are seeking a new order where democratic participation and human respect are recognized and accepted. The *chaebol* refuse to accept that. Instead, they seek the traditional way out: tag the union as communists, "radicals," "impure elements" and then call in police, baikgoldan, kusadae and squads of land, sea and air assault troops.

Goldstar

The first Goldstar[21] products to hit the market were women's cosmetics in 1947. Four years later, Lucky tooth paste and tooth brushes claimed a market monopoly which to a large degree they hold even today. In 1958, the company expanded into electric appliances. In the sixties, oil refining and the new sector of electronics were added to the business. Today, the Goldstar Group is one of the world's best known producers of chemicals, electric and electronic equipment and it offers a wide variety of financial and engineering services as well. In 1981, it was listed by Fortune magazine as having sales of $5.26 billion. By 1986, that had expanded to more than $11 billion. Goldstar and its export arm, Bando Sangsa, claim offices throughout the Asia–Pacific area and in Canada, the U.S.A., South America, and most countries of West Europe. Goldstar has production facilities in U.S.A., West Germany and Saudi Arabia.

Unlike the founders of the other super–*chaebol*, the man who created Lucky–Goldstar is little known in Korean society. He was Koo In Hwoi. After his death, his son, Koo Cha Kyung, took over leadership. He also avoids the limelight, seldom is seen in public, and even less frequently are his words or picture seen in the newspaper. The Koo family's motto is "Human Harmony". In its application to labor relations in Goldstar plants, the motto is said to mean that "our employees are our most valuable assets. Their creativity, loyalty and productivity can be fostered only through personalized management, a comfortable working environment and maximum benefits."[22] Unlike the other super-*chaebol*, one gets the impression that these words have some base in the actual practice of labor relations.

Goldstar has a long history of unions in their plants; some date back to the early 1960's. When the 1987 fury hit, 16 of the Group's 27 member companies already had union organizations. Though prior to 1987 all of the unions could be described as "o'yong," nevertheless the structures were there and the process of union–company negotiation was well practiced. In the latter half of 1987, all 27 companies and their 57 subsidiaries experienced worker uprisings and strikes. The two big demands made by workers in each place were wage increases and recognition of democratic unions.

Goldstar management came through the 1987 union assault fairly well. In May, unions and *chaebol* had agreed on a healthy wage increase. So when the big organizing drive came in the latter part of the year, Goldstar workers were already at the top of the wage ladder. Furthermore, top management in the Goldstar Group had read the omens correctly. In 1986 a corporate decision was made that shifted responsibility for labor relations to each company in the group away from corporate headquarters. If conflicts arose local management was to resolve them and not depend on a centralized decision–making system. To strengthen the position of the member companies, corporate management made available to them some extra funds that could be used for bonuses or wage increases if they were needed to bring about quicker resolution to labor demands. The strategy worked. Most of Goldstar labor problems in 1987 were settled within a week. While Hyundai and Daewoo were being buffeted about by the new union movement, Goldstar was able to continue with minimal interruption.

The milder level of conflict at Goldstar was reflected in the events at one company, Goldstar Electronics, which employs about 4,000 workers in three plants, one each in Anyang, Kumi and Kunpo. The strike there lasted eleven days. It was provoked more by the political flow of the times than by managerial mistreatment. Wages were good. Hours were under control. Nevertheless, the winds of democratic unionism were strong and the workers at Goldstar Electronics joined forces with them. Two demands were made: a wage increase, and recognition by the company of a new democratic union rather than the established o'yong union. The first demand was quickly settled. A small increase, in addition to the one given in the spring, was granted. The second demand was not so easily handled. Technically, of course, the company could take no action on union recognition. That was an internal affair that only the workers could resolve. In reality, however, everyone knew that the company called the tune for the union leadership. It had over the years regularly inserted itself into the decision–making processes of the union and had in an indirect fashion designated the choice of union officials. So the workers' demand that the company recognize a new democratic union was not off target.

At first, only a third of the workers joined the strike action, but soon the rest of them followed suit. They demonstrated mostly inside the plant walls, but on the few occasions they did go to the streets, violent confrontations took place with the police. Many were injured on both sides and ninety one unionists were arrested. Throughout the eleven days, negotiations went on and finally an agreement was reached. The pay raise was officially granted, and in some unofficial way, it was agreed that thereafter union officials would be elected by direct vote of the union members. The old indirect method, which the company so easily manipulated, was discontinued. When agreement on the direct election system was reached, Goldstar Electronics returned to normal operations.

1988 was a peaceful year for Goldstar. Not one major work stoppage occurred during the entire year. The storm broke in 1989. During the first six months for approximately one hundred and seventy days, strikes and demonstrations shook the Goldstar *chaebol*. When the union leaders, imprisoned in 1987, were released, they immediately established their own dismissed workers' association, and began to publish a newspaper that circulated news, ideas and plans for coordinated action among workers in Goldstar Electronic's three plants. In October of 1988 the "prison graduates" and their newspaper were instrumental in having Kim Sang Ho elected as president of the Electronics' Union. Kim was heavily committed to the democratic movement. He and the other elected officers immediately published a set of demands: a 30% increase in pay, a 44 hour work week, a progressive severance pay system, a family allowance, and equal union membership on the company personnel committee which administers discipline against employees. The company made little response. Lower echelons of management were sent to the bargaining table, but the company president, who is the only one with authority to make decisions, attended only sporadically and even then, from the union perspective, offered nothing of substance. The company was "stonewalling." It met with union representatives, but made only superficial gestures toward bargaining.

On January 7, 1989 union representatives from the three plants voted to go on strike. They set January 16 as the date for the membership vote. One last meeting with management was held, but that too was of no avail. Management did, however, deliver a sobering message. They told the union representatives that unlike the practice in other companies, Goldstar would not pay wages to workers while they were on strike. The company slogan became "No work, No pay!" This threat gave everyone cause for hesitation, but when the vote was taken eighty five percent voted to strike. Expecting a long struggle workers carefully cleaned and oiled the machines. The company removed some of them for safe-keeping, and then discontinued food and transportation services.

To gather support for the strike, the union hosted a shamanistic ritual, where sacrifice for a union victory was offered. Union leaders from around the entire Anyang and Seoul areas were invited. They brought words of encouragement and envelopes of money for the Goldstar union to use as a strike fund. In his welcoming address Kim Sang Ho thanked everyone for their generous contributions and challenged the workers in all Goldstar companies to join the Electronics' Workers in striking against Goldstar and forming one united union throughout the entirety of the *chaebol*.

To sustain solidarity among workers at Anyang, Kunpo and Kumi the union organized mobile teams that serviced the workers at each place. If morale began to drag, or an item of strategy needed to be explained or a demonstration had to be planned, a mobile team would be dispatched to help the local union leadership. The teams also visited other Goldstar plants to incite their workers to join in the action. Their success was startling. Workers in eighteen Goldstar plants around the country joined Electronics either in strike or threat of a strike. A Goldstar Group Association of Labor Unions was formed. Worker demonstrations were held in the plants, on the streets and in front of the *chaebol*'s ultra–modern, skyscraper headquarters on Yoido Island in Seoul.

In one demonstration 5,000 members of "Kyungki Noryun" took part. The Kyungki Noryun is the Association of Labor Unions for the Province of Kyungki, which includes the city of Seoul. As the new democratic labor movement began to grow, locals began to reach out to other locals that had the same goals and philosophy. As a result, over the nation regional associations of minju unions came to be formed. The Kyungki Noryun was one of the most important of those regional associations. The government had early on declared such regional organizations to be illegal, but that had little effect. They continued to grow. The union at Goldstar Electronics was associating with Kyungki Noryun at the same time that it was busy forming an alliance of unions within the Goldstar *chaebol*.

This multidimensional character of the new unionism generated much anxiety in the government. It was getting out of control and going in directions that the government found hard to control. Officialdom's anxiety was heightened even further when the Goldstar unions joined representatives from other democratic unions in support of worker action at Hyundai in Ulsan. They gathered in front of Hyundai's corporate headquarters in Seoul and read a statement demanding democratic rights for workers at Hyundai and workers everywhere. A new nationwide solidarity was being born and the authorities did not like it.

The Goldstar *chaebol*, however, kept to its game plan. It assumed a low profile. It continued to meet with the union but offered no concessions and made little effort to compromise. It urged the workers to return to work and to continue negotiations while they worked. At the same time it reminded them that there would be no pay if there was no work. Toward the end of March both sides were ready to make a deal. Union and company reached an accord that included a 19% wage increase, a 44 hour work week, 15% bonus, a few allowances and payment of fifty percent of wages during the time of the strike. On vote by the rank and file, the accord was rejected by a small majority, but after that the center of strike action at Goldstar moved south to the city of Changwon. Changwon is another of Korea's new, industrial cities. It is the location of Korea's weapons' industry and much of the military research and development is done there. Consequently it is designated by the government as an area vital to national security in which work stoppages are forbidden. Workers at Changwon were first infected with the minju labor movement when in 1987 workers at Hyundai's Precision Instrument Company joined the strike action of their brother unions in Ulsan. Hyundai workers in Changwon struck despite the government's decree forbidding it -- without dire consequences to either them or the company.

In 1987 when the explosion in union organizing took place, women workers in Masan, a city adjacent to Changwon, organized one hundred or so plants at the Masan Free Export Zone. These young and militant women challenged the older, more conservative and much better paid male workers in Changwon to join the union movement. The result was that workers in the two cities formed the "Ma-Chang" Labor Alliance (Ma-Chang Noryun) to coordinate their struggles for independent unions and pay raises.

Goldstar plants in Changwon joined in with the Ma-Chang Alliance. In 1989 an Alliance-led campaign resulted in a confrontation with employees and police that lasted several months. Workers from sixty plants in the two cities took part in the daily demonstrations. The Alliance formed two bodies to carry out the campaign. One coordinated the immediate actions of the workers in Masan and Changwon. The other was a long range planning group that connected the Ma-Chang Alliance with similar worker organizations across the country. Front line leadership of these two bodies were arrested early in 1989, but that only made the Alliance members more militant. Release of their imprisoned comrades became their strongest rallying cry.

Goldstar workers in Changwon were active in, and part of, the leadership of the Ma-Chang Alliance. At the same time they were tied to the association of unions within the Goldstar Group. The militancy of Ma-Chang reinforced the hand of the activists throughout the Goldstar *chaebol*.

On April 25, twenty five thousand workers over the twin cities rallied first at their respective places of work and then paraded through the streets of Masan and Changwon. Late into the night bands of workers marched and shouted their demands that the imprisoned leaders be freed, that each of the companies grant a wage increase and that the work week be reduced to forty four hours. Among the banners and slogans were also political messages such as "Overthrow the

Roh Tae Woo Dictatorship," "Withdraw all U.S. Troops," and "Yankee Go Home." At one large intersection in Changwon the demonstrators were met by police who were showered with bricks and molotov cocktails. The police responded with tear gas and a frontal attack that dispersed the crowd and ended the demonstrations for that night. Scenes similar to this one were repeated over and over again during the first months of 1989.

The parades, demonstrations and demands for collective bargaining were coordinated by the Ma-Chang Alliance, but unions at each company were responsible for their own negotiations. The union at Goldstar shops demanded a fifty three percent wage increase. The company offered nineteen percent, which had been accepted by some of the other unions in the Goldstar *chaebol*, but rejected at Changwon. After many parades and fights with the police, the union agreed to submit the issue to arbitration by the Central Labor Committee of the government. The three public representatives on the Board made the findings on April 29. Their decision included a twenty four percent wage increase and a variety of added benefits such as a family allowance and seniority pay. While both sides were legally required to accept the decision, when the arbitrators implied that there had been outside political influence involved in the union's actions, the union rejected the arbitrators' report and continued the strike. As a result seventy union leaders were arrested for illegal activity.

After another month of more sit-ins and street demonstrations, on June 3, Koo Cha Kyung, Goldstar's president took the unprecedented action of directly entering the dispute. The company, he proposed, would pay workers' wages for the period of the strike and it would arrange with the police to have the seventy labor leaders released from prison. In return, he called upon the union to accept the arbitration decision of the Labor Committee and return to work. Koo's compromise was accepted and the strike was over.

Summary of Super *Chaebol*

The industrial relations system at Korea's super *chaebol* has three major actors: the *chaebol*, the government and the union. In each case referred to above the interaction among the three has taken on a distinctive configuration. Certain patterns of authoritarianism dominate in all four, but at the same time significant differences are apparent.

The Hyundai *chaebol* is likened unto the "street fighter" who intends to crush the enemy, no holds barred. Company commandos under James Lee are sent to attack the enemy by surprise; police are manipulated and the marines are rallied. Hyundai will negotiate if forced to, but only until an advantage is gained. Then the attack will be renewed. At Ulsan the government, through the Ministry of Labor tried at first to act as a neutral party, a mediator, to bring the two sides to compromise, but its efforts were weak and irresolute. It quickly deserted that posture and instead assumed its more usual role of colluding with the company. At the local level, the police authorities helped to put together the James Lee escapade. At the national level a massive attack by police was used to finally subdue the workers.

The union at Hyundai is characterized by strength, heroism and determination, but also by poor planning and broken solidarity. Hyundai unions have been strong in their faithful pursuit of democratic unionism. The determination and heroism of leaders like Kwon Yong Mok have repeatedly rallied the workers and forced Hyundai management to deal with the union. Yet the workers have never been able to sustain the solidarity and organization needed to overcome the stubborn hostility of Chung Ju Yong.

At Samsung the company-government pattern is not too much different from that of Hyundai except Samsung has much more finesse and sophistication. Samsung isolates and dismisses any pro-union worker; it sneaks to the labor office and registers "ghost unions"; it quietly kidnaps its own employees; and it utilizes the best trained kusadae there are. All of this is well coordinated with the police and other government authorities. The Samsung name does not come out in the news associated with the violence that characterizes Hyundai. Samsung's public image is kept clean. The union movement at Samsung generally has been unsuccessful in generating any sustained enthusiasm among the workers. In most cases the company's ploy of registering a ghost union or kidnapping a couple leaders is enough to defeat the movement. Even in the case of Samsung Heavy Industry where there were hundreds of workers involved in union action, it could not be sustained nor organized. Some observers say worker attitude toward unions at Samsung is different because of three factors: fear, anti-union indoctrination and a comparatively high standard of wages. Whatever the cause, Samsung stands out as the lone example of a *chaebol* without a labor union.

Daewoo is known as the "opportunist". Though it likes to be seen as the company that uses modern, scientific methods of management, in its labor relations at Daewoo Motors and the Okpo Shipyards, its management seems to vacillate and seek temporary gains rather that moving toward basic resolution. Daewoo's opportunism, unfortunately, eventuates in a reliance on police and kusadae just as do the harsher attitudes of management at Hyundai and Samsung. Workers at Daewoo shipyards have exercised an amazing amount of solidarity in the midst of heavy political and financial pressures. Union leadership has been there with the skills and courage to chart the course through the many difficulties. At Daewoo Motors, though a hard core of about three hundred workers maintain solidarity and continue to be loyal to the minju ideals, they have not been able to persuade the majority. Solidarity has escaped them so the union experiment there resembles an internecine battle rather than a clear minju labor movement.

The government's contributions to the confusion at Okpo have been several. Under the guise of the Korea Development Bank the government is the chief financier and also the party chiefly responsible for the company's huge indebtedness; at the level of the Ministry of Labor government went back and forth from claiming its neutrality, to offering itself as mediator, to making a variety of threats and exhortations. And, of course, the government was also present in the form of a massive police force held ready for a take over of the shipyards. The government's lack of consistent policy and its unwillingness to support democratic processes leads it into self contradictions.

Goldstar's pattern of industrial relations is considerably different from the other three. It has been more pragmatic in its dealings with the union. Prior to 1987 Goldstar factories had many unions most of which were company dominated. As the democratic unionism exploded on to the scene in 1987, Goldstar management seems to have gone with the flow, compromising and consenting to minju nojo demands for independence and direct elections of union officers. It has not relied on kusadae violence. Police have become involved usually as the workers left company grounds and moved into street marches.

The unions at Goldstar Electronics illustrate that a contest of economic power can end in compromise. That is a critical lesson in the context of Korean industrial relations where the *chaebol* want to have nothing less than absolute victory. Another significant pattern comes out of Goldstar in Changwon. The unions there are bound together by an association within the *chaebol* and at the same time are members of an alliance that cuts across lines of employer and industry. The Ma–Chang Alliance is representative of regional organizations that have been formed all over the country. These regional organizations are the structural side of the nation–wide minju nojo movement. The intent is to form a national federation of regional minju associations as an alternative to the FKTU. Therefore the regional alliances like Ma–Chang are involved not only in strikes for economic demands, but also in campaigns for political change.

In the Goldstar disputes the government role has also been of a different nature. The police have mostly played the role of keeping order on the city streets. The government's Central Labor Committee played an important role in acting as arbitrator. The Labor Committee has existed since 1947, but seldom used with any seriousness because neither labor nor management trusts one another enough to go that way. It is significant that the one dispute to be helped by arbitration was one at Goldstar.

It will take much more research to confirm the accuracy of these generalizations about patterns of behavior among *chaebol*, government and union, but for the present a tentative set of hypotheses might look like this:

144

authoritarianism still prevails in the minds and practices of the *chaebol*; government agencies play their roles according to the directions of the *chaebol*; and unions have moved to a new level of democratic consciousness that will continue to confront the authoritarian powers of both management and government.

DEMOCRATIC UNIONS IN SMALL FIRMS

About 33 percent of Korean workers are in small firms that employ between 5 and 100 people. Another 24 percent are in medium sized companies where the workforce numbers from 100 to 500.[23] One clear pattern that emerged early in the 1987 labor eruptions was that the small and medium sized plants were being organized at the same rapid rate as the big *chaebol*. Riding along on the political fervor released by Roh Tae Woo's 6.29 policy statement, workers at these firms stretched out their courage and their consciousness and took the risk. Subsequently, a good portion of them have maintained themselves by organizing regional associations for mutual protection. Unions in the city of Inchun are an interesting case in point.

Like many cities in Korea, Inchun has undergone tremendous change. Within a decade and a half, its population has grown from around 500,000 to roughly 2 million. In early years its factory area, huddled in one northwest section along the harbor, was dominated by heavy industry, steel, machines, electric equipment, railroad running stock, glass, textiles and flour mills. The big firms employed a thousand to fifteen hundred workers. Smaller firms of a few dozen to a couple hundred workers were scattered throughout the area. As the industrial expansion of the 1970's took shape in Inchun, new industrial areas were opened up to the north and east. Three industrial estates were established, and where there were once salt beds next to the Yellow Sea, a maze of factories manufacturing everything from garments to electronics to steel products was constructed. These newer shops employ many fewer workers on the average than factories in the older part of town. One estimate is that the average plant has around one hundred workers, the range being from ten to about 600.

When the flood of union action took place in July and August of 1987, it included most of the workers of Inchun. Estimates are that four hundred or more work places had strikes or some form of protest. Workers at a large steel mill employing around 3,000 moved heavy equipment several miles to the plaza in front of the railroad station to take part in a city-wide demonstration. For three months, there was at least one protest demonstration everyday, and at times there were as many as thirty.

After the initial enthusiasm subsided, however, a clear pattern of differences emerged between the workers in the older part of Inchun and those in the newer sections. Unionism in the old part of town goes way back, even to the post liberation years of 1945–50. Many of the shops in the old district had been established by the Japanese and no doubt participated in Japan's sampo movement of 1943–45. After liberation, the struggle between Chun Pyung and No Chong took place in some of these same factories. Under Syngman Rhee, in the 1950's, unions in Inchun factories were retained, but under government control. Even during the 1960's, most of them would have qualified for the stigma, o'yong. The companies blatantly interfered in the internal decision-making processes of the unions. Even so, several of the unions in "old" Inchun had registered disputes and had exercised their right to strike. All of these unions were charter members of the FKTU, system. The workers tend to be men with families. Their ages are on the average about ten years above the workers in the new areas. The initial protests in 1987 provided a vent valve for the workers in these older plants, but the unions were not easily persuaded toward reform. After September, 1987 most of them returned to the organization and the processes they had used over previous decades. The unions in "old" Inchun have not subsequently become part of the democratic labor movement, though it is claimed that there are vigorous "democratic" factions among their members.

The democratic labor movement has taken root in the newer sections of town where there is no history of unionism. Most of the workers are young and many are women who work under conditions that, on the whole, are much worse than those in the older and bigger plants. Workers in these plants are committed to the expansion of union militancy and have formed an Inchun association of labor unions, independent from the FKTU structures. FKTU and the more staid unions in "old" Inchun are identified as part of the problem, part of ruling class, that is preventing democratization and independent unionism. About one hundred new unions have been formed and sustained in Inchun. Accounts of the formation of two of the new unions illustrate their enthusiasm for the democratic labor movement.

Namil Kumsuk

Namil Kumsuk is one of the larger plants in "new" Inchun. It employs six hundred, mainly male, workers who produce a stainless steel kitchen utensil, most of it for export. As is not an unusual pattern, the owner is brother-in-law to a national assemblyman. The plant which started production in 1973 was not unionized. In 1986, the workers were bold enough to form an association, the chief purpose of which was to elect members to the Joint Labor-Management Council in the plant. The workers elected four of their own candidates as delegates to the Joint Council. Only one "company man" was chosen. Management refused to call the Joint Council to session. Three hundred workers protested. They had matters of safety, work process and general supervision that

146

they wanted to resolve. The company's only response to the protest was to fire five of the protest leaders.

By the time June of 1987 came around, the workers were ready for action. They determined to organize a trade union. The company followed the example of Samsung by having a few foremen and several pro-company workers register a union with the labor department before the bonafide unionists could do so. Outraged, the unionists took the fight back to the workers. They denounced the company's actions and demanded direct elections of union leadership, restoration of dismissed workers and an increase in wages. Workers were asked not to put their faith in management, nor in an assemblyman, but in themselves. The speeches were followed by the thunderous singing of songs and chanting of slogans. Namil workers were solidly behind the union.

Then came the kusadae. They waded in with pipes and clubs and beat the workers until many were seriously injured and had to be sent to the hospital. Others were held captive in a room at the plant, and the union leaders were fired on the spot. The union appeared to be defeated. There was little enthusiasm left. Then the unexpected took place. Wives of the hospitalized workers became so incensed at seeing their husbands clubbed into submission that they marched on the factory with several of the injured men limping behind them. The outraged women rallied support as they went. By the time they arrived at the front gate, they were joined by a large contingent of workers. Together, they broke into the plant and made their demands: direct elections for union leadership; rehiring of the dismissed comrades; and indemnity for the injured workers. The kusadae made an appearance but this time they stood by and watched. The anger of the people was too obvious for them to risk their necks. With no other options management agreed to the workers' demands. An election for union president was held. The workers' candidate won 386 to 132.[24]

Cosmos Electronics

The Cosmos Electronics Company, which is part of a larger firm that is famous for its department store in downtown Seoul, produces black and white and color TVs for export. Its 450 workers are mainly young women who live in the crowded quarters of the company dormitory.

In 1985, the first movement toward worker solidarity took place when one of the new workers, a college student, pointed out to the other workers how their rights were being violated by the company. She also initiated discussion among the workers about how to improve their lot by organizing and demanding improvements. Most of the workers who had come straight from the farms were quite unhappy with their crowded living quarters, the bad food, the hard work and the arrogant attitude of their supervisors. The college student had merely

147

voiced the grievances which most of the workers felt. They were not, however, familiar with her proposed solution -- a labor union.

When the company heard about a meeting of some of the workers which took place in December (1985) the college student was fired and several other workers were put under surveillance. Two other things happened soon afterwards that the workers interpreted as retaliations for their meeting. One line of production was shut down and some union sympathizers lost their jobs. In addition wages were not paid in April 1987. The company did not respond to worker protest, and though the wages were finally paid, the company's refusal to explain the nonpayment further roused the ire of the employees.

By August of 1988, workers all over the Bupyong area of Inchun where Cosmos Electronic is located were forming unions. Banners calling for increased wages and for struggle to organize unions were flying over many of the neighboring plants. The company announced to their employees that it would provide a 5% increase in wages for the coming year. The strike banners over other plants were calling for 25 percent increase, 37 percent and even 53 percent. Five percent was humiliating. That evening, thirty-seven of the women workers met at a Chinese restaurant to form a union. They had studied the legal requirements and followed each of them carefully.

The next day during lunch hour, in the company yard the decision to form a union was announced to management and workers. A flurry of emotional speeches was followed by a song-fest that included recently composed songs like "Raise Our Wages," "The Fire and the Butterfly," and "The Old Workers' Ballad." One hundred and fifty workers signed up immediately and a sense of solidarity among the workers took root.

On August 21, the company declared a general shut down, with no food service until things were resolved. A large number of workers quickly gathered in the factory yard. At first, the company stood firm. Only a five percent increase was possible. All day, the workers sat in the plant grounds. Off and on, talks took place between representatives of the company and the new union. Night came and went. Finally, at around five in the morning, a break was declared. A raise of 10 percent would be granted, and bonuses would be paid when the company was able. The company also promised to improve the quality of the food.

The union president told the gathered workers, "We did not win everything we needed, but this is a first step. As long as we stay united we can create democracy even in this factory." The union at Cosmos Electronics has continued to play an important role in the Association of Democratic Unions in Inchon.[25]

Each of approximately one hundred new unions of the Inchon area has its own unique story. As of June 1989, thirty-six of them are participating in the

Inchun Area's Association of Democratic Unions, which, though not a legal entity, is being used by its members to coordinate activities, strategies and information.

Similar associations have been organized in industrial districts all around the country. In Puchun, a town next to Inchun, there is an industrial area of about fifty factories. Unions in these shops have organized an association with the formidable title "The Headquarters to Struggle for Wage Hikes and Revision of the Present Labor Law." In April of 1989, unions in 35 of these plants participated in a one day general strike. On the agreed upon day, 6000 workers stayed off the job to march to the Puchun City Hall where speeches were made demanding democratic labor unions and pay increases. Worker solidarity was affirmed through songs, chants, dances and drama. The day after the march the unions of Puchun began a coordinated spring offensive for increased wages.

Like the workers of Masan, Chongwan, Inchun and many other industrial areas the workers in Puchun formed an alliance of minju unions independent from the FKTU system. Together these many alliances plan to organize a National Federation of Labor Unions (Chunnohyup).

The government has determined that such a nationwide organization shall not be formed. Democratic leadership in all regions are kept in prison or under close scrutiny. It is estimated that from the middle of 1987 to mid-1989, six hundred leaders of democratic unions have been imprisoned. While that tactic might slow down the process, in the long-run it is not likely to alter the direction in which the democratic union movement is headed. Already there is conflict between the democratic unions and the FKTU at the local levels and within FKTU itself. The establishment of a nationwide headquarters for the democratic unions will up grade the conflict to one of national and even international competition.

WHITE COLLAR UNIONISM

Successes at economic planning brought many changes to Korea's industrial structures. One change that went unnoticed until the union outbreaks in 1987 was the expansion of the "white collar" sector of the economy. One study concludes that by 1980, 38.2 percent of the employed workforce were white collar workers.[26] They too were activated by the events of 1987 and quickly became an important part of the minju labor movement. Overnight, unions were formed in such unlikely workplaces as insurance companies and brokerage houses. Researchers at government and private laboratories and think tanks formed their own separate unions. Even the employees of the government's Korean Institute of Science and Technology took the step of organizing. Newspaper reporters and employees in other media got together. Hospital workers, who for many years had tried to improve their lot, now found the impetus to win organization drives in hospitals and health care units all over the country. Bank unions had a similar experience of resurrection, and last but not least, school teachers joined the ranks of the white collar service sectors that joined the labor movement.

Bank Workers Union

A union has existed among bank employees for many years. It was already one of the national federations recognized in the union reorganization of 1963. Its claimed membership in 1971 was 23,549. By 1986, it had expanded to 92,084 members in 83 local unions. Two years later, as a result of the 1987 fervor, membership had increased to 126,407 in 168 branch unions.[27] The branches now embrace most foreign banks and even the Korean National Bank which is the counterpart to the American Federal Reserve Bank is organized.

In June of 1989, new unions at six commercial banks entered into wage negotiations with their employers. A tentative agreement was reached which would provide a 21.7% increase in wages and certain benefits. Before the agreement could be effected, however, the Ministry of Finance supported by the Economic Planning Board, indicated that it was returning to a policy of permitting only single digit wage increases. Therefore, the 21.7 percent proposal was not acceptable. The negotiators would have to start over again. To make the point clear, the Finance Minister added that if banks raised wages in excess of ten percent, they would forfeit further financial assistance from the Bank of Korea. The Minister suggested binding arbitration by the Central Labor Committee as an alternative to strike or lockout.

The union responded that the Finance Minister had violated the declared government policy of non-intervention in labor-management affairs. Furthermore, since the six banks in question are all private banks, the Finance Minister had injected himself as a third-person into the collective bargaining process. That is clearly an illegal act. The union went on to say that if the Finance Minister insisted on his way, it would bring a law suit against him. To the matter of a wage increase the union spokesperson reminded the Minister and the Bank president that their wages had been virtually frozen for eight years.[28]

The union organized at the Bank of Korea (the Nation's central bank) added its support. The Bank of Korea should not, it claimed, be used as a club over the heads of those trying to negotiate a settlement in the private sector.[29]

Technically, unions at banks are forbidden to strike since they are defined as a public utility. Union leadership, however, saw the issue as primarily a showdown between the government and unions in general. Was government interference in labor-management disputes to be tolerated? Union leaders said they would be willing to go to prison, if necessary, to make their witness on that question. At the same time, the union consulted with the FKTU. That body had been waiting for an opportunity to flex its muscle. Here was an opportunity to show that it had reformed its old practices and now stood with the workers. A press conference was called and it was announced the FKTU would, if necessary, ask its 20 federation members to join a general strike in support of the bank workers.[30]

In the end the Finance Minister won. The bank presidents were sobered by the thought of no credit from the Bank of Korea. They refused any bargaining with the union. The union representatives accepted what they thought was unavoidable: a wage increase of 9.9 percent. Perhaps more than the immediate settlement to this dispute, two other matters will be important for the long-run. The issue of a government agency acting as an outside, third party was raised for the first time. The Roh Tae Woo administration has boasted that it supports a liberalization of labor-management relations without government involvement. Here, as the union so clearly pointed out, it was violating its own policies. That point is bound to be reiterated by other unions in the future.

The other item of importance relates to the role of the FKTU. It is in search of ways to break out of its image as kept houseboy of the ruling party. The bank dispute was probably not a good one on which to build a new image. After threatening to call a nation-wide strike, it backed off and did nothing. FKTU's image was further damaged.

For the Bank Workers' Union the defeat was not a disaster. It emerged from the battle much more knowledgeable about the government powers arrayed against it. It also had built up a solidarity of effort that will strengthen its hand when the next round of bargaining begins in 1990.

National Teachers' Union

It was a surprise to most everyone when the teachers in the public school system began to join the minju labor movement. There are some 300,000 elementary and secondary school teachers in Korea. They find themselves in a unique quandary between the old authoritarianism and new ideals of equality and democracy. Traditional culture is deeply ingrained in education, and as could be expected, hierarchical values are perpetuated by the system. Teachers work under a chain of command that lays heavy teaching and extra-curricular loads upon them, but provides little opportunity for teacher participation in the decision-making processes. They are given high social status, but low levels of income.

Most teachers, however, are graduates of teacher colleges where the ideals of democracy and teacher participation in policy and curriculum are central premises. These progressive ideas clash with the realities of the system in which they work. A teachers' labor union is one way by which the clash can be ameliorated. One survey found that eighty four percent of teachers favor the idea of organizing a labor union.[31]   The movement toward the actual organization, however, was slow. Not until 1989, two years after the minju union eruptions in industry did the teachers make the decision to act.

On May 28, on the campus of Yunsei University 130 teachers from around the nation met to organize a teachers' union. The government had ordered police to prevent such a gathering, but the teachers out-maneuvered the police by announcing that they would meet at Hanyang University while in fact they gathered at Yunsei. By the time the police caught on, it was too late. The formation of the union had taken place and the legal documents for union registration were completed. Afterwards the newly elected leaders proceeded to the offices of the Reunification and Democracy Party (RDP), the opposition party led by Kim Yong Sam. There they carried out a nine day fast to demonstrate the "rightness" of their actions and to elicit support from the RDP.

The government refused to accept the union registration documents, and the Ministry of Education warned the teachers that a union would not be tolerated. It was illegal according to existing law for teachers to organize or form a labor union. Besides, they reminded the teachers, a union is quite contrary to the cultural traditions of education and unacceptable to the people. Unions furthermore would inject conflict into the school system and disturb the teacher-student relationship.

The union retorted that as citizens and employees, teachers had the same rights as do all others. Those include the rights to organize, bargain and take collective action. The education system, furthermore, is in dire need of reform. Teachers must have more engagement in the decision-making processes. Only a union, they claim, will ensure that. Teachers will still be teachers and students will still be students. That relationship will not be hindered. In fact it will be improved because the students will see the teachers participating in a democratic fashion and thus learn democracy rather than authoritarianism.

The government is not persuaded. It has arrested union leadership and threatens to both dismiss and prosecute any and all of the 5,166 teachers whom it says have joined the union. The union counters that the government underestimates. The number of members, it claims, is closer to 26,000. If the government insists on persecuting its members, the union says it will call for mass resignations.[32]   The Minister of Education says he intends to recruit 10,000 new teachers and that will more than cover any who might resign. However, the Minister says he will recruit only those who do not have "impure" backgrounds, meaning those who have not been activists in college or have any "leftist thoughts."[33]

At the end of 1989 the situation is at an impasse, but with the government holding the stronger position. Most of the union leadership is in prison. Many have been dismissed from jobs and others are under constant surveillance. Yet if past experience is any guide, a teachers' labor union movement is not likely to fade away. It is more likely to incubate for awhile more and reappear at a later date.

CHAPTER NOTES

1. Young-ki Park, "Labor Relations in Korea: Recent Developments and Prospects," Sogang University, Seoul, 1987, p. 3, 4.

2. Ibid.

3. Far Eastern Economic Review, September 3, 1987, p. 47.

4. *Saebyu'ku'r Yo'nu'n Hamso'ng* (Dawn of the Battle) Han'guk Nodong Yu'nguso, 1988, p. 31.

5. *Han Kyurae* Newspaper, March 21, 1989, p. 11.

6. *Saebyu'ku'r Yo'nu'n Hamso'ng*, p. 37.

7. Korea Times, January 14, 1989.

8. Korea Times, January 12, 1989.

9. Korea Times, January 14, 1989.

10. Korea Times, April 1, 1989.

11. Samsung does have one union. It bought the Chosun Ilbo which had a union when taken over.

12. Personal letter to the author.

13. *Chosun Worgan*, "Samsung. Yuryong Nojo Siljai" (The Real Situation of the Ghost Unions at Samsung), February, 1989, p. 208.

14. Ibid., p. 206.

15. Ibid., p. 207.

16. Ibid., p. 212.

17. Ibid., p. 212.

18. Vital Speeches of the Day, October 1, 1985, p. 756.

19. Woo Choong Kim. "Labor-Management Disputes and a Businessman's Reflections," *Tonga Ilbo* Newspaper, December 8, 1987. Found in Byong Kuk Kim. *Kim Woo Choong*, Bobmum Sa, 1988, p. 210.

20. Vital Speeches, p. 756.

21. *The official name of the chaebol is Lucky-Goldstar. The original company was called Lucky Chemical. For the sake of brevity, we will refer to the Group as Goldstar.

22. "Lucky-Goldstar," Yearly Report, 1988, p. 3.

23. *Han'guk Sahwei Nodongja Yu'ngu I* (A Study of Workers in Korean Society) Han'guk Sahwei Yu'nguso, Seoul, 1989, p. 117.

24. Information for this story came primarily from an unpublished book printed by the Committee for the Formation of Democracy in the Inchun Area (*Inchu'n Jiyu'k minjunojo Ku'nsu'r Kongdong Silchu'n Wiewonhwei*). The book is entitled <u>1987 Inchun Area: July and August Labor Disputes</u> (*1987 Inchu'n Jiyu'k, 7,8 Wor Nodong Tojaeng*, p. 53 ff.

25. Ibid., p. 92 ff.

26. Yong Hi Lee, "Study of White Collar Workers in Large Industry" in *Han'guk Sahwei Nodongja Yu'ngu I*, published by Han'guk Sahwei Yu'nguso, Seoul, 1989, p. 277.

27. Figures taken from Mario F. Bognanno, <u>Korea's Industrial Relations at the Turning Point</u>, Korea Development Institute, Seoul, December 1988, p. 63.

28. <u>Korea Times</u>, June 23, 1989.

29. Ibid., June 24, 1989.

30. Ibid., June 27, 1989.

31. <u>Korea Times</u>, May 18, 1989.

32. Ibid., June 4, 1989.

33. Ibid., July 15, 1989.

VII. LABOR'S ROLE IN KOREAN DEMOCRACY

The story of organized labor has gone on for eighty years. It is a story of men and women seeking dignity and equality. Much of the story is sad. Brutality and suffering has punctuated every chapter. The brutality has been inflicted by Japanese, American and Korean, whichever nationality happened to be in the ruler's seat. Yet the entire history of organized labor in Korea has been also a story of amazing endurance and persistence on the part of the workers. Under the Japanese, there was the instinctive coming-together to protect themselves against the common enemy. When the Japanese were banished, workers immediately threw off their shackles. They took over plants and ran them as both managers and workers; they formed unions; they joined with the Peoples' Committees to create a better land. That dream , however, was never fulfilled. The cold war between the Soviet Union and the United States delivered South Korea into the hands of the political right wing. Unions were given over to a native oppressor, Syngman Rhee. He held them captive for thirteen years. After Rhee was driven out and a new constitution promulgated in 1963, the reaction of workers repeated the model of 1945: they organized; they engaged employers in negotiations; they became active members of society. Pak Chung Hee's first version of government (1963-71) protected workers' rights to organize, to bargain and to take collective action. Workers responded with enthusiasm. Union membership grew. Collective bargaining began to be practiced. Work stoppages were seldom, and worker productivity grew each year, launching South Korea on its way to an economic miracle. Freedom, this time, lasted eight years.

1971 opened a new chapter of the story. This chapter was Pak's second version of government. The resulting military dictatorship lasted for sixteen years. It was a chapter characterized by one outrage after another. The ruler's seat was occupied by a consortium of military generals, *chaebol* and foreign financiers. They created a subsystem of enforcement that outdid the earlier rulers in systemic cruelty against the nation's working people. Yet even in the midst of that cruelty, a cry for justice was heard. In the earlier part of the period young women held the banner and suffered the indignities inflicted upon them by police and KCIA. In the mid 1980's, the men came forward to join their sisters. Beginning in 1985, and reaching crescendo in 1987, a brand new chapter in the story of organized labor in Korea has begun. New, independent unions have emerged and the economic giants of the land, the *chaebol*, are being challenged. This chapter of the saga is only now beginning to take shape. It will be different from the previous chapters. A new dynamic is present now that did not exist prior to 1987. Korea's workers are calling an end to the authoritarianism that has for so long tried to crush their spirits. Both white collar

157

and blue collar workers demand a new social egalitarianism, a democratic style of economy. It is this call for egalitarianism that exploded so resoundingly onto the scene in 1987. It has been there all along, under the surface, waiting. That which broke forth in 1987 is kin to the earlier revolts of the Tonghak in 1894, to the Wonsan dock workers of 1928, the People's Committees of 1945 and the resistance of Kwangju in 1980. 1987 brought industrial workers of Korea to a new awareness of their own role in history.

One worker at an automobile factory said, "Prior to 1987 I was just a worker doing my job. I was shocked by the company violence against us when we demonstrated for a wage increase. I became aware of the realities in which I work."[1] Individuals became caught up in the wider movement and began to see that their individual predicaments had wider, social significance. All of a sudden they became conscious that they were facing not just their line foreman, but also an entire economic political system that oppressed them. Simultaneously they were taking part in mass action to counter those powers. Unions were formed where previously there had been none; company unions were being thrown out; and workers were forming associations across industrial and geographic lines. The new egalitarianism took shape and became institutionalized in what has come to be called the minju nodong oondong, or the democratic labor movement. The minju (democratic) labor movement is a new ingredient in Korean history. It challenges the system of authoritarianism crafted by the innovators, and it creates new possibilities for South Korea to move beyond the militarized authoritarianism that has dominated it one way or the other through this entire century.

With the emergence of the democratic labor movement, new possibilities for democracy have become visible:

o It is possible for all unions to become democratic.

o It is now possible to change the outmoded, authoritarian attitudes of employers.

o Worker participation in the planning for economic growth has become a possibility.

o The minju labor movement provides a viable democratic model for reunification.

DEMOCRATIC LABOR MOVEMENT AND THE FKTU

Korean labor unions have been in captivity since 1947. Once Chun Pyung was eliminated all debate ended in regards to what a union should do or be. At the local level they became instruments of employer control. At the national level the FKTU was made subservient to government policy. In those rare instances, like Dongil or Wonpoong, when workers attempted to maintain an independent local, the FKTU, acting as a proxy for government, withdrew the local union's charter and dismissed the leadership. Throughout the Pak–Chun era FKTU was unfailingly loyal to the dictatorship. Almost alone among social organizations, it declared public support for Pak's *Yushin* system. In 1987 when the national debate raged between the democratic forces that demanded direct presidential elections and the Chun Doo Hwan forces that intended to perpetuate the dictatorship, FKTU backed Chun Doo Hwan.

Thus when the 1987 explosions occurred, FKTU was listed along with the *chaebol*, police and government as an enemy of democracy. As workers in Hyundai, Daewoo, Goldstar and other *chaebol* rose up and demanded the right to organize and bargain, FKTU was not there to support them. Workers in many of the smaller shops had earlier been betrayed by the FKTU so when they made their move to unionize in 1987, they did not expect nor want FKTU assistance.

The minju labor movement demands that either the FKTU be dissolved, since in its view the FKTU is irredeemable, or that a second confederation organized by the minju unions be allowed to legally exist. The democratic unions have organized themselves into regional associations. Women workers, who have suffered many grievances at the hands of FKTU, are pivotal in many of these associations. At the right time, a national organization called the National Federation of Labor Unions, parallel to FKTU, is to be formed. Even though it is now illegal to do so, it is the intention of the minju movement to challenge the FKTU at local, regional and national levels. The monopoly of the FKTU over labor organizations must be broken, they contend, if democratic participation is to survive. The web of control spun by the coterie of management, government, police and the FKTU has too long a history and is too ingrown to be left intact. Though the FKTU has since 1987 attempted to reform its leadership, its basic institution with traditional ties to government, *chaebol* and ruling party remains unchanged. Electing a few honorable men for positions of top leadership is not enough to undo the collusive practices of the past. Democracy requires new institutions and new processes that can carry a new flow of information and action. The old will not do. It is time for new skins that can carry new wine.

The minju labor movement's break with the old is illustrated in two particular ways. As in the cases of Hyundai and Daewoo, minju unions demand that union officers be elected directly by the rank and file. This one new policy signifies the workers' determination to shake off decades of company control. The move toward ratification of contracts by union membership is another step in the same direction. The heart of the minju initiatives is to turn decision-making over to the workers and curb company interference.

The next step in becoming independent from the company is practicing financial freedom. In the present system the company provides office space, remunerates union officials and even pays the wages of union leaders at the industrial federation and FKTU levels. If independence from company interference is necessary in a democratic system, then workers must pay for their own union and employ their own union staff.

In addition to the particular changes in process and structure, however, the minju labor movement confronts the FKTU with a more fundamental challenge. Though FKTU may come around to accepting rank and file participation and perhaps even financial responsibility, it seems hopelessly bound to a concept of unionism inherited from the American military government of 1945–48. The Americans structured unions around the concept of "economic unionism." There were two parts to this American pattern: first, union concerns were restricted to wages, benefits and working conditions; and secondly, the union leaders were required to give loyalty to the political and economic policies of the government. For more than forty years the various dictatorships have manipulated this two-tiered system for their own benefit. The minju labor movement now calls it into question. "Economic Unionism" is a subterfuge used by dictators and innovators to control unions and prevent workers from participating in society. The minju labor movement rejects FKTU's political subservience. It intends to integrate the economic interests of workers into a political philosophy of its own making, independent from the *chaebol*, independent from the government and independent from the ruling party. To that end some of the new regional labor associations have joined a social–political group called the chunminryun (National Democratic Federation). Chunminryun is a broadly based coalition of workers, farmers, religious groups, women's associations and other political groupings. It provides a new entry onto the political scene for the minju labor movement.

It is at this point where the clash between minju and FKTU is most dramatic. FKTU has not been able to declare its independence from government or company. Its dependence is too deep. The minju labor leaders reject the FKTU because of that dependence.

In the 1989 situation, the minju unions are at a definite disadvantage. A coterie of authoritarians still hold legal and economic power. The minju unions use of work stoppages and demonstrations is the only means whereby their message can be brought to the people. Strikers at Goldstar or Daewoo, or in the smaller firms of Puchun City, shout slogans that demand a wage increase followed by slogans that call for the overthrow of the government or withdrawal

160

of American troops. The mixture of economic and political messages illustrates the minju philosophy of integration between the economic and the political. It is also the only way that the minju unions can get the ear of the people. Other than strike action the unions have no access to the public. Media basically ignores them; the politicians are afraid of them; and the government attacks them. To have workers shout slogans and carry banners that communicate a political message causes consternation and frustration among the *chaebol* and the politicians, but that frustration may be a road leading to democracy.

The minju labor unions have opened up the labor movement as never before. The goals and strategies of unions are for the first time being debated by workers, and also for the first time workers, on a large scale, are acting to set up their own organizations. The strength of the new unionism now opens up the possibility that all of Korea's labor organizations will become more democratic. Even the FKTU now has the chance of breaking its political bondage.

DEMOCRATIC LABOR MOVEMENT VS. AUTHORITARIANISM

The Kwangju massacre was the calamity that laid Korea's authoritarianism open on the table for all to see, and it has become the analogy through which much of labor's sufferings have been interpreted. The kusadae are like the soldiers sent to Kwangju. They are organized to beat and even kill their fellow workers. Employers encourage groups of ex–marines, or ex–navy men or ex–MP's to use their military skills to intimidate and commit violence against their brothers and sisters. Korea's militarization has turned in on itself. Those skills learned to supposedly defend against communist aggression are used to subdue workers and citizens who seek a democratic homeland. The mammoth weight of military force used against South Korean society over the last two decades is incredible. The rationale of anti–communism is used to justify a police force estimated at 300,000; endless numbers of soldiers acting as riot police; the formation of special swat teams called "baikgoldan;" the ubiquitous presence of spies and plain–clothes men; and the secretive and brutal KCIA. The rulers of Korean society have ruled, and continue to rule, primarily by force. The kusadae used in the nation's factories is but one logical extension of this institutionalized violence.

Facing that violence are, as it were, the people of Kwangju. They are the ones who are committed to an egalitarian and democratic reform of society. Kwon Yong Mok, president of the union at Hyundai Engine gave voice to the democratic movement in his speech the night he was released from prison.

We formed the union because we believe the land wants to be democratic....our task is an inescapable task of history. (p. 121)

161

Indeed a turning point in history is being experienced. It is that sense which carries men like Kwon and others into conflict and eventually to prison. At the factory level, it is still too early to say that there has been change in authoritarian ways. Where unions are strong enough, employers must bargain, but there is little indication that there is any significant change of mind. Violence alternating with paternalism are still the dominant attitudes. Some plant managers have ordered their lower management to spend their leisure times drinking with the workers as a means of restoring harmony to the work place. Managers report back that their stomachs are having a hard time digesting the large intake of rice wine. Little else has changed.

Conversation with some men at the corporate headquarters level indicate an analysis of events not too dissimilar from that made by labor leaders. Yet little insight is expressed regarding the depth of institutional and personal authoritarianism in which they themselves play such critical roles. Following is a paraphrase of ideas expressed by several men in positions of top corporate management:

A revolution has taken place. We are at a turning point in history. In the past, especially in the 1970's and early 1980's, we have been too authoritarian. We were so busy building up the economy, we were reckless about labor relations. We put the least qualified persons in that job. Now we realize that that was not wise. We now need to accept unions and workers as equals and resolve our problems through rational collective bargaining. The problem, however, is that the unions now have all the power. Everyone is on their side. Union leaders are too radical. They do not play according to the rules of the game. They make political demands in the middle of a strike over wages. They act illegally and ignore the law. How can we solve our mutual problems when they act in such an irrational manner. They have to realize that we are all in this together and the company is ours -- management and labor together.

These ideas were spoken with sincerity and suggest the possibility of a more democratic relationship with workers, but it will take much more than sincerity and good intentions. Interviews with corporate management took place in spacious offices atop skyscrapers with a panoramic view of Seoul's natural beauty. Interviews with laboring people and unions most often took place in small, cubbyholes situated in a back alley. These two locations symbolize the distance between labor and management. Labor sees the dilemma from its perspective of the underclass that has long been humiliated. Now they see their position as strong enough to seize some economic benefit, but perhaps more importantly social–political benefit as well. On the other hand the company people see the increase in worker strength as a threat to all that management has built over the years. They fear that big wage increases will put the company at a competitive disadvantage; they fear communists are behind the unions.

Perhaps more than anything else, the idea of equality injects fear into the hearts of the rulers of society and business. Confucius taught that social order depended on the inequalities of superior–inferior, the morally powerful and the morally recessive. To do away with inequality, or to establish equality, he thought, would result in chaos and barbarism. Over and over again spokespersons for government and corporations contend that unless the workers "cooperate," chaos is inevitable, or if the worker does not act as a family member should, it will bring anarchy to the nation. There is no alternative: either obedience or chaos. The term, "equality," conjures up the fears of social chaos, class conflict and personal disaster.

This adds up to a modern type class struggle. Both sides seek to humble the other. Management wants unions to forget all the humiliations and class differences and now "play" according to reason and legality where management holds the upper hand. Labor is more interested in cutting down management power at the work place and in society so that workers can increase their power. Thus the act of making management kneel down in front of the workers at Daewoo Motors takes on class and political symbolism.

The democratic initiatives of unions have not substantially changed the power balance in Korea. The elite of the rich, the foreign financiers and the military still wield the iron hand. They still do not recognize the legitimacy of unions. In 1986 a government paper had these words, "The basis of labor–management relations rests on mutual cooperation and peaceful settlement between labor and management rather than the class struggle which characterized the development process in the Western nations.[2] In July of 1987, just as the big wave of union organizing was to begin, five management groups issued a statement that reiterated this same inaccurate assumption about management–labor relations in Korea. In part it said: "...the existing labor–management cooperative system should be activated with added momentum to prevent any serious dispute."[3]

Management's lack of insight into its own class dominance is the central obstacle to resolution of management–labor conflict. To assume that the labor policy of the innovators has been a "cooperative system" is not only inaccurate, it reflects a social callousness that will be hard to correct. Labor policy has been cooperative only in the sense that "cooperative" was the word the innovators gave it. In actual practice it has always been authoritarian. The challenge that management faces is how to modify its dominance to accommodate worker demand for equality and participation. Until the Chung Ju Yong's who work in the plush skyscraper offices come outside and sit down with the Chun Tae Il's and Kwon Yong Mok's of the workforce, the clash between management and labor will continue. Both sides will be violent. Management's superior force can continue to dominate workers and unions, but in so doing management will only create the emotional ground for the next round of worker revolt.

DEMOCRATIC LABOR MOVEMENT AND
ECONOMIC DEVELOPMENT

For the last 25 years the economic development plans, as put together by the innovators, have guided the nation's economy. Worker demands for democratization now challenges those plans at several points. The low labor cost policy of the innovators is most in question. Not only has it caused economic stress, it has also been a badge of continuing servitude. The low–cost labor policy carries both an economic and political impact. Likewise, the worker demand for wage increases of 50 percent or more also carries a dual message: more money and more power.

There are other questions about the necessity for low labor–cost policies also. In the 1960's Korean labor already was out–working and out–producing workers in other countries of the world. Wages were low. Everyone, including labor, understood that such was a necessity. Yet there was no *Yushin*, no KCIA, no kusadae around to oppress the workers. Union organizing was a legitimate operation. In the 1970's under *Yushin*, EPB threatened to cut off credit to employers if they did not keep wages down, and the KCIA swarmed around workers to dissuade them from demanding wage increases. Yet government statistics show that the rate of wage increases exceeded productivity gains in five years of the decade –– with brilliant economic success. Furthermore, during the turbulent years of 1987 and 1988, when wages rose an average of twenty two percent, the overall indices for economic growth continued to spiral upward. GNP grew around 13%, five points more than planned. Exports increased substantially and employment figures saw an increase of from 15.5 million in 1986 to 16.3 million in '87. Consumer prices were stable.[4] The economic escalator is apparently more elastic and adaptable than thought. Perhaps survival–scale wages are not a necessity. Perhaps the horrendous suppression of workers and unions is not required at all in order to get positive economic results. Perhaps economic and political oppressions stem more from the mentality of class domination than from economic necessity.

It is now being said that since development has shifted to higher levels of technology the low–cost labor policy may no longer be necessary. The point of comparative advantage now has moved from labor to technology. That Korea has successfully switched to higher levels of technology is correct. To suggest that high tech will in some way resolve labor problems and improve management–union relations is hardly persuasive. Despite successes in high technology, labor intensive industries are going to be around for a long while, and Korea will continue to depend on the labor of young women workers.

164

Furthermore, the major union disputes of the last three years have been in precisely those industries which are the most technologically advanced. As the economy does move to higher stages of technology, it is also quite likely to require increasing amounts of foreign capital. Already restrictions on ownership by direct investments has been eliminated and the rates of foreign investments are increasing. The foreign factor will probably exacerbate management–union problems even further. High tech will solve none of the basic disputes between management and labor.

The time is overdue for the EPB and the other innovators to formulate a new labor policy and eradicate the subsystem of enforcement. Too much unnecessary damage has already been done. Now is the time to promote labor participation at all levels. Unions should have the freedom to form their own organizations and associations, without government or management interference. If unions wish to receive help from other unions, experts or church, why should they not? The democratic union movement can contribute much to the liberalization of the economy, if it is permitted to form its own natural confederation with the same legitimacy as the FKTU. A legitimate national confederation of democratic unions can move into the mainstream of society and provide the ideas and new directions for which Korean society now is calling.

Furthermore, it is now essential for the EPB to include representatives from the democratic wing of labor in its planning processes. As the nation goes through the new tensions at higher development levels, it is to everyone's advantage that unions be a genuine partner in planning for the future.

DEMOCRATIC LABOR MOVEMENT AND UNIFICATION

The June 29 Declaration made by Roh Tae Woo in 1987 not only lit the flame for the democratic movement but also for the reunification movement. Though the 1945–imposed division of the country was never acceptable to Koreans north or south, the suffering of people during the years of the power struggle, the pain experienced during the Korean War and the strict anti-communist laws had for decades kept the lid on any movement for reunification.

Following the 6.29 Declaration, reunification emerged openly as a priority concern. Fueled by a spirit of nationalism, students carried out protests at most of South Korea's 115 colleges and universities. Some even stabbed and burned themselves to death after writing letters calling for reunification. Workers, farmers, urban poor, dissidents, opposition politicians, women's groups, and Christian and Buddhist leaders joined the students, forcing the Noh government to place reunification at the top of its agenda.

On July 7, 1988 Roh Tae Woo made a Special Declaration on North-South Relations stating, "We have now come to a historic point when we must achieve a breakthrough toward a lasting peace and the reunification of the

Korean peninsula." Stating that north and south should develop relations "as members of a single national community to achieve common prosperity," Noh promised to actively promote exchanges between the people of north and south from all sectors of society. He promised to promote the reunion of the ten million separated family members, to open doors for trade between north and south and to encourage South Korea's allies to improve relations with North Korea.

Roh Tae Woo's actions in the year and a half following the July 7, 1988 Declaration have not been in keeping with the Declaration. The Noh government refused to grant permission to students who applied to go to the Pyungyang International Youth Festival in July 1989 and arrested Im Soo Kyung who attended without permission as South Korea's student representative. Others who have visited North Korea and any accused of supporting their visits or even knowing about their visits have been arrested. The National Security Law which is still in place is being used by the Noh government to discredit the opposition parties.

Since June of 1987 formerly secret study groups have expanded, and for about a year books about North Korea and reunification were available in the book stores. A new wave of nationalism ironically has selected its key word from the philosophy of Kim Il Song who for forty years has been the leader of North Korea. The word is *juche*, or self reliance. Kim Il Song has held stubbornly to the idea that Korea should develop on its own strength with minimal help from foreigners, even other communist states. The north has in its own stiff and regimented communist way achieved some remarkable success. It claims it has full employment with a fair distribution of income and food for everyone. It has universal, free education and free health care. It has rebuilt its cities and industries all laid waste by the war. It is no match for South Korea in technology and industrialization, but what it has done, it has pretty much done on its own. That is what now appeals to so many in the south. Pride in self-achievement has become a point of honor, so the example of North Korea and the philosophy of juche have strong appeal to many in the south.

Unfortunately the government of Roh Tae Woo is proving to be as anachronistic as was Chun Doo Hwan's government. Rather than applauding the new birth of independence and channelling it as a resource, Noh and the innovators have all risen up to condemn it and hurl at it the epitaphs of "Communist!, Radical!, Traitor!." The once dreaded word, "communist," however, has lost its sting. Despite Noh's attempts over the last years to whip up some anti-communist hysteria, the philosophy of juche expands. The appeal of unification, independence and self-reliance grows. Shrieking out, "The communists are coming, the communists are coming!," has an unreal, hollow sound in 1989.

The world has changed. Everyone knows it except the military and some of the older generation who want to stop the clock permanently at June 25, 1950, the day the Korean War began. That type of mentality cannot prevail. The Soviets and Chinese have changed. Neither of them are hostile to South Korea. Both are trading with South Korea's *chaebol*. Neither is going to enter a war to assist North Korea should it use force against South Korea. North Korea itself has changed. It knows better than anyone that a war would bring instant disaster and lay waste its beautiful cities, locks and dams and industries. Though North Korea could inflict heavy damage, it has fallen so far behind South Korea in economic development and technology that there is no way it could win a war. The factors that once propelled North Korea into the war of 1950 no longer exist.

Things have changed in the south as well. The Korean people realize that, in spite of the rhetoric of their military ally, the U.S.A., the people of the United States would be no more supportive of a new conflict in Korea than would the Soviets or Chinese. The love affair between South Korea and the United States has ended. Ever since Kwangju a new class analysis has taken hold of the minds of many. It sees the U.S. military and business interests as the main powers propping up authoritarianism in South Korea. The United States is also identified as the primary obstacle to unification between the north and south. In student and worker demonstrations the two slogans, "Withdraw U.S. troops" and "Unify the Motherland," are often seen together. Discussions with workers and democratic union leaders indicate that both ideas are widely accepted.

In addition, a good portion of Koreans are just plain tired of having American soldiers, American bankers, American businessmen and American tourists around. Prostitute villages around some forty U.S. military installations are still an insult to Korean pride. The United States Embassy and the American CIA are thought to be the power behind the hated Korean CIA. The time has come when independence from the foreigner is being demanded. American presence is seen as an affront to nationalistic pride and a hindrance to unification with the north.

Most significant of all, the people of South Korea have changed. The war has been over for thirty six years. Over half the population has no direct recollection of it, and for many others the fires of hate have died away. Despite attempts by the military and some of the older generation to keep those fires stoked up, the old fervor is just not there. Even Chung Ju Yong, who screams "communist" at his striking employees at Hyundai, is willing and eager to do business with the north. Prior to the hysteria whipped up by the right wing of Noh's party in the summer of 1989, Chung had made two trips to North Korea. He met with Kim Il Song, praised Kim's great accomplishments, and worked on

167

arrangements to do construction work for the North Korean government. The other big *chaebol* have been sending their representatives on a regular basis to China, the Soviet Union and Eastern Europe. The old anti-communist heat has moved from the heart to the tongue. It is no longer a controlling emotion for the vast majority of Koreans.

In all these ways the world inside and outside Korea has changed. A war is unlikely. The old battle lines of communist vs. anti-communist have at long last broken down. Now is the time when the government and other innovators in South Korea should be focusing their considerable skills and resources on the questions of unification. Among those questions perhaps one with highest priority should be this: how is democratic participation by workers to be assured in any industrial-political arrangement that might come about? Some assume that unification in and of itself will resolve all issues. Others are certain that any accommodation with the North will result in communist style dictatorship. Neither of these is likely to happen, but unless there is a better democratic model to interface with the communist model of the North, the result of unification could well be an authoritarianism of a type not yet seen. Though at some levels communism and capitalism are contrary to each other, both have a core of authoritarianism.

North Korea and South Korea are examples of their respective models of development: one, guided capitalism and the other, guided communism. Both have relied heavily on low cost labor and authoritarian styles of management-labor relations, albeit with obvious differences of methodology. Labor in the North has always been under the tight control of the communist party. There is no free or independent union in the North, no history or experience of such. The worker organizations they do have are used as instruments to maintain party control and improve labor productivity. They are, in other words, vehicles of the communist party.

Unions in the South have for most of their history been reduced to a similar function. Workers in South Korea have been under a labor policy that results in a pervasive web of control over workers and their unions. Though the South Korean system has permitted a protest every once in a while, it was not until 1987 that the minju union movement broke the old mode of suppression. For the first time, workers in South Korea have an independent voice. Within the context of corporate capitalism they are demanding democratic participation in company and government, and equal distribution of national income. South Korea now has a model of independent, free unionism that is different from both the traditional models of North Korea and South Korea.

The emergence of the minju labor movement at this point in time is critical. As the two parts of the peninsula begin to inspect each other with the intent of drawing closer and eventually moving toward unification, labor, labor organizations, and worker participation are bound to be central points of negotiation. To have no model for labor other than the one devised by the South Korean innovators or the North Korean communists is to invite a continuation of authoritarianism and oppression into the future. The minju system provides a legitimate option that can insert a model of democratic freedom into the exchanges between two basically authoritarian governments. It also has the advantage of expressing many of the ideas and values of the young people of Korea which will be important in any interchange between the one time adversaries.

CHAPTER NOTES

1. Paraphrase from an interview in a magazine called *Jayu' O'rlon* (Free Speech), "So'nohyu'b Changnip kwa Nodong Undongu'l Hyu'nan," Seoul, July 15, 1988, p. 48.

2. Statement on Labor and Management made by Embassy of the Republic of Korea, Washington, DC, Fall, 1986, p. 20.

3. <u>Korea Times</u>, July 24, 1987.

4. Young–ki Park, "Labor Relations in Korea: Recent Developments and Prospects." Sogang University, Seoul, December, 1987, p. 20.

Until the last decade Koreans saw the U.S. and its Western allies as liberators, perhaps even saviours, of their nation. Many remembered that the World War II allied victory resulted in liberation from imperial Japan. The UN participation in the Korean war had thrown back the north Korean communists. There was also a recognition that billions of dollars of foreign aid had been pumped in to help south Korea recover from the destruction of war, and that financial investments and technology from the West and Japan had played a big part in the subsequent economic miracle.

Then one dramatic event changed that, perhaps for ever. Since the atrocities perpetrated in Kwangju in May of 1980, the United States and other Western nations are seen through different eyes. New questions are being asked. Why would the United States act in collusion with a hated military dictator to put down a people's demonstration for democracy? Whose side was the U.S. on anyway? From those initial questions a whole series of other questions came rolling out. The answers reduced the previous friend to the status of probable enemy. Why over the last two decades have presidents and diplomats visiting Korea never denounced the Pak and Chun dictatorships? Why did President Reagan invite Chun Doo Hwan to the White House and call him a great democrat soon after Chun had committed the Kwangju massacre? Was keeping Korea subservient under dictatorships all a part of a U.S. plan? Were Pak and Chun only puppets of U.S. policies?

The reconsideration of the U.S. role in Korea is extended backward in history. Why was the U.S. military so quick to put down the People's Committees in 1945? Did the Americans crush genuine democratic organizations so that they could keep control? Was not the division of the country forced on to the Koreans primarily by the Americans? And even further back, did not the Americans agree to the Japanese takeover of Korea in 1905? The Taft–Katsura Treaty of that year was tantamount to a swap between the U.S. and Japan: the U.S. took the Philippines and Japan got Korea.

Seen from Kwangju it all seems to fit a pattern, a pattern of sellout and then domination by the United States. Students, workers, religious groups and ordinary citizens now speak openly, even matter–of–factly about American imperialism. Korea is a land of ironies, but no irony is so dramatic as that of the transformation of the image of the U.S.A. from hero to enemy. To hear young Koreans shout "Down with the U.S.A.!" "Save Korea, put out the Americans!" "Yankee go home!" is a shock to American ears accustomed to warm praise and expressions of gratitude.

History has been rewritten. To those who do not share this perspective, the rewriting is a distortion of historical fact. The point to be made here, however, is not one of determining historical accuracy, but rather one of discerning the messages within the new Korean nationalism.

MESSAGE TO THE MILITARY

The first and most obvious of the messages is addressed to U.N. and American policymakers. The time has come to end the Korean War. The clock is no longer frozen at June 25, 1950. Thinking of Korea in terms of war is an anachronism that only does damage. Having the military formulate policy in Korea is obsolete and perpetuates the militarization of Korea's governments.

Koreans, north and south, are looking toward peace and reunification, not war. Now American and U.N. ingenuities must be centered on how to make peace and encourage north and south as they move closer together.

Many groups of Koreans are calling on the U.S. and the U.N. to participate in negotiations to replace the 1953 Korean War Armistice with a peace treaty and establish with the governments of north and south Korea, mutually acceptable time tables for troop reductions on both sides of the D.M.Z. They urge the removal of all foreign troops and nuclear weapons, and the termination of the U.S. military command function in South Korea.[1]

In addition, the U.S. and Europe need to improve their relations with north Korea in the same way that south Korea has improved its relations with China and the U.S.S.R. Even President Roh Tae Woo in his well known July 7, 1988 "Declaration on New Policies toward the North" urged the U.S. and Japan to improve relations with north Korea. The voice of north Korea must be heard and their proposals tested.

The West can also encourage democratization in Korea. It is important to recognize that the voice of the Korean people cannot be heard clearly until the National Security Law is abolished. Under the National Security Law people can be arrested for advocating a peace treaty or calling for removal of U.S. troops or nuclear weapons. Since the leaders of the democratic labor movement have frequently been labelled "communist" and arrested under the National Security Law, they are especially concerned that it be abolished.

MESSAGE TO FOREIGN INVESTORS

The second message is directed toward foreign corporations and banks that invest in South Korea. Part of the responsibility for the dictatorship and for the abuse of Korean workers lies squarely on their shoulders. As part of the team of innovators, the foreign business men helped meld together the low labor–cost, anti–union, pro–authoritarian policies of the last couple decades. The small American firm, Oak Electronics Company, began the practice in 1969 and since then foreign firms have been free with advice as to how Korea must not permit unions and how it must keep wages low. To enforce the point, the threat

172

of close–down and withdrawal to Taiwan or Hong Kong or Singapore has been liberally used. As the innovator with the needed ingredient, namely capital and technology, the impact of the American, Japanese and European investors has been great. Their labor policies and their financial support perpetuated the dictatorships. Gulf Oil alone contributed four million dollars to the 1971 election campaign of Pak Chung Hee.

Since 1987, actions of some American firms have added considerably to the persuasiveness of the re–written history. Rather than accept the minju unions, a few companies have been willing to close their doors. The Tandy Corporation's behavior is notable. After having done a lucrative business in Masan for twelve years, it abruptly left town without notifying the Korean government or its 1,500 employees. When its employees formed a labor union, Tandy was so offended it discontinued its operations. Another United States' firm out did Tandy. It left Korea without even informing the Korean managers of the company. It left without paying its debts and made no provision for paying the workers' last month wages or severance pay. The employees were mostly middle–aged women. The $6.20 a day wages they earned kept them living on the brink of poverty. When they formed a union, Pico Products, Inc. walked away. Even though Korean workers followed the Pico company to its headquarters in Syracuse, New York seeking a settlement, Pico's president treated them only to verbal abuse refusing all compromise. The case may now go to American and Korean courts.

To many Koreans,however, Motorola is the firm that has come to represent the foreign attitude toward Korean workers. One of the world's leading manufacturers of electronic components, Motorola has done business in Korea for more than twenty years. On several occasions during those years it has defeated worker attempts to unionize. In 1987 workers again attempted to organize. There are variations in reports of what took place, but the version told here, which comes from the union leaders, is not likely to be forgotten by Korea's workers.

Motorola employees had long–standing grievances against the company. Wages, they claimed, were always lower than those of workers in comparable firms. The management was harsh and arbitrary. When the wave of union action began in mid–1987, the five thousand workers at Motorola were also affected. A union was formed and registered with government authorities. Management, however, instead of recognizing the union, "kidnapped" the workers who had taken the lead in the union. They were taken on "trips" to hotels, hot baths and resort areas. They were wined and dined. And back at the factory word was spread that the union leaders had sold out to the company. Other rumors were circulated that unless the union nonsense stopped, Motorola would close its doors and pull out of Korea. The company attack prevailed. After only a month, the union was disbanded.

Instead of getting better, however, the atmosphere at work got worse. Management became paranoid. Everyone was suspected and put under surveillance. Discipline and reprimands were handed out freely.

In December of 1988 some workers decided to try once more to form a union. One hundred and fifty of them held a rally on company grounds. They proclaimed a minju union and called upon all the workers to unite. The company, alerted ahead of time that a rally was to be held, formed a kusadae group for the occasion. The kusadae attacked the leaders of the rally and herded them (mostly young women) into the dining room of the factory. The doors were barred shut. Water, electricity and heat were cut off and the air conditioning was turned on. It was December. For three days the employees were locked in the cold dining room. On the third day they finally broke out through an unguarded window in the back. Once out of the building they were again attacked by the kusadae and driven out of the company compound.

The next day a message was delivered to the unionists saying that unless they reported to work in four days they would be dismissed. Each time they tried to enter, however, the guards or kusadae would drive them off. On the last day, the unionists stormed the gate by surprise and gained access to the company grounds. Their intent was to report to work to save their jobs, but before they could reach the plant building they were cut off by the kusadae led by a department supervisor. They were told to leave. They would not be permitted to enter. Five of the young men workers foreseeing something like this, had brought a can of paint thinner with them. They doused each other with the fluid and threatened to light a match if they were not let through. The supervisor, it is reported, laughed. He produced a cigarette lighter and said he would be glad to assist. With that he set one of the men on fire. Then followed the macabre sight of the young man being surrounded by the kusadae while he burned to unconsciousness. He did not die. His body, however, shall never be free from the incinerating pain.

As this tragic spectacle was taking place on the grounds in front of the factory, a figure was seen on the roof. It is said that the person was an American who had come to Korea from the corporate headquarters not many days before. He had a walkie talkie and acted as though he were directing the show below.

The image of the burning young Korean worker and the "commanding American," safely distanced on the roof, reenacts in the minds of many the events of Kwangju. Like the American military, the foreign corporations have had too long and too close a connection with events of the last two decades to claim innocence or detachment. Motorola is an American company, managed in Korea primarily by Koreans, but under the control of the home company. From the beginning its labor policy has conformed to the policy of the innovators: keep labor costs low and unions out. When the union finally broke through, the American company followed the same pattern of authoritarian response as did Hyundai and Samsung.

One foreign business man once told the author, "All I came to Korea for was to make a buck. I don't want anything to do with their politics or unions." To the foreign businessman that may sound pure enough, but, of course, it is just the opposite. "Making a buck," is not a simple matter. It is a highly political–social–personal affair as well as a production system. The Korean economy has become a complex, modernized process within which the workers have "come of age." They are no longer willing to play the role of docile serfs. They demand not only improvement in wages and working conditions, but also the right to organize their unions and be recognized as equals with the company. That is not a radical demand. It is a fundamental statement of human rights and democracy. In the 1990's as Korea's technology continues to expand, direct foreign investments are predicted to increase rapidly. Corporations making those investments hopefully will learn something from the minju labor movement. Instead of authoritarianism, they might try a labor policy of cooperation with the workers and their unions.

MESSAGE TO INTERNATIONAL LABOR

The third message of the Korean minju labor movement is directed toward labor unions in U.S.A. and Europe. Where were you in the 1970's when we needed help so desperately? Where were you in 1980 when the guns of Chun Doo Hwan forced his dictatorship on us? Where were you when so many of us were being taken away to "purification" camps? The International Confederation of Free Trade Unions (ICFTU) has had contact with the Korean labor movement for decades. The AFL–CIO established its Asia–American Free Labor Institute (AAFLI) in Seoul in 1971. For the next sixteen years it cooperated actively with the KCIA–appointed leaders of the FKTU. It provided thousands of United States AID dollars to the FKTU. Never was it recorded, however, that the ICFTU or AAFLI stood with the workers or unions against oppression. In the 1970's when the women workers at Dongil Textile were being beaten and humiliated, they were silent. In the early 1980's when the male unionists were being thrown in prison or beaten by the kusadae, not a word was heard from international unions. Workers in Korea know little or nothing about ICFTU, and have come to believe that AAFLI is an agent of the American government, not a legitimate union operation at all.

At the same time, however, the minju movement is sharply aware of the need for genuine solidarity among Korean and international unions. Union movements everywhere are being attacked by international corporate capitalism, and unless unions learn to exercise solidarity across nationalistic lines, they all are apt to be destroyed. The struggle of the Korean labor movement against the innovators and their enforcement systems is the same struggle that unions are undergoing in the United States, England, Latin America and South Africa. Militantly anti–union corporations, protected by anti–union laws and anti–union government agencies, attack every effort of workers to organize, or consolidate their strength. In the U.S.A. unions have already lost half their members and for over a decade wages, health care, pensions and safety have been declining at a significant rate. Low–cost labor plus authoritarian structures are eating up the American union movement as they have the Korean. Korean unions in recent years, for example, have been able to rely on strike action more than their American counterparts. Theoretically, the right to strike is still on the books in the U.S.A., but the use of the "replacement team" has made it tantamount to suicide. Striking unionists find themselves permanently replaced by non–union people. This is America's style of kusadae.

The same basic pattern of anti–unionism prevails in other parts of the globe: giant corporations (*chaebol*) attack workers who are organized, or attempt to organize; the legal apparatus supports the attacks.

Workers in the Korea, however, have responded to these attacks quite differently from their Western counterparts. Most dramatically Korean workers have gone on the offensive. American and European workers, by comparison, seem more resigned to a future of dwindling income and deteriorating political status. Korean workers have suffered enough. They now demand that the *chaebol*'s power be conditioned by the democratic and humane demands of the workers. Instead of retreating and permitting worker rights to be disregarded, as is being done so often in the U.S.A., Korean workers are claiming that human rights, including the rights to organize and bargain and strike, have pre–eminence over the *chaebol*'s right to rule like kings. In Korea corporate attacks against unions are often violent, using police, kusadae and thugs. In the West the violence, by and large, is absent. Its absence, however, is probably not because Western corporations are more civilized, but rather because they have other means of achieving the same end.

Another characteristic of the Korean workers' response to corporate attack is rejection of the official union apparatus (FKTU). The uprisings over the last three years have been spontaneous worker movements. For four decades official unions had been manipulated by KCIA–corporation–government collusion. FKTU had come to accept a posture of subjugation. Since 1987 Korean minju workers have refused to play the game according to government and corporation rules.

Some unions in the U.S.A. have been in a bondage similar to that of the FKTU. Though not faced with the truncheons of a KCIA, yet they have become bound to a legal system in which they seldom win. The laws, the courts, and the NLRB are hostile to workers' rights. The corporate, or *chaebol*, influence prevails as much within the legal system that controls labor–management relations in the U.S. as it does in the Korean system. The minju labor movement of Korea sidestepped the whole morass of institutional unions and legal processes. Without reference to either, the workers spontaneously initiated their own movement. Though a people's movement like the Korean minju labor movement cannot be programmed ahead of time, it would appear that the unions in the Western nations once more need a minju–style uprising of working people.

For the minju movement of Korea to be free from the bondage of the innovators they must create a new philosophy of unionism that integrates the economic, political and social aspects of work in a modern internationalized world. Economic unionism is no longer sufficient. In today's international economy, economic unionism hands over leadership of the nation and economy to the rich, their corporations and banks.

A political–social minju philosophy that interprets the internationalizing process in terms of human rights and social justice for workers and the poor of the world is desperately needed. Western labor can no longer live to itself, or consider itself as somehow superior to others. It's submissiveness to capitalist values and nationalistic foreign policies place it in the predicament of having no philosophy to guide it through the process of economic internationalization. Corporate capitalism has the upper hand. Economic unionism imprisons workers in the narrow confines of self–interest, which in today's global markets leads to weakness, instead of strength, division, rather than solidarity.

The example of the Korean minju labor movement suggests an alternative. It proclaims a renewal of democratic, independent unionism that acts according to the demands of workers. It suggests an internationalizing of the union ideals of social equality, a just distribution of goods and political participation. Four specifics of a minju philosophy are:

1. The economic system controlled so tightly by the innovators (the economic planners, the *chaebol* and the international bankers) must be restructured. The resources of the world and the wonders of technology should serve the poor and the laboring classes around the globe. Corporate governance and ownership must be reconsidered. The claim of the few to unregulated ownership of the world's economic organizations and institutions must be put

under public scrutiny. Structures of worker participation and governance need to be invented.

2. The priority of labor over capital has to be reasserted. Pope John Paul II speaks to the point: there is an obligation on employers "to consider the welfare of the workers before the increase in profits. They have a moral obligation not to keep capital unproductive and in making investments, to think first of the common good."[2]

Such policy direction would lead to a high-wage, full employment economy, with continuing investments in development of communities and human beings.

3. International trade and international capital must be linked to international worker rights. Oppressed labor should not be for sale to foreign capital nor should it be the crutch upon which so called domestic "comparative advantage" is built. Fundamental rights of organizing and bargaining fairly without threat of beatings or tortures are minimal human standards that both trade and capital investment must accept.

The ILO's international standards of worker rights should be dusted off and the international community should begin to enforce those standards.

4. Democratic union movements must clearly make the distinction between the interests of international labor and the nationalistic interests of their own country. International solidarity requires that unions and workers in the so-called "First World" identify their futures more closely with the interests of labor in Korea and the "Third World" than with the interests of corporations headquartered in their respective homelands. Unions huddled each in their own country colluding with government and *chaebol* are only instruments of authoritarianism. There must be a break-out, an act of defiance that declares union independence and solidarity with workers in other countries.

Without active international solidarity it is unlikely that Korea's minju labor movement can prevail in its struggle against authoritarianism. The help that is needed is immediate and physical -- not just money, exhortations, or letters to the heads of state. They need American, Japanese and European union leaders, who will join their picket lines, who will put physical pressure on

Korean companies operating within their respective countries. They need union solidarity that will boycott Hyundai, Samsung and Daewoo products until union contracts are achieved. Korean unions too must learn this lesson of international worker solidarity now that the *chaebol* are expanding into nations much poorer than Korea.

International union solidarity is the only way Korean workers will be able to maintain their march toward democracy. It is also the only way that Western unions will survive with integrity.

At the beginning of Chapter IV, the lives of two men were contrasted: Chung Ju Yong, president of the Hyundai Corporation and Chun Tae Il, a laborer at the Peace Market, who burned himself to death. Chung Ju Yong is the symbol of success, power, industrial greatness. Chun Tae Il represents the workers of the world who have been consumed by the success of the powerful, but even in death he claims a dignity for himself and his sister workers. Western labor has for too long set up the Chung Ju Yongs of the earth as its model to emulate. The Korean minju labor movement is now calling it to switch identities: to claim Chun Tae Il as brother, to proclaim a solidarity with the workers for whom he died.

CHAPTER NOTES

1. Declaration of the Churches of Korea on National Reunification and Peace.

2. Taken from Union, September 1988, p. 9.

SELECTED BIBLIOGRAPHY

Adelman, Irma. _Practical Approaches to Development Planning, Korea's Second Five-Year Plan_. Johns Hopkins Press. 1989.

Baker, Edward J. "Within the Scope Defined by Law: the Rights of Labor under the Yushin System." Harvard Law School. September 1, 1979.

Bognanno, Mario. "Korea's Industrial Relations at the Turning Point." Korea Development Institute. Seoul. 1988.

Cho, Sung Hyuk and Whang Yong Whan. _Nodong Johap Erani Mat Jom Bwayagaitgun_ (This is a Labor Union. I'll Take a Taste of It!), Korean Christian Industrial Development Center. Seoul. 1987.

Choi, Bong-youn. _Korea, a History_. Charles Tuttle. Tokyo. 1971.

Choi, Jang Jip. "Interest, Conflict and Political Control in South Korea: a Study of the Labor Unions in Manufacturing Industries," 1961-1980, a Ph.D. dissertation. University of Chicago. 1983.

Chung, Chung-kil. "The Ideology of Economic Development and Its Impact on Policy Process," a paper. Seoul National University. 1987.

Clive, Hamilton. _Capitalist Industrialization in Korea_. Westview Press. Boulder, Colorado. 1986.

Cumings, Bruce. _Child of Conflict_, University of Washington, 1983.

Cumings, Bruce. _The Two Koreas_, Foreign Policy Association, New York, 1984.

Forbes, "How South Korea Surprised the World," April 30, 1979. p. 54.

"Foreign Equity Investment in Korea," a paper prepared by the U.S. Embassy. Seoul. 1989.

Halliday, John and Bruce Cumings. _Korea, the Unknown War_. Pantheon, 1988.

Han'guk Nodong Undongu'i Enyum (The Theory of the Korean Labor Movement), Korean Christian Industrial Development Center. Seoul. 1988.

Han'guk Sahwei Minjuhwa Banghyung kwa Kwajai (Directions and Tasks of Making Korean Society Democratic), Korean Christian Industrial Development Center. Seoul. 1987.

Han'guk Sahwei Nodong Tongjai (Control of Labor in Korean Society). Korean Christian Study Center for Social Problems. Seoul. 1984.

Han'guk Sahwei Nodongja Yu'ngu I (Study of Korean Workers). Han'guk Sahwei Yu'nguso (Center for the Study of Korean Society). Seoul. 1989.

Harvard Business School Case Studies. "Hyundai Heavy Industries and the Shipbuilding Industry." Harvard University. March 1986.

Henderson, Gregory. Politics of the Vortex, Harvard University, 1968.

Jacobs, Norman. The Korean Road to Modernization and Development, University of Illinois Press, 1985.

Jones, Leroy and Il So Kang. Government, Business and Entrepreneurship in Economic Development: the Korean Case, Harvard University Press, 1980.

Kim, Byong-Kuk, *Kim Woo Choong*, Bobmun Sa, Seoul, 1988.

Kim Dae Jung. Mass Participatory Economy, University Press of America, Boston, 1985.

Kim, Seok Ki. "Business Concentration and Government Policy: A Study of the Phenomenon of Business Groups in Korea, 1945–1985," doctoral thesis, Harvard University, 1987.

Kim, Soo Kon. "Labor Economics and Industrial Relations in Korea," working paper #7801 in Korea Modernization Series, Korea Development Institute, Seoul, 1978.

Korea's Economy, "Debt-financed Growth and Foreign Banks: the case of Korea," Washington, D.C., August, 1987.

Major Statistics of the Korean Economy, Korean Foreign Trade Association, Seoul, 1988.

McCune, George. Korea Today, Harvard Press, 1950.

Meacham, Stewart. "Korea Labor Report," Report submitted to the Secretary of Labor, Seoul, November 1947.

Michell, Tony. From a developing to a newly industrialized country, the Republic of Korea, 1961–82, ILO, Geneva, 1988.

Nodong Hyunjang kwa Ju'ngo'n, (Witness and the Condition of Labor), Published by Han'guk Kidokkyohwei Hyubu'ihwei, Seoul, 1984.

Pak, Chung Hee. Our Nation's Path, Donga, Seoul, 1962.

Pak, Young Ki. "Changes in Industrial Relations in Korea," Sogang University, Seoul, 1988.

Pak, Young Ki. "Industrial Labor in Foreign Invested Firms in Korea," Sogang University, Seoul, 1988.

Pak, Young Ki. "Labor Relations in Korea: Recent Developments and Prospects," Paper for International Metal Workers' Federation, December 1987.

Saebyu'ku'r Yo'nu'n Hamso'ng, (Dawn of the Battle), Ha'nguk Nodong Yu'nguso, 1988.

Steinberg, David. The Economic Development of Korea, Unites States AID, Washington, 1982.

Stephens, Bernard. "Labor Resurgence in South Korea," the Nation, September 19, 1988.

Sullivan, John and Roberta Foss. Two Koreas -- One Future?, University Press of America, 1987.

Sumiya, Mikio. "Growth Economy and Unstable Society: Mechanisms of the South Korean Economy," University of Tokyo, September 1977.

Wade, L.L. and B.S. Kim. Economic Development of South Korea, Praeger, 1978.

Westwood, J.N. Russo-Japanese War, Henry Regnery, 1974.

Woronoff, Jon. Korea's Economy: Man-Made Miracle, Si-sa-yong-o-sa, Seoul,   1983.

Index

188 *Index*

International Labor Rights Education and Research Fund

The International Labor Rights Education and Research Fund was established in 1986 to promote worker rights in connection with United States foreign trade, investment and aid policies.

Associates of the International Labor Rights Education and Research Fund are united by a common commitment to the rights of working people in all countries to freely organize and bargain to more fully share in the fruits of their labor, and to economic development strategies that promote broad based economic growth and equitable distribution of wealth.

To receive further information on the Fund or about this and other Fund publications, please write to the Fund at:

Box 28074
Washington, DC 20038–8074 USA